"This work is a readable and balanc_ ... 15:1-17, arguing that its central theme is that of communal hol... believes that the notion of covenant, with its associated ideas of holiness and corporateness, underlies John's metaphor; while the Johannine understanding of the people of God, in his view, stems from the biblical motif of the covenant with Israel. This intriguing presentation will provide a fresh and helpful contribution to the field of Johannine studies, and I commend it to you warmly."

Stephen S Smalley
Dean Emeritus of Chester

"This book is a valuable reminder of the New Testament's focus on the community of faith as the locus for holy living, an important corrective to Western individualist readings of Scripture. By bringing together a focus on the covenant motif, via the vine metaphor, with insights into ancient communal concerns by reference to his own Bantu tradition, Kunene presents a compelling reading of John that opens a fresh window for contemporary Christian interpretation and church practice."

Dwight D Swanson
Senior Lecturer and Senior Research Fellow in Biblical Studies
Nazarene Theological College, Didsbury, Manchester

"Studies on John 15 have either focused on its background or on the notion of the believer's individualistic abiding in Christ. Dr. Kunene's work fills a gaping hole in the interpretation of the vine metaphor in John 15 by ably demonstrating its implications for the understanding of communal holiness, situated in the context of Trinitarian theology. His work also shows that the teaching on holiness or sanctification is not to be confined to John 17 as is often done by those within the holiness movement. This book is important not only for its academic grounding of its thesis but also for its relevance to the life of Christian congregations as they continue the pursuit of holiness that is demanded by their covenant relationship with God."

Prof. J. Ayodeji Adewuya,
Professor of New Testament
Pentecostal Theological Seminary, Cleveland, Tennessee

Communal Holiness in the Gospel of John

The Vine Metaphor as a Test Case with Lessons from African Hospitality and Trinitarian Theology

Musa Victor Mdabuleni Kunene

Langham

MONOGRAPHS

© 2012 by Musa Victor Mdabuleni Kunene

Published 2012 by Langham Monographs
an imprint of Langham Creative Projects

University of Manchester, Dissertation 2010

Langham Partnership
PO Box 296, Carlisle, Cumbria, CA3 9WZ
www.langham.org

ISBNs:
978-1-907713-23-1   print
978-1-907713-24-8   Mobi
978-1-907713-25-5   ePub

British Library Cataloguing in Publication Data

Kunene, Musa.
  Communal holiness in the Gospel of John : the vine metaphor
  as a test case with lessons from African hospitality and
  Trinitarian theology.
  1. Bible. N.T. John XV, 1-17--Criticism, interpretation,
  etc. 2. Metaphor in the Bible.
  I. Title
  226.5'06-dc23

  ISBN-13: 9781907713231

Cover and Book Design: projectluz.com

Contents

Dedication

To Sinenkhosi,
my daughter diagnosed with
Myasthenia Gravis
in the process of writing this work,
for resilience.

And to my parents (now late),
Mr Petros Magotolwane and Mrs Janet Jabhile Kunene,
Who taught me to persevere and, as dad would say,
"keep your [my] mind straight"

Acknowledgments

This thesis is a fruit of the communal efforts of many. I thank the faculty, staff, and students at Nazarene Theological College, for every support: especially the intercalations, encouragement, and prayers when my daughter was unwell. Special thanks to Dr. Kent E. Brower, my supervisor, for his patience, encouragement, guidance, and support throughout the writing of this thesis. He alone knows how far we have come. His quick and informative responses to my work kept me busy. I especially thank him for believing in me at times when I did not believe in myself. I am also grateful for the many expressions of hospitality he and his wife showed to my family, including the many hospital visits to my daughter.

I wish to thank my friends, Dr. Dwight Swanson, Dr. Ayodeji Adewuya, Dr. Tom Noble, and Dr. Jirair Tashjian, who have read parts of this work and offered constructive criticism. I owe special thanks to Rev. Dr. Deirdre Brower-Latz, for her painstaking proof-reading of the manuscript. I thank the Pastoral team and congregation of Longsight Church of the Nazarene for the love, care, generosity, and support they have given me and my family, including opportunities for ministry. I thank Mr. Bill Graham for proof-reading parts of the manuscript.

I am grateful to the organizations and individuals that have supported my studies: The Africa Region Church of the Nazarene, The Hynd Fellowship, The Souter Charitable Trust, Hiram F. Reynolds, Dr. Bruce Tailor, and the Margaret F. McLaren Memorial Scholarship. This thesis would not have been possible without these donors. I also wish to thank Dr. Arseny Ermakov, who kindly offered his IT skills. I thank my brother Mr. Themba

Kunene and his wife LaMahlalela for their support, especially sending Themba to Manchester at their expense at the height of Sinenkhosi's illness. Finally, I would like to thank my wife Prudence, our daughters Sinenkhosi, Phesheya, and Tiyandza, for their love, patience, and support throughout the writing of this thesis.

Abstract

This book contends that communal holiness is the central theme of the vine metaphor in John 15:1-17. It draws on background information on the vine and its metaphorical usage in the ANE, OT, and 2TP to illuminate the Johannine vine metaphor and to suggest understanding in light of the communal holiness of the covenant people of God. It juxtaposes the themes of holiness and corporateness pertinent to the covenant and attempts to reflect the covenant with Israel in relation to John's understanding of the people of God. The notion of covenant, which embraces reference to the people of God as vine/vineyard in OT and 2TP, underlies John's vine metaphor.

The book begins with an examination of recent studies in the vine metaphor showing how it has been interpreted in recent scholarship. It then elucidates some gaps that this research will close. Scholars concur that the background for the metaphor is OT and 2TP passages on Israel as YHWH's vine but seldom use these passages to illuminate interpretation of John 15:1-17. The book researches ANE viticulture to determine the context(s) of when the vine was used to refer to Israel in a covenant relationship with God. What becomes apparent is that the vine is used as a social and religious symbol with strong relational implications. Both in OT and 2TP the metaphor is used as a polemic against Israel's unhealthy vertical and horizontal relationships, by which she betrayed the covenant. When these relationships were healthy, the people sat "under the vine and fig tree."

In this historical context the Johannine vine metaphor receive fresh meaning and relevance for the people of God. In continuity with early

Jewish usage, motifs pertinent to a covenant relationship, such as unity, corporateness, mutuality, hospitality, and holiness will be explored. The book draws on this matrix of motifs to underpin ideas of communal holiness embedded in John's corporateness. The mutual abiding motif, central to John's vine metaphor, is postulated as John's redefinition of covenant relationship and explained in relation to John's corporate metaphors. John's interest in the Trinity opens a window into the perfect example of mutuality while anthropological insights from the Bantu illuminate mutuality from a current human perspective. Finally, the conclusion is drawn that John's emphasis is not individualistic holiness but "holiness-in-corporateness."

List of Abbreviations

Primary Sources

1 En.	*1 Enoch (Ethiopic Apocalypse)*
1-2 Macc	1-2 Maccabees
1QH	*Thanksgiving Hymns*
1QM	*War Scroll*
1QS	*Rule of the Community*
2 Bar.	*2 Baruch (Syriac Apocalypse)*
4QM	*War Scroll*
11QT	*Temple Scroll*
Ag. Ap.	*Against Apion*
A.J.	*Antiquitates Judaicae*
Ant.	*Jewish Antiquities*
Apoc. Mos.	*Apocalypse of Moses*
Apoc. Bar.	*Apocalypse of Baruch*
Apoc. Ab.	*Apocalypse of Abraham*
b. Šabb	*Bavli Šabbat*
CD	Cairo Genizah copy of the Damascus Document
DSS	Dead Sea Scrolls
GOJ	Gospel of John
Jub.	*Jubilees*
J.W.	*Jewish War*
L.A.B.	*Liber antiquitatum biblicarum* (Pseudo-Philo)
m. Sanh.	*Mishnah Sanhedrin*

NT	New Testament
Odes Sol.	Odes of Solomon
OT	Old Testament
Pss. Sol.	*Psalms of Solomon*
Sib. Or.	*Sibylline Oracles*
Sir	Sirach/Ecclesiasticus
T. Ab.	Testament of Abraham
T. Benj.	*Testament of Benjamin*
T. Gad	*Testament of Gad*
T. Iss.	*Testament of Issachar*
T. Jud.	*Testament of Judah*
T. Levi	*Testament of Levi*

Secondary Sources

AB	Anchor Bible
ABD	*Anchor Bible Dictionary.* Edited By D. N. Freedman. 6 vols. Berkeley, 1971-1980
AJ	*Asbury Journal*
AnBib	Analecta Biblica
ANET	*Ancient Near Eastern Texts Relating to the Old Testament.* Edited by J. B. Pritchard. 3d ed. Princeton, 1969
ANTC	Abingdon New Testament Commentaries
BAB	*Bulletin of Applied Botany*
BBR	*Bulletin of Biblical Research*
BJRL	*Bulletin of the John Rylands Library*
BTB	*Biblical Theology Bulletin*
CAUSSR	*Comptes rendues Academy of Science U. S. S. R.*
CBQ	*Catholic Biblical Quartely*
CBQMS	Catholic Biblical Quarterly Monograph Series
CHBP	Christian Holiness in Biblical Perspective
DUJ	*Durham University Journal*
EAAE	*Encyclopaedia of the Archaeology of Ancient Egypt*
EC	Epworth Commentaries
HTR	*Harvard Theological Review*

JBL	*Journal of Biblical Literature*
JSNT	*Journal for the Study of the New Testament*
JSNTSup	Journal for the Study of the New Testament: Supplement Series
JSOT	*Journal of Studies in the Old Testament*
JSOTSup	Journal of Studies in the Old Testament: Supplement Series
LSTS	Library of Second Temple Studies
NDBT	The New Dictionary of Biblical Theology
NICNT	New International Commentary on the New Testament
NIGTC	New International Greek Testament Commentary
NovT	*Novum Testamentum*
NovTSup	Supplements to Novum Testamentum
NSBT	New Studies in Biblical Theology
NTS	*New Testament Studies*
OTL	Old Testament Library
SBL	Society of Biblical Literature
SBLDS	Society of Biblical Literature Dissertation Series
SBLMS	Society of Biblical Literature Monograph Series
SBLSymS	Society of Biblical Literature Symposium Series
SP	Sacra pagina
TBST	The Bible Speaks Today
TDNT	*Theological Dictionary of the New Testament.* Edited by G. Kittel and G. Friedrich. Translated by G. W. Bromiley. 10 vols. Grand Rapids, 1964-1976.
TNCBC	The New Century Bible Commentary
TNTC	Tyndale New Testament Commentaries
TWFS	The Wine and Food Society
TynBul	*Tyndale Bulletin*
UBS	United Bible Societies
WBC	Word Bible Commentary
WTJ	*Wesleyan Theological Journal*
WUNT	*Wissenschaftliche Untersuchungen zum Neuen Testament*
ZNW	*Zeitschrift für die Neutestamentliche Wissenschaft und die Kunde der älteren Kirche*

Others

2TL	Second temple literature
2TP	Second temple period
APC	Africana Publishing Company
BBH	Baker Book House
BHPKC	Beacon Hill Press of Kansas City
BIP	Biblical Institute Press
DG	Downer's Grove
DLT	Darton, Longman & Todd
EBL	Evans Brothers Limited
EPIB	Editrice Pontificion Instituto Biblico
FF	Faber and Faber
GBP	Gordon and Breach Press
GHDC	George H. Doran Company
GR	Grand Rapids
HRW	Holt, Rinehart & Winston
IVP	InterVarsity Press
JKP	John Knox Press
JONLC	Jesus of Nazareth Lord and Christ
KC	Kansas City
NKP	New Kregel Publications
NTS	Nazarene Theological Seminary
NY	New York
RKP	Routledge and Kegan Paul Ltd
SAP	Sheffield Academic Press
SLMC	Sampson Low, Marston & Co. Ltd
SPP	Sheffield Phoenix Press
TPI	Trinity Press International
TR	Teacher of Righteousness
VSP	St. Vladimir Seminary Press
WBP	Word Books Publisher
WJK	Westminster John Knox

Foreword

It is only in the recent past that the discussion of holiness has moved from a minority interest of those chiefly concerned with personal piety to a wider discussion amongst biblical scholars. In theological discussions, holiness was too often relegated to the periphery, an issue concerned with "ritual purity." In popular discourse, it was readily linked with "works righteousness" or even legalism.

But a growing awareness of the social dynamics of holiness within community has changed this. The seminal work of Mary Douglas on the related topic of purity and the insights of Jacob Milgrom on Leviticus contributed to this renewed interest. Enhanced understanding of late second temple period Judaism, fuelled in part by attention to the Dead Sea Scrolls and the Qumran community, gave further impetus to a re-reading of the importance of holiness and social identity. Holiness was shown to be a live and controversial issue in the late second temple period all tied to the question of Jewish self-definition as the people of God. Israel's sense of call to be a holy people as articulated in Scripture was re-read by New Testament writers in terms of the identity of the new people of God. For them the people of God were all those called to be saints, the holy ones, by virtue of their identity with Jesus Messiah. The result is that holiness is now widely acknowledged as the central identity of the people of God throughout Scripture.

Several recent studies have explored the social or communal dimension of holiness in Scripture. These studies have resisted the individualism through which biblical texts have often been interpreted, particularly in popular piety, and have recovered something of the corporate dynamic of this identity as God's holy people. Detailed studies on specific scriptural passages have enhanced this picture. Kunene's work is an important contribution to this discussion.

Kunene examines the vine metaphor of John 15:1-17 which, he argues, is a call to communal holiness. He establishes his case by placing the vine metaphor against the backdrop of ancient viticulture. This allows Kunene to show the real-life context in which this metaphor would have been heard and read. Its textual background in the Ancient Near East, the Old Testament, and Second Temple Period literature is also explored. Several scholars acknowledge this literary background but do not make the intertextual connections to John 15 that Kunene hears. When combined with the viticulture backdrop, the metaphor takes on greater depth and color, enhancing the reading of John 15. The vine metaphor is used as a social and religious symbol with strong relational implications.

What makes Kunene's study particularly interesting is the unique way in which the standard tools of Western historical and social criticism are wielded by a scholar firmly rooted in African culture (in Kunene's case, Swazi culture). He hears and reads the text in ways that are illuminating to Western scholars who are, perhaps unconsciously, tied to the individualism of the Enlightenment paradigm. In his section on hospitality Kunene draws explicitly on the notion of hospitality in Swazi culture. This is different from the practice of hospitality often on display in Western cultures, where it is commercialized or restricted to family and friends. For Swazi culture, hospitality lies at the heart of the culture. Boundaries are porous; kinship is elastic and a person is really only a person in community. Kunene argues that all of this resonates with the Johannine language of mutual indwelling and participation in the life of the divine family. It is within this hospitable life of mutual indwelling that the holy community has its existence and from which it derives its mission. Kunene rounds out his discussion with a convincing intratextual examination of the communal aspects of holiness in the Fourth Gospel. This book is a worthy contribution to the discussion on communal holiness in Scripture.

Kent Brower Ph.D.
Vice Principal and Senior Research Fellow in Biblical Studies,
Nazarene Theological College

CHAPTER 1

Introduction

1.1 The Project

The purpose of this research is to show that communal holiness is at the heart of the vine metaphor in John 15:1-17.[1] Johannine holiness is portrayed as the participation of humankind in the mutual abiding of the Triune God,[2] which has strong implications for the ethical life of the new covenant people of God.[3] In 15:1-17 the disciples, who represent a

---

1. All references to the Gospel of John are hereafter cited with chapter and verse only. Thus, for example, 15:1-17 = John 15:1-17.

2. There is on-going scholarly debate on whether the GOJ is Trinitarian. Recently, David Crump, "Re-examining the Johannine Trinity: Perichoresis or deification," SJT 59 (2006): 395-412, argued that "the Johannine Spirit does not share in such mutual indwelling" and that John's pneumatology offers "no insight into the Spirit's eternal or essential place within the Godhead." However, others such as Jürgen Moltmann, *The Trinity and the Kingdom: The Doctrine of God* (London: SPCK, 1981), Royce Gordon Gruenler, *The Trinity in the Gospel of John: A Thematic Commentary on the Fourth Gospel* (GR: BBH, 1986), Cornelius Plantinga, Jr., "The Fourth Gospel as Trinitarian Source Then and Now," in *Biblical Hermeneutics in Historical Perspective* (Eds. Mark S. Burrows and Paul Rorem; GR: Eerdmans, 1991), 303-321, Clark D. Pinnock, *The Flame of Love* (DG: IVP, 1998), David S. Cunningham, *These Three are One: The Practice of Trinitarian Theology* (Oxford: Blackwell, 1998), Stephen Smalley, *John-Evangelist & Interpreter* (2nd ed.; Carlisle: Paternoster, 1998), Kent E. Brower, *Holiness in the Gospels* (KC: BHPKC, 2005), treat the Johannine Holy Spirit in a thoroughly Trinitarian context and with enormous practical implications. This writer concurs with the latter school of thought and will argue that the Johannine Spirit is an integral part of the Johannine Trinity and plays a significant role in the perichoretic reciprocation.

3. For a concise discussion of the disciples' community as the new covenant people of God see Rekha M. Chennattu, *Johannine Discipleship as a Covenant Relationship* (Peabody: Hendrickson, 2006), 41-49. Chennattu identifies Old Testament (OT) covenant motifs in

holy community and the new covenant people of God, are portrayed as participants in the mutual abiding of the Holy Triune God. They are holy insofar as they participate in the life of the divine family. They are called to reflect the life modelled by the divine family by rejecting all individualism and practising communal holiness expressed in hospitality and sharing of God-given resources.

Recent studies on the vine metaphor in 15:1-17 and on the GOJ as a whole show that Johannine metaphors, particularly the vine metaphor, have strong corporate aspects to their interpretation.[4] However, the call to communal holiness that is so integral to the vine metaphor has conspicuously been neglected. This research provides a fresh look at John's corporate metaphors, unearthing the holiness emphasis embedded in them. These metaphors are read in the light of the covenant theme in the OT and 2TP including its strong emphasis on holiness.

Taken at face value, the vine metaphor appears to have nothing to contribute to the subject of holiness. The term "holiness" does not appear in 15:1-17. However, the language the writer uses with reference to the disciples demonstrates that he regards them as the holy people of God: 1) the use of OT covenant motifs suggests that the disciples are in a covenant relationship with God. In the OT and 2TP the vine/vineyard is a covenant motif used with reference to the holy people of God (Ps 80:8-18; Isa 5:1-7; Jer 2:21; *Jub.* 1:16; *1 En.* 10.18, 19). 2) The description of the disciples as branches mutually indwelling Christ, the holy one of God (6:69), suggests that the disciples are holy in relation to Jesus' holiness. Jesus' holiness is a contagious power that cleanses and transforms those around him, bringing them into the new holy people of God. 3) The description of the disciples

---

the call stories in John 1: 35-51. She highlights the significance of the verb "abide," a key motif in 15:1-17, in the covenantal language of the OT (LXX). See also John Pryor, *John: Evangelist of the Covenant People: The Narratives and Themes of the Fourth Gospel* (London: DLT, 1992), 157; Charles H. Talbert, *Reading John: A Literary and Theological Commentary on the Fourth Gospel and the Johannine Epistles* (London: SPCK, 1992), 213, who identifies the domination of covenant structures of thought in 15:7-10.

4. See Craig S. Keener, *The Gospel of John: A Commentary* (2 vols.; Peabody: Hendrickson, 2003); Craig R. Koester, *Symbolism in the Fourth Gospel: Meaning, Mystery and Community* (Minneapolis: Fortress, 2003); Jey J. Kanagaraj, "Mysticism" in the *Gospel of John: An Inquiry into its Background* (JSNT 158; Sheffield: SAP, 1998). See the section on Johannine individualism and corporateness in this research.

as those who are already made clean by Christ's word (15:3) suggests moral purity[5] in line with receiving the words of Jesus (3:34; 6:63; 14:10). As early as the first chapter they believe in the "Word" of God and are identified as "children of God" (1:12).[6] 4) The presentation is of the disciples as fruit-bearing branches. Fruit-bearing is understood in relation to holiness in early Judaism.[7]

A close examination of the verb "sanctify" in its context, used elsewhere (17:17, 19) with reference to Jesus' disciples, shows that the GOJ treats the holiness of the disciples' community as a significant theme closely related to the holiness of God.[8] This thesis, therefore, argues that John's vine metaphor is a picture of the renewed people of God centered in Jesus and is an appeal to the people of God to live in holiness and bear fruits befitting their new status. Holiness is an obligation of the people of God because God is holy.

However, a common feature in contemporary scholarship is that it makes no connection between the intimacy described by mutual indwelling and the holiness of the people of God. In this research we draw this connection and further elaborate it by highlighting its connection to John's Trinitarian theology. We show how John's Trinitarian hospitality functions at different levels, emphasizing how the hospitality modelled by the divine family can be reflected by the new people of God. We further elucidate hospitality by showing how it works within the context of the African Bantu communities. The ideas of communality, kinship, and ubuntu, which are pertinent to Bantu culture and tradition, though not idealized, are postulated as human models. The underlying thought is that John 15:1-17 clearly describes

---

5. On a literal level the language of cleansing used here refers to the pruning of the vine, but on a symbolic level it means that the disciples have been purified from sin by his word. It harks back to the symbolic washing of the disciples in 13:10.

6. See John Bogart, *Orthodox and Heretical Perfectionism in the Johannine Community as Evident in the First Epistle of John* (Missoula: Scholars, 1977), 62-91 for an in-depth discussion of the disciples' community as believers and children of God and what the implications of that are.

7. See our discussion of the motif of fruit-bearing in chapter 5.

8. Richard Bauckham, "The Holiness of Jesus and His Disciples in the Gospel of John," in *Holiness and Ecclesiology in the New Testament* (ed. Kent E. Brower and Andy Johnson; GR: Eerdmans, 2007), 95 (hereafter called HENT). Also, according to 6:69 the disciples have believed and have known Jesus to be "the holy One of God" and they are determined to follow him at all costs.

the divine-human intimacy and its implications for the ethical life of the people of God.

1.2 Problems and Necessity of Research

Five problems are identifiable in current scholarship on the vine metaphor.

First, the wealth of background knowledge on the vine in ancient Near Eastern (ANE)[9] viticulture and religion has not been adequately considered. As a result the metaphor is often removed from reality and fails to invite change in its hearers. If patterns of viticulture were properly investigated and allowed to illumine our understanding of the metaphor, the metaphor may retain its initial power to call readers into action. The works of Goodenough, Seltan, and the recent works of McGovern and Unwin are helpful in providing historical background.[10] However, few of the scholars use this background when interpreting the Johannine vine metaphor. Where attempts are made,[11] some historical details are lacking and there is no effort to invite response from readers.

Second, although there is a scholarly consensus on the importance of the OT vine image for interpreting 15:1-17 there has been no significant effort to investigate the relevant texts or the ANE religious system as the milieu of those texts.[12] The relevant OT texts are cited without attempts

---

9. In this research ANE designates the region from the Aegean coast of Turkey to central Iran and from Northern Anatolia to the Red Sea, including Egypt. Nevertheless our primary interest is the Bible lands whose culture and influence extended over shifting zones in different periods.

10. Erwin R. Goodenough, *Jewish Symbolism in the Greco-Roman Period* (13 vols.; NY: Pantheon, 1956); Charles Seltan, *Wine in the Ancient World* (London: RKP, 1957); Patrick E. McGovern, *Ancient Wine: The Search for the Origins of Viticulture* (Princeton: Princeton University Press, 2003); Tim Unwin, *Wine and the vine: An Historical Geography of Viticulture and the Wine Trade* (London: Routledge, 2003).

11. See Keener, *Gospel.*

12. See Krijn van der Jagt, *Anthropological Approaches to the Interpretation of the Bible* (NY: UBS, 2002), 21, who rightly suggests that the religious system of the ANE is the most powerful reading scenario for the OT. See also Adrian Curtis, ed., *Oxford Bible Atlas* (4th ed.; Oxford: Oxford University Press, 2007), 37, who states that "The story of Israel and of Judah and of the beginnings of Christianity, as recounted in the Bible, is set in the ancient Near East. . . ."

to show how they impact on the interpretation of John's vine metaphor. Thus it is not clear how the vine image in John relates to the vine image in the OT and 2TP and whether lessons can be learned from the negative portrayal of the vine in the OT and 2TP. Present scholarship does not show how scripture takes readers from the vine that bears injustice and cries of pain to the true vine that bears justice and right living (Isa 5:7; John 15:1).

Third, interpretation of the vine metaphor as an appeal for the communal holiness of the people of God as they live in union with the holy God through the holy One of God remains fertile ground for research. Although some scholars identify the vine as a covenant metaphor,[13] the holiness issue that is so pertinent to a covenant relationship with God has been neglected. John 15:1-17 contains important motifs that the writer uses in relation to the holiness of the disciples: branches, mutual abiding, fruit-bearing, pruning, cleansing, and love. No scholarly work identifies these motifs as John's chosen language of referring to the holiness of the new people of God.

Fourth, although mutual abiding is properly identified as the main theme of John's vine metaphor,[14] scholars do not interpret it within the context of Trinitarian theology. As a result they miss the implications for shared life suggested by the metaphor's mutuality. Mutual abiding suggests the participation of one in another and has significant implications for hospitality and caring for the poor and marginalized of society. The theme of hospitality that is illustrated by the image of mutual abiding is introduced in the prologue and runs through the Gospel as Jesus is hospitably received by some and rejected by others. The failure to employ the Trinity as an important interpretative context for the metaphor equals the failure to see in the metaphor an emphasis upon hospitality and a polemic against injustice.

Fifth, current scholarship does not engage with relevant inter/intratexts of the key motifs of 15:1-17. When interpreting the metaphor scholars seldom allow scripture to interpret scripture; as a result they do not show

---

13. See especially Chennattu, *Discipleship.*

14. Kanagaraj, "'Mysticism'"; J. Massyngbaerde Ford, *Redeemer, Friend, Mother: Salvation in Antiquity and in the Gospel of John* (Minneapolis: Fortress, 1997), 147-167.

how the various aspects cohere and fit into the overall plot of the Gospel.[15] An inter/intratextual approach to the text of 15:1-17 will, therefore, show that themes addressed in John's vine metaphor are coherent with other themes raised in the Gospel and they all together contribute to the purpose of John.

1.3 Methodology

A brief statement of methodology will clarify how this research will achieve its aims. At least three methodologies will be juxtaposed.

First, the thesis follows a historical-cultural approach to the Johannine text. It is "historical" not in the sense of concern for historical accuracy or recourse to details of composition such as authorship, source, and dating. Rather, the Johannine vine metaphor is interpreted in the light of its historical cultural background in the Mediterranean world where it was first heard. Like other Johannine images (e.g. water and sheep/shepherd) the vine imagery is alive and developed over time in Jewish culture and usage. Indeed "the fourth evangelist and his readers were also surrounded in their day by a Mediterranean world in which syncretistic, pagan religions, themselves influenced by the orient, flourished."[16] It is in this religious culture where the vine metaphor was particularly active in various ways.

To some extent we follow Keener, who interprets the GOJ in the light of its socio-historical context, which he defines as the eastern Mediterranean cultural, social, political, religious, and ancient literary settings in which the GOJ would have been originally read. Keener asks historical questions in order to reconstruct John's text in keeping with his ideal audience in the ancient Mediterranean context. He maintains that "the more familiar a reader [is] with the circumstances of a document or speech, the better

---

15. See R. Alan Culpepper, *Anatomy of the Fourth Gospel: A Study in Literary Design* (Philadelphia: Fortress, 1983), 79-98; Fernando F. Segovia, "The Journeys of the Word of God: A Reading of the Plot of the Fourth Gospel," *Semeia* 53 (1991): 23-54.

16. Smalley, *John*, 48.

the reader [will] comprehend it."[17] It is in the "supply of specific social data" that Keener makes his "contributions of the longest range value."[18] For this he must be given credit. However, this thesis differs in two distinct ways: 1) it does not include specific historical details (i.e. date, authorship and composition) that the historical critical method includes. Also, although occasionally referencing cultural traditions outside 2TP Judaism our scholarly contribution draws heavily upon 2TP Judaism. 2) While offering a similar contribution to scholarship in regards to specific cultural data, we go beyond Keener by answering the question that Keener does not address: so what?[19] Like Keener, however, this thesis treats the GOJ as a coherent whole.

The importance of reading the text in the light of the cultures within which it developed is acknowledged by other scholars. Indeed it is necessary to read the text in conversation with the demands of its own world.[20] Kysar writes about the "secularity" of John's metaphors in that "they speak of the mundane, daily reality of their hearers, lifting up the most common activity or occurrence."[21] The vine metaphor and its images "draw on common realities of the first century world and use ordinary commonsense knowledge as the occasion for new meaning."[22] The implied reader, a first century reader with specific cultural assumptions, can identify with the metaphor and probably attach to it a culturally nuanced meaning.

Second, we follow the narrative critical approach. According to Smalley, "narrative criticism adopts a synchronic stance, and treats the material concerned as a unified whole."[23] Smalley stresses the need to distinguish narrative criticism from redaction criticism and composition criticism. While redaction criticism and composition criticism are preoccupied with the

---

17. Keener, I:xxvi.

18. Keener, I:xxv.

19. Nicholas. T. Wright, *Jesus and the Victory of God* (London: SPCK, 1996), 117.

20. Gail R. O'Day, "Toward a Narrative-Critical Study of John," Interpretation 4 (1995): 344.

21. Robert Kysar, "Johannine Metaphor – Meaning and Function: A Literary Case Study of John 10:1-8," Semeia 53 (1991): 100.

22. Kysar, "Johannine Metaphor," 101.

23. Smalley, *John*, 121.

theological perspective of the writer, narrative criticism focuses on the story and the response of its readers, thus embracing reader-response criticism.[24] It is not in the interest of this thesis to discuss the process of redaction and accretion that resulted in the present text of the Gospel. Rather, we take the GOJ synchronically as a coherent and unified whole, a product of creation and a piece of literature in its own right. The narrative world of the text, its characters, values, norms, conflicts, and events which constitute the plot of 15:1-17 are considered key to the meaning of John's vine metaphor. We take Kysar's suggestion seriously that the text itself creates a new world and has the power "to invoke and summon a new reality and to invite the reader to a new way of seeing the world."[25] The text represents a threshold into a new dimension and an introduction into a new world. Thus by reading the text as a whole and making the mental moves the text calls its reader to, we may see the world in a new way.

Still within the parameters of narrative criticism, we will engage in reader-response criticism and in discerning intertextuality.[26] The reader takes an active part in the construction of the meaning of the text; meaning is a result of a negotiation between the text and the reader.[27] The reader is competent; able to interact with the text and in the process recognize clues to the reading encoded in the text.[28] In the process of interacting with the text the levels of inter/intratextuality in the text are discerned, and bring a fresh understanding to the metaphor. Two levels of intratextuality, the GOJ and the letters of John, illuminate the themes of the vine metaphor and

---

24. Smalley, *John*, 122.

25. Kysar, "Johannine Metaphor," 81-111, emphasizes the importance of reader-response criticism whereby the reader reads the text with care and sensitivity and allows himself or herself to become vulnerable to influence, where the text is experienced more as an event than an object.

26. Elizabeth Struthers Malbon, "Ending at the Beginning: A Response," Semeia 52 (1990): 177-178. See also George J. Brooke, *The Dead Sea Scrolls and the New Testament* (London: SPCK, 2005), 72-73, who gives an overview of the origins and development of intertextuality and suggests that "all texts present their meanings only in as much as they are in dialogue, primarily with other texts."

27. Segovia, "Journey(s)," 24.

28. See Richard A. Burridge, "Who writes, why, and for whom?," in *The Written Gospel.* (eds. Markus Bockmuehl and Donald A. Hagner; Cambridge: Cambridge University Press, 2005), 109.

show how the metaphor fits into the whole plot of the Gospel. Discerning intertextuality will enable us to place the metaphor into the larger plan of redemptive history by relating it to the OT, NT, and other 2TP Jewish literature. It is here that we will make a significant contribution to scholarship.

Third, we will draw upon African[29] anthropological insights to illuminate the interpretation of the vine metaphor. The *Bantu* (Bantfu)[30] share many features in common with ancient Israelite culture, including a corporate view of human existence, emphasis in mutual dependence/interdependence, and a strong concept of kinship. We shall show that these features are embedded in the hospitality implied by the mutuality in the Johannine vine metaphor. The question of whether "encounter with a non-Western culture, especially one that reminds us of biblical times, [can] really help us understand the Bible" is critical.[31] Following Evans-Prichard,[32] who used the OT to explain some African beliefs and ritual customs, Lang argues that African society can also illuminate biblical studies.[33] After reviewing anthropologists who engage in participation observation and comparative ethnography in various cultures, Lang sees a potential for anthropology to "widen horizons for biblical scholars."[34] Our use of comparative ethnography in this thesis is a "widening of horizons" for Johannine studies. While this is not our primary methodology, it is another area where a significant contribution to Johannine research is made.

---

29. The researcher is a Swazi scholar. Examples in this research will reflect how the concept of ubuntu works among the Swazi.

30. Bantu, literally "human/person," is a linguistic label derived from the root *ntu*, "human/person," and the plural prefix, *ba*. The proper SiSwati word is Bantfu, in which case the root source is *ntfu*. There are over 400 Bantu languages and many dialects, but their structure is sufficiently characteristic and distinctive to postulate a common origin.

31. Bernhard Lang, "Introduction: Anthropology as a new model for Biblical Studies," in *Anthropological Approaches to the Old Testament* (ed. Bernhard Lang; London: SPCK, 1985), 1.

32. E. Evans-Pritchard, *Nuer Religion* (Oxford: Oxford University Press, 1956).

33. Lang, "Anthropology," 7.

34. Lang, "Anthropology," 17.

1.4 Scope and Limitation of Research

The focus of this research is communal holiness, a neglected aspect of 15:1-17. Other modern terms such as social justice, racial discrimination, and economic imbalance will be used to refer or allude to communal holiness or absence thereof. The research, however, is not a general study of holiness either in the NT or the Johannine corpus but is a narrative-critical reading of 15:1-17. The primary scope of the investigation is 15:1-17 and other texts are referred to as they are considered for background and inter/intratextuality. Where we use comparative ethnography, our interest is limited to three specific aspects of Swazi culture: community, kinship, and *ubuntu* (buntfu).[35] Importantly, this research is not a word study of "vine" or a study of the vine in general. Although including background information on viticulture, the focus is metaphorical usage of the vine particularly within the context of 2TJ and the Johannine community at the end of the first century C.E. Uses of the vine metaphor in other contexts are referred to as they add to clarity.

1.5 Definition of Terms

1.5.1 Relational Holiness

In this research relational holiness is perceived as the holiness that God's people possess by virtue of their covenant relationship with the holy God through the Holy One of God. Like anything belonging to God they are holy since they belong to God as his new covenant people. It is this right relationship of belonging-ness that confers on the people of God the status of the holy; "in essence, relational holiness is based on belonging-ness."[36] In this research relational holiness is primarily used in its basic sense of the believers' holiness by virtue of their right relationship with the holy God through Jesus Christ. A right relationship with God, however, necessitates a right relationship with humankind in imitation of

---

35. See Charles G. Haws, "Suffering, hope and forgiveness: the ubuntu theology of Desmond Tutu," *SJT* 62 (2009): 478, who defines *ubuntu* as "the understanding that all human life is interconnected according to the reconciling love of God."

36. J. Ayodeji Adewuya, *Holiness and Community in 2 Cor 6:14-7:1: Paul's View of Communal Holiness in the Corinthian Correspondence* (NY: Peter Lang, 2003), 9.

God. According to Petersen, "the holy people of God are then called to live in a way that demonstrates the reality of their relationship with God and with one another."[37] Therefore, in relational holiness the locus is the believer's relationship with God and the degree to which that relationship affects the believers' relationship with each other and with other people. This is where relational holiness overlaps with communal holiness.

1.5.2 Communal Holiness

In this thesis communal holiness is envisaged as the holiness which characterize God's people as they live not only individually but corporately as a community of faith. It embraces a corporate view of life and emphasizes the responsibility of one believer to another or to others. It is unfortunate that most definitions for holiness narrow its focus to individual holiness. Communal holiness calls for an embrace of and participation in the truth that "God is not just making individuals holy . . . but making a people holy."[38] Like relational holiness it emphasizes belonging-ness but not so much to God as to one another as the corporate people of God. It consists in taking responsibility and accountability for each other including empathy and acting to meet the physical needs of other members of the corporate family. Indeed, "it is the holiness which believers collectively manifest in every sphere of life rather than an inward-looking individualistic, and, quite often, self-centered holiness."[39] It is others-centered and embraces participation in one another's lives so that when one has a problem "we have a problem" rather than "he/she has a problem." It excludes every attempt by Christians to be "holy solitaries." Communal holiness is akin to what John Wesley described as social holiness: "the gospel of Christ knows no religion, but social; no holiness, but social holiness."[40] It is best modelled by the life of the divine family, the Father, Son, and Spirit and is possible when the human community shares the life of the divine community in mutual indwelling.

---

37. D. G. Petersen, "Holiness," *TNDBT*, 544-550.

38. Adewuya, *Holiness and Community*, 9.

39. Adewuya, *Holiness and Community*, 10.

40. John Wesley, *The Poetical Works of John & Charles Wesley* (13 vols.; Collected and arranged by G. Osborne; London: Parternoster-Row, 1868), 1:xxii.

1.6 Working Assumptions

1.6.1 The Trinity as the Model of Holiness in the GOJ

Within this research a primary interpretative context is the assumption that the Trinity is the ruling motif in John's theology. "John's theology involves God in all his fullness, as Father, Son and Spirit; it is Trinitarian in character, if not yet in definition."[41] Echoing this, Brower suggests that the Trinity is the ruling motif in John's theology and any studies in John whether Christology, Pneumatology, or ecclesiology must begin from there.[42] It is not possible to address adequately the theme of communal holiness in John outside the Trinitarian model. The Trinitarian approach is an important backdrop for understanding Christian holiness as corporate and as participation in the perichoretic reciprocation of the divine family.

1.6.2 Johannine Discipleship as Covenant Relationship

Another interpretative context is John's portrayal of discipleship as a covenant relationship with God through Jesus, the covenant Lord. The writer's use of OT covenant motifs clearly puts the new people of God in the position of covenant partners akin to Israel in the OT, suggesting an understanding of the holy people of God as existing in a covenant relationship with God.[43] As demonstrated, this covenant relationship context functions as the basis for the disciples' relational holiness. They are the true eschatological people of God gathered by their covenant Lord. From the early chapters of the Gospel where Christ is portrayed as creator of a new community and descending-ascending revealer, covenant language dominates the Gospel.

---

41. Smalley, *John*, 271.
42. Brower, *Gospels*, 142.
43. Pryor, *John*; Chennattu, *Discipleship*.

1.7. Outline

The research opens with a survey of literature on the vine metaphor from scholars of the OT, 2TP, and NT. While the scholars selected make significant contribution, it is postulated that they do not see the importance of communal holiness in vine metaphorical speech. Although scholars cite the OT texts where the vine metaphor is used, they seldom interpret these texts. As a result they miss the connection between John's use of the metaphor and its usage in the OT and 2TP to describe divine-human and human-human relationships. Also conspicuously missing is the backdrop of the notion of "sitting under the vine and fig tree,"[44] which holds clues for interpreting the metaphor as a device for peace with God and peace with fellow humankind. We have attempted to close these scholarly gaps by reading the metaphor against this backdrop in the OT and 2TP.

In chapter 3 we investigate viticulture and the vine metaphor in the ANE and the OT. Following Jagt,[45] who suggests the religious system of the ANE as the context for understanding the OT, we explore the extent to which ANE viticulture influenced OT vine language. Was viticulture practiced in the ANE? If so, is there possible connection between viticulture and vine metaphorical language in the ANE and the vine metaphor in the OT? The underlying objective is to gain insights into a culture that gave birth to a plethora of vine speech in the OT, both metaphorical and regular. This objective is met by the discovery of the overwhelming importance of viticulture and vine metaphorical language in the ANE, particularly in matters of religion. It is this backcloth of the vine in the ANE that then becomes useful for interpreting the vine metaphor in the OT, 2TP, and the NT in this research. The discovery made in this thesis of the important place of viticulture and vine metaphorical speech in ANE religion provides clues for understanding the voluminous vine language in the Bible.

---

44. See Walter Brueggemann, "'Vine and Fig Tree': A Case Study in Imagination and Criticism," *CBQ* 43 (1981): 188-204. Cf. Mic 4:1-5; 1 Kings 4:25; Zech 3:10; 1 Macc 12:14.

45. Jagt, *Anthropological Approaches.*

Chapter 4 investigates the vine metaphor in 2TP Jewish literature with the purpose of finding how the Jews used the metaphor in this period. The concern here is determining if the trajectories of divine-human and human-human relationships still persist as interpretations of the vine metaphor. That is, does the use of the vine metaphor in the ANE and OT as a theo-social device subsist in the 2TP? The findings of this chapter show that this is indeed so. 2TP literature supports the use of tree metaphors including the vine for the covenant people of God. The social implications of a right relationship with God are also prioritized. As a result where the people fail in their covenant relationship with God the vine is represented as spoiled. The notion of "sitting under the vine and fig tree" is postulated as the vine metaphor par excellence since it combines social, political, economic, and religious aspects of the lives of the people of God.

Chapter 5 is an exegesis of John's vine metaphor (15:1-17). Here each of the images of the metaphor is interpreted in the light of the established cultural background and the context of John in the late first century C.E. Each image is also given a further dimension, bridging the gap to the twenty-first century. At the fore here is the intra/intertextual links in keeping with the narrative-critical method. The conclusion is reached that John's vine metaphor, including its images, centers on the work of God in creating a new people in Christ as well as God's call to his new people to participate in God and his purposes for the world. The new people of God are made clean by the words of Christ; they are called upon to perceive life corporately and share in the social needs of others; they are to live in selfless and outward looking love.

Chapter 6 is an in-depth study of the theme of mutual abiding that is at the center of the Johannine vine metaphor. That the theme of abiding is central to John's vine metaphor is rightly advanced by some Johannine scholars.[46] Here we build on Kanagaraj's work while differing from him in that we are not interested in the background of mutual abiding; we are interested in how the motif was possibly interpreted and how its interpretation might make sense to a twenty-first century reader. We identify the

---

46. See, especially, Kanagaraj, "'Mysticism'"; Ford, *Redeemer*.

three levels of mutual abiding in the text and then interpret the motif in relation to other new covenant motifs in John, particularly the new temple motif introduced early in the Gospel (1:14; 2:14-21). We also relate to motif to its early interpretation in its intertexts in OT, NT, and 2TP Jewish literature.

Chapter 7 advances suggestions for mutual coinherence and shared life raised in chapter 6. Here we focus on the giving of room and sharing of space in mutual abiding, emphasizing hospitality as modelled by the divine family. Still upholding the centrality of mutual abiding we treat the vine metaphor as a climax anticipated by the hospitality language throughout the GOJ. To illuminate our emphasis on hospitality we draw upon anthropological insights from the Swazi, a *Bantu* tribe in Africa with a culture similar to ancient Jewish culture. Like any human culture, however, Swazi hospitality can only be an imperfect model. Thus having drawn upon insights from the Swazi we discuss the perfect model of the Trinity and show how in the GOJ Trinitarian hospitality is extended to humankind, to believers and to lapsers. The chapter ends with an application where we show how the new covenant people of God can possibly reflect the perfect hospitality of the Trinity.

Chapter 8 is an argument for holiness in John's corporate theology. First, we build upon the arguments advanced by others, such as Smalley[47] and Rensberger,[48] that John's theology is corporate. Second, we argue that John's theology of holiness cannot be separated from his theology of corporateness—it is holiness in corporateness. Our case for holiness in John's theology is based upon recent contributions by Brower and Bauckham[49] who argue that the GOJ does refer to the holiness of the disciples in relation to that of the Trinity. The chapter ends with a postulation of aspects of holiness in John using motifs already raised in the thesis. This is another area where this thesis makes a contribution to Johannine studies.

---

47. Stephen S. Smalley, "Diversity and Development in John," NTS 17 (1971): 276-292.
48. David Rensberger, *Johannine Faith and Liberating Community* (Philadelphia: Westminster, 1988).
49. Brower, *Gospels*, 63-81; Bauckham, "*Holiness*," 95-113.

1.8 Preliminary Conclusion

Proper interpretation of the Johannine vine metaphor must consider at least three important factors: first, the historical-cultural background in which the metaphor developed and was initially used; second, intertextuality of the metaphor including how it fits within the complete work of the Gospel; third, how the metaphor can speak to the contemporary reader. It is as we consider these factors that we become aware of the need for a new interpretation of the metaphor in relation to the theme of holiness in John. While we stand on the shoulders of others in many aspects of this thesis, the contribution we make to Johannine studies is very significant.

CHAPTER 2

The Vine Metaphor in Recent Scholarship

2.1 Introduction

Scholarly research on the Johannine vine metaphor has been meagre of late. This is true in spite of a surging interest in the GOJ.[1] Such interest has led to numerous investigations into aspects of the Gospel such as Christology and the historical situation of the Johannine community. Scholars who have attempted to study the metaphor rarely reconcile it with its background in the OT and 2TP. The result of this is that scholars miss the real-life circumstances and call of people to action as intended by those who first used it, such as OT Prophets. Brueggemann and Chaney provide significant information on OT use of the metaphor, which we

---

1. David Asonye Ihenacho, *The Community of Eternal Life: The Study of the Meaning of Life for the Johannine Community* (Lanham: University Press of America, 2001); Tricia Gates Brown, *Spirit in the Writings of John: Johannine Pneumatology in Social-scientific Perspective* (ed. Stanley Porter; JSNTSup. 253; London: T&T Clarke, 2003); Armand J. Joe Gagne Jr., *The Testimony of the Fourth Evangelist to the Johannine Community: We Know His Witness is True* (Crewe: Trafford, 2004); Alexander S. Jensen, *John's Gospel as Witness: The Development of the Early Christian Language of Faith* (Aldershot: Ashgate, 2004); Chennattu, *Discipleship*; Richard Bauckham, *The Testimony of the Beloved Disciple: Narrative, History, and Theology in the Gospel of John* (GR: Baker Academic, 2007); Edward W. Klink III, *The Sheep of the Fold: The Audience and Origin of the Gospel of John* (Cambridge: Cambridge University Press, 2007); Emmanuel O. Tukasi, *Determinism and Petitionary Prayer in John and the Dead Sea Scrolls: An Ideological Reading of John and the Rule of the Community* (1QS) (ed. L. Grabbe; London: T&T Clarke, 2008).

use as a source for interpreting the vine metaphor in John. Seven other scholars, working in the last three decades, are selected to represent those who worked the Johannine vine metaphor. The scholars selected are in no particular chronological order. They all make a contribution to this research either by the content of their discussion or their approach to the topic.

2.2 The Vine Metaphor in the Old Testament

In his article, "Vine and Fig Tree,"[2] Brueggemann juxtaposes Mic 4:4 and 1 Kings 4:25, interpreting the prophetic material within its socio-political context in the eighth century B.C.E. According to Brueggemann, the prophets' words "every man under his vine and under his fig tree," inaugurates "a new world of social possibility."[3] The metaphor is designed to decry the present social order and at the same time lead Israel to an alternative reality. Reading the vine metaphor in light of the prophetic tradition (Jer 1:10), Brueggemann understands it to describe "a transformed public policy and a transformed human consciousness."[4]

For Brueggemann, Mic 4:1-5 reflects a personal agrarian dream of Israel to be secure enough to produce and enjoy produce unmolested—either by lawlessness or by usurpation of the state due to its social policy of consumerism and its public policy of war. He puts the metaphor in the socio-historical setting of Micah where the royal economy practiced a surplus-value (cf. Mic 2:1-5; 3:1-3). This politics of war and the consumerism of the royal household made the people (peasants) in Micah's time live in fear and so look forward to a dream time when they will "dwell in safety" and when there will be "peace on all sides."[5]

While Brueggemann reads the Micah passage as positive and promissory, his reading of 1 Kings 4:25 is negative and critical. Solomon's

---

2. Brueggemann, "Vine," 188-204.

3. Brueggemann, "Vine," 189.

4. Brueggemann, "Vine," 192.

5. Brueggemann concludes that both passages draw on the "tradition of blessing" in that they both appeal to the promise of Lev. 26:5-6, where the blessing is "peace on all sides" and "dwell in safety."

achievement of peace by his public policy of war made him a threat to the peace and safety of others and his state policy left them unsure and terrified. In 1 Kings Brueggemann sees "criticism couched in subtle and high irony, subtle enough to escape the vigilant censors and high enough not to be missed by those who hold other visions."[6] He identifies irony in three different points: first, "they ate and drank and were happy" (v. 20), which suggests a high standard of living and a degree of consumerism. Those who benefited were the minority of royalty and first class citizens, which implies that others paid the price, thus linking affluence and security to oppression and domination. Second, the uncritical realized eschatology, "peace on all sides" (v. 24), suggests that we ask: Who benefits? Who eats well? Who has peace? Third, the statement about "vines and fig trees" (v. 25) is placed in the utterly incongruous context of Solomon's arms and oppression. The force of the irony is in the state's practice of greed, usurpation and exploitation, all of which impinge on personal well-being.[7]

According to Brueggemann, "Micah 4:1-4 shows deep, irrevocable opposition between swords and spears on the one hand, and vines and fig trees on the other."[8] For Micah swords and spears do not cohabit with vines and fig trees. Thus the poem (Mic 4:1-5) must be read as "an example of imaginative use of concrete and anticipatory metaphor to evoke an alternative world in the consciousness of Israel."[9] Israel is invited to imagine a better future that is beyond human engineering, one that God alone can give. The imagined future will be characterized by residence and presence of YHWH (vv. 1-2), and the supremacy of his word and will (vv. 3-4), which for Brueggemann is "a new ordering in heaven that makes possible a new arrangement on earth."[10] This new arrangement suggests a new society, a disarmed society that will reject consumerism and will embrace peace and welfare for all.

---

6. Brueggemann, "Vine," 196.

7. Brueggemann, "Vine," 198.

8. Brueggemann, "Vine," 197.

9. Brueggemann, "Vine," 189.

10. Brueggemann, "Vine," 191.

Brueggemann's rendering of the vine metaphor here is important. First, the hallmark of his interpretation is the centrality of divine-human and human-human relationships. Regarding the divine-human aspect there is the dethronement of other gods and the enthronement of YHWH, which, when properly articulated, occasions proper human-human relations. On the human-human side there is the call to the wealthy and powerful to treat the poor and powerless with compassion, hospitality, and dignity. The metaphor speaks to governments and individuals who thrive on policies and systems that oppress and dominate the weak and voiceless. Such systems hold some as royal and first class citizens while others are second class citizens subject to slave-labor policies.

Second, the metaphor supports a new arrangement on earth with a new society/community where the peace and welfare of everyone is prioritized. This suggests a link with other renderings of the vine metaphor in the OT and NT, especially including that of 15:1-17. Such a rendering of the metaphor carries strong covenant nuances. The idea of a peaceful community also carries the notion of corporateness and solidarity which are implied elsewhere where the vine metaphor is used (Isa 5:1-7; Zech 3:10; John 15:1-8). The peace in view embraces primarily the meeting of social needs and is not personal or individualistic but is shared in a deep sense of community. This realization of peace, blessing, and safety in abundance is the most common Jewish understanding of the vine imagery in the 2TP (cf. *1 En.* 10:18-19; *Jub.* 13:6; 4 QM 1:3-5).

Third, Brueggemann's realization that the peace and welfare so central to the vine metaphor can only come from God is significant. It is only the enthronement of YHWH that will bring about an alternative social system. This means that the new people of God depend entirely upon God for life and vitality. Also strongly connected to the enthronement of YHWH is walking according to Torah (1:5), which is an important theme in the NT where the metaphor is used.[11]

Chaney's article[12] on Isa 5:1-7 is a social-scientific study of the vine metaphor in respect to the political economy in Isaiah's time. Chaney

---

11. See 15:7, 10, 12-17.

12. Marvin Chaney, "Whose Sour Grapes? The Addressees of Isa 5:1-7 in the Light of

compares the sour grapes of Isa 5:1-7 to the aristocracy and the ruling dynastic houses of Judah and Israel instead of the general populations of Jerusalem, Judah and Israel. Reading the parable in light of the rapid agricultural intensification[13] of Judah and Israel in the 8th century B.C.E., Chaney argues that the parable cannot refer to artefacts and activities that were routine in Israel and Judah.[14] Instead, he claims that the audience in mind cannot be the masses since these were victims of viticultural injury. For him the indictment of guilt in the parable refers to aristocratic and urban élite who, as absentee landlords, engaged in international trade and pressed for regional specialization of agriculture and land consolidation. This impoverished many peasant farmers and left them with no alternative but survival loans at high interest rates.[15]

Chaney, therefore, concludes that while vineyards were proud symbols of economic progress and prosperity to the élite, they did not symbolize this to the peasants whose land had been expropriated and combined as sites for these new vineyards. Thus he argues that "vineyard" was not a neutral word.

Chaney's argument that the parable refers only to royal or élite figures can be misleading. Although the propensity towards aristocrats is sometimes clear where the vine metaphor is used in the OT, in most cases the aristocrats-as-leaders are representative of the whole nation of Israel.[16] There is a sense in the prophets in which the vineyard is the people of God who are in many ways caused to suffer. The aristocrats who cause the people to suffer are sometimes accused of devouring or ruining the vineyard and having grazed the vineyard bare (Isa 3:14). In this case the aristocrats

---

Political Economy," Semeia 87 (1999): 105-122.

13. The eighth century B.C.E. saw an increase in international trade, in which the leaders imported luxury goods and military material. These imports were paid for by exports of wine, which meant that the peasant farmers had to work harder to produce more wine. However, the beneficiaries of this agricultural intensification were not the peasant majority but the élite minority.

14. Chaney, "Sour Grapes?," 106.

15. Chaney, "Sour Grapes?," 107.

16. Cf. Ps 80:8-18 where the nation of Israel is elevated to the position of "son of man" and "vine" or "stock" is used synonymously. These are interpreted as referring to the king or kingdom. The vine of Ps. 80:8 brought out of Egypt is the whole nation.

cannot be the vineyard. The metaphor is used to describe the whole life of the people of God including their religious, socio-political, as well as socio-economic life.

Two aspects of Chaney's essay are helpful: First, his social-scientific approach led him to a wealth of background information on the use of the metaphor by the prophets who coined it. His essay is an important window into the circumstances that gave rise to the metaphor, especially its negative use (sour grapes). Second, his classification of the vine metaphor as a polemic against social injustice shows the metaphor lends itself to use in the context of social injustice, especially where there is a strong dichotomy of power and powerless, and rich and poor. The use of the vine metaphor as a social critique forms an important backdrop for interpreting the vine metaphor in the NT.

2.3 The Vine Metaphor in John 15:1-17

In his article on the vine metaphor,[17] Burge presses for interpretations that take into consideration the cultural weight of the metaphor and how it served the communities who first used it. He acknowledges various interpretations of the vine metaphor in the OT and 2TP, especially with regard to wisdom (Sir 24:7) and the Messiah (2 Apoc. Bar. 39:7). Burge finds the thrust of the metaphor to be "a concern about The Land and place and sacred space so central to the Jewish consciousness."[18] He suggests that this was possibly at the center of Jesus' thinking in this passage. For Burge the metaphor is the fourth Gospel's "most profound theological relocation of Israel's holy space."[19] He sees in the metaphor a description of rooted-ness in the vineyard, a land that is a source of life, hope and future. According to Burge, John shifts the content of Holy Places to Jesus Christ who is the

---

17. Gary M. Burge, "Territorial Religion, Johannine Christology, and the Vineyard of John 15," in *Jesus of Nazareth Lord and Christ: Essays on the Historical Jesus and New Testament Christology* (eds. Joel B. Green and Max Turner; GR: Eerdmans, 1994). Hereafter called JOHNLC.

18. Burge, "Territorial Religion," 391.

19. Burge, "Territorial Religion," 392.

Holy Place and the one in whom "God the Father is cultivating a vineyard in which only one life-giving vine grows."[20] Jesus is this only vine and attachment to him alone naturally leads to fruit-bearing (2:1-2).

Burge identifies the vine metaphor with the replacement motif that he finds at work in the GOJ. Burge, alongside other exponents of this motif, suggests that in John "Jesus replaces what is at the heart of Jewish faith."[21] Here Jesus is understood as replacing Jewish festivals and institutions such as the Passover (John 6) and the temple (John 2). Since for Burge the vineyard is the land, in John 15 Jesus critiques the territorial religion of Judaism and spiritualizes the land—pointing away from vineyard as territory to himself. In this case Jesus rather than The Land has become "the sole source of life and hope and future."[22]

Certain aspects of Burge's essay are useful. First, his treatment of the vineyard, The Land, as the source of rooted-ness, hope, and life, and the transference of that to Jesus in John, connects well to John's Christology. Indeed John portrays Jesus as the life (1:4; 3:15-16; 5:21, 26, 40; 6:48; 11:25; 14:6), and that is made clear in John 15 where branches must remain intact to the vine in order to live and bear fruit. John also suggests that Jesus is now the new place of revelation and blessing for the people of God. For instance in 1:51 he is the new Bethel, the new house of God's presence. In him Jerusalem is no more the holy space designate, and, all pilgrimages to the "holy land" are now rendered futile. In this the Johannine Jesus becomes both the vineyard and the vine of life that grows in it. Some difficulty, however, may arise when this interpretation is placed in the context of colonialism and the usurpation of land. To say "Christ is the space of God's promise"[23] does not imply the negation of geography for the people of God, who must still invite their neighbors under their own vines and fig trees. Nevertheless, we concur with Burge that territorial religion comes under serious scrutiny in the GOJ.

---

20. Burge, "Territorial Religion," 394.
21. Burge, "Territorial Religion," 394. There is no scholarly consensus that this motif is at work in the GOJ.
22. Burge, "Territorial Religion," 395.
23. Burge, "Territorial Religion," 389.

Second, Burge's view that the vine metaphor encompasses both the people of God and the land allows for its emphasis upon the notion of abiding. In this case, the call to "abide in me" would be interpreted as an invitation to occupy the new "dwelling place" which God has provided in Christ. This view of the vine metaphor is particularly important in contemporary scholarship when studies on "the land" as the "place of promise" and the place where God's blessings are realized have received fresh considerations.[24] However, Burge does not make the connection between the notion of abiding in the vine and the land as vine. The notion of abiding in Christ, the new dwelling space, has great implications for hospitality and is central to the vine metaphor as will be demonstrated later. It is important to understand the vine metaphor to refer not only to the people of God but to all that is pertinent to them as well, including their land.

Beasley-Murray[25] suggests that the chief theme of the vine metaphor (15:1-17) is the relationship of the Son to the believer.[26] For him while the vine is at the fore, the vine dresser remains in the background throughout, allowing the Son to play his mediatory role. Beasley-Murray reads the metaphor against its OT background and emphasizes the depiction of Israel as a corrupt and fruitless people who are under the judgment of YHWH (Isa 5:1-7; Jer 2:21). He sees the depiction of Jesus as the true Vine as "primarily intended to contrast with the failure of the vine Israel to fulfil its calling to be fruitful for God."[27] Against this failure Beasley-Murray places Jesus who, as the Son of God-Son of Man, is the one who dies and rises, that in union with him a renewed people of God might come into being and bring forth fruit for God. The union emphasizes that the branches are in the vine as part of the plant. The figure of Christ and the disciples becoming one

---

24. Wright, *Victory*; W. D. Davies, *The Gospel and the Land: Early Christianity and Jewish Territorial Doctrine* (Berkeley: U of California Press, 1974); Sean Freyne, *Galilee, Jesus and the Gospels: Literary Approaches and Historical Investigations* (Dublin: Gill and Macmillan, 1988); Sean Freyne, *Galilee from Alexander the Great to Hadrian: A Study of Second Temple Judaism* (Notre Dame: Notre Dame University Press, 1980).

25. George Beasley-Murray, *John* (WBC 36; Waco: WBP, 1987), 271-275.

26. Beasley-Murray, *John*, 271.

27. Beasley-Murray, *John*, 272.

is comparable to the figure of Christ as the body in Paul's teaching (1 Cor 12:12-13, 14-27).

At least two aspects of Beasley-Murray's interpretation are important for our research. First, reading the metaphor against its background and usage in early Judaism and in the OT, especially with regards to Israel's failure to produce fruit. However, it is not enough to cite the link to the OT polemic. Beasley-Murray might have been clearer if this polemic was extended to include details on what sort of fruit was expected. This failure to elaborate on the polemic, which is common among interpreters of the vine metaphor in the NT, creates ambiguity in the application of the metaphor. We will suggest that there was no speculation with regard to the ethical implications of the metaphor in the 2TP and in late Judaism.

Second, the idea that the disciples in union with Jesus are the renewed people of God is important for this research. Such reading allows the metaphor to function as covenant renewal and takes a view of the disciples of Jesus as God's new covenant people. However, like others, Beasley-Murray has missed the holiness message at the heart of the metaphor. If the disciples are in union with a holy God through the holy one of God, and this union implies a covenant relationship with a holy God, it follows then that they are the holy people of God. This relationship with God carries countless implications for holy living.

Keener's commentary[28] offers a more comprehensive socio-historical study of 15:1-17 in recent research. Emphasizing the use of the vine metaphor in the OT[29] and 2TP,[30] and in ancient Mediterranean viticulture in general, Keener includes detailed cultural data to help readers understand the text in its own context. Focussing on the primary image of branches dependent on the vine, he suggests the metaphor implies the "sense of community the Jewish believers inherited from early Judaism in general."[31] In describing this community, Keener distinguishes between the rigid hierarchical structure expected of Qumran covenanters and early Jewish

---

28. Keener, II:988-1016.

29. Ps 80:14-15, 17; Isa 5:1-7; 27:2-6; Jer 2:21; Ezek 15:2-6; 17:5-10; 19:10-14.

30. *2 Bar.* 39:7; Sir 24:13-17.

31. Keener, II:993.

and Christian communities who associated for common worship and need, where structures were less rigid. That the early Christians associated for common worship and fellowship is important for this research.

Interpreting each of the images within 15:1-17, Keener provides background information and intertextual links, allowing scripture to interpret scripture. For instance, he suggests that "John's vine image functions in the same way that Paul's olive tree image does,"[32] with both images stressing the breaking off of unfruitful branches (15:2, 6; Rom 11:17). Another intertextual link made is between the notion of abiding (union) and Paul's adaptation of the ancient body image for the church (Rom 12:4-6; 1 Cor 10:16; 12:12; Eph 4:12-16). This will be explored in chapter 5.

Keener also makes a connection between the notions of abiding and dwelling places (14:2-3, 23). The notion of abiding is perceived as suggesting that disciples become the dwelling place for the Triune God, whereas emphasis on mutuality shows that the opposite is also true. He does not, however, draw out the connection between the notion of abiding and the temple theme. Also missing is the theme of mutual hospitality. Keener does not show that mutual abiding suggests mutual hospitality, and that this is an important theme that runs through the GOJ.

Keener does not give attention to the holiness theme that this thesis will show is central to the metaphor. This can, however, be developed from his emphasis on the centrality of community, since this new community is built around and by the holy one of God. Does the metaphor have anything to say concerning relationships within the community of faith? How are the people of God to live in the light of their new status? Keener does not draw together holiness and community in his reading of the metaphor, although the writer's reference to the community as "clean" should suggest a relationship between cleansing and the holiness of the community.

Keener's suggestion that the "image could involve judgement or difficulty"[33] must be pursued. His references to *1 En.* 106:17, where the flood is described as "a cleansing of the earth," and *Pss. Sol.* 17:30, where the Messiah is pictured as "cleansing Jerusalem to restore it in holiness," are

---

32. Keener, II:993.
33. Keener, II:996.

important. Still more could be said on how 2TP Jews associated difficulty with discipline and how they encouraged endurance[34] and perseverance in the face of chastisement. We shall encourage, however, a positive interpretation of pruning.

Koester[35] puts the entire GOJ in the context of community by suggesting that it "was written in and for a community of faith."[36] For him the Gospel bears the marks of the social setting in which it was composed. Like the hands of the risen Jesus it displays transcendent realities through scars incurred in earthly conflict. He suggests that since the GOJ is rich in symbolism, it is important to ask the right questions when interpreting symbolism. Such questions include "asking about what the symbol does as well as what it means, about its role in community life as well as its theological significance."[37]

Koester disagrees with reading the Gospel as "a closed system of metaphors whose meaning is clear to insiders but opaque to the uninitiated."[38] According to Koester, a number of the Gospel's symbols, including the vine, are Christological reinterpretations of common Jewish symbols and have several social functions within the community: First, they provide an element of continuity during a period of social change. Second, they contribute to the community's sense of its own legitimacy. Third, they are integral to Johannine apologetics.

Koester suggests that the imagery "describes a community of believers rooted in Jesus, yet is accompanied by exhortations to be and become this kind of community by abiding in the vine."[39] For him there is no hesitation that John's audience would perceive the vine as a symbol for God's people.

---

34. The Jews cultivated a positive attitude towards difficulty. They viewed it as the Lord's chastisement and encouraged all who experienced it to persevere to the end. It was seen as a means of cleansing from sin and protection from evil (see Pss. Sol. 10:1-2).

35. Koester, *Symbolism*, 247-286.

36. Koester, *Symbolism*, 247.

37. Koester, *Symbolism*, 247.

38. Wayne A. Meeks, "The Man From Heaven In Johannine Sectarianism," JBL 91 (1972): 68. Others in this camp include John Ashton, *Understanding the Fourth Gospel* (Oxford: Clarendon, 1991), 451, 455 and Tom Thatcher, *The Riddles of Jesus in John: A Study in Tradition and Folklore* (SBLMS 53; Atlanta: SBL, 2000), 104-108.

39. Koester, *Symbolism*, 248.

The unity of the community expresses Jesus' own unity with God, and is one of the Gospel's most important social issues.[40] We will expand on the archetypal unity of the Father and the Son and its implications for the unity of the new people of God.

Koester also picks up the idea of ongoing pruning as a way of cleansing for the community. Pruning becomes the way of dealing with sin in the community and is crucially important if friendship with the vine will be maintained. Sin continues to become an issue in the community and the "word" is a means of dealing with it. Koester's contribution is important for this research and will be useful in many parts of this thesis.

Segovia,[41] in an article focussed on the theology and provenance of the vine metaphor, suggests that the focus of 15:1-17 is "love". He takes 15:9-17 to be an explanation of the vine imagery (vv. 1-8) and suggests a link between "Abide in me" (v. 4) and "abide in my love" (v. 9). Placing the metaphor in the *Sitz im Leben* of 1 John, Segovia shows that the metaphor addresses problems within the new community. He dissociates the metaphor from the ongoing debate or controversy with the synagogue or any outside circumstances. For example, "true vine", which according to Segovia places a strong emphasis upon the adjective, addresses believers who were facing the danger of abandoning the vine; the call to bear fruits implies that some branches were not bearing fruits and were behaving as if they were not branches.[42] The command to love is directed to an inner-Christian problem that has strong ethical connotations: "The disciples are failing in their love for one another."[43]

Several aspects of Segovia's essay are crucial for this research. First, the metaphor addresses a new community whose life is patterned after Jesus' sacrificial love. Second, this new community lives in unity with the Father and the Son. Third, and importantly, the emphasis on "love" as the proper interpretation of the metaphor places it at a cutting edge. From the

---

40. Koester, *Symbolism*, 248.

41. Fernando F. Segovia, "The Theology and Provenance of John 15: 1-17," JBL 101 (1982): 115-128.

42. Segovia, "Provenance," 121-122.

43. Segovia, "Provenance," 124.

onset the metaphor invites action and calls hearers to align their lives with its demands.

Segovia's rendering of the vine metaphor, however, leaves several gaps. First, Segovia does not give any background information. Has this metaphor been used elsewhere other than in John? Second, the absence of the cultural setting leads Segovia to conclude that the vine is the word of Jesus by which the disciples had been cleansed. While this may be true, it is clear that this is not what Jesus meant here. There is more to the vine metaphor than just "the word of Jesus," especially when it is read within its context and when its background in the OT and 2TP is properly considered. It is not clear why Segovia leaves out the rich background and heritage of the "vine" when his essay focuses on provenance. Fourth, Segovia also avoids aspects of the metaphor that would have been helpful in discussing the theology embedded in the metaphor. For example, examination of mutual abiding would have shown that Jesus and the Father are a hospitable community in which humankind can participate through union with Christ. Also, consideration of "he prunes" (15:2) and "clean", (15:3) may have led to interpretations regarding the disciples' holiness. This research will fill some of the gaps left by Segovia.

Ford,[44] who takes 15:1-17 as a feminine text, suggests that the vine is the symbol for "abiding, immanence, and friendship."[45] Stating that "the image of the vine is a brilliant image for expressing mutual indwelling,"[46] she argues from the feminine gender of the noun "vine" that the metaphor must be treated as feminine. Her argument is further strengthened by the OT renderings of Israel as feminine in her relationship to God (Ps 128:3). Ford associates friendship with fellowship which she thinks is demarcated by seeking what is beneficial to others. She stresses that the metaphor does not "apply to the individual but to the community."[47] To strengthen her point on community, she uses the sacraments of baptism and the Eucharist, both of which are community experiences. This community is the new

44. Ford, *Redeemer*, 147-167.

45. Ford, *Redeemer*, 159.

46. Ford, *Redeemer*, 160.

47. Ford, *Redeemer*, 162.

covenant people of God who are the branches of the vine. As true vine, the Son "is the fulfilment of the prophetic promises for the eschatological salvation community of God. The Son is the new people of God."[48]

Several aspects of Ford's interpretation contribute considerably to this research. First, mutual abiding is at the center of the metaphor, including its implications for immanence and community. Second, Ford identifies the vine with OT covenant motifs and properly postulates the new covenant as the main point in the GOJ. That the disciples are the new covenant people of God gathered by their covenant Lord is not only a thread that runs through our research but forms the basis for the conclusions that we make. Third, Ford's emphasis on friendship and "seeking what is beneficial to others" is also important for our argument for hospitality and practical holiness. Fourth, that the figure of the vine is feminine and is in accordance with the portrayal of God's people Israel in the OT is an important point. We shall show throughout our research that humankind is equal before God despite differences in gender, ethnicity, social status, and age. Discrimination of any kind is antithetical to the vine metaphor and has no place in John's understanding of holy community.

2.4 Conclusion

The work accomplished by these scholars offers a wide range of contributions to vine metaphor scholarship. Can anything further be done with the Johannine vine metaphor? Does anything remain to be unearthed regarding the author's intentions in using this metaphor? Evidently, some ground remains unbroken in interpreting the metaphor. The following section will outline some interpretative problems we encounter and further suggest a way forward.

First, the usage of vine symbolism in the NT must be explained in light of the vast background available in OT and 2TJ without rejecting possible

---

48. Ford, *Redeemer*, 164.

influences from the Hellenistic world. Any interpretation that disregards these contexts is potentially misleading.

Second, there is scholarly consensus on the community aspect of the vine as a symbol for Israel. The disciples in Christ, including those who will believe their message, are the new covenant people of God. Therefore, any treatment of the vine metaphor that excludes community life and relationships is inadequate. The metaphor functions within the community and has theological as well as social significance, necessitating investigation.

Third, scholars agree that the hallmark of John's vine metaphor is the notion of mutual abiding. There is a mutual indwelling and interpenetration between the vine and its branches which is a condition for fruit bearing. Interpretations of this remain shallow especially where the unity of the disciples is concerned. We will suggest a more practical interpretation of mutual abiding: mutual hospitality patterned after the archetypal hospitality of the Father and the Son. It is not clear why scholars seldom link the notion of mutual abiding to hospitality, yet the mutuality suggested consists in reciprocal giving and receiving of life and possessions of one by another.

Fourth, current scholarship leaves out the connection between the vine metaphor and the holiness of the people of God as they live in covenant relationship with God. While scholars agree that the vine metaphor is a covenant metaphor, they do not show how the people of God in John function as an embodiment of Israel. Consequently they do not show how the terms of the covenant with Israel apply to the renewed people of God in John, including the requirement for holiness and its daily expression. The language John uses should point to that. For example, "cleansing" (13:10; 15:2, 3) is a covenant term pertinent to the holiness of the people of God in the OT and 2TP.

In the next chapter we attempt to close the scholarly gap by researching the background of viticulture and the vine metaphor in the OT and its backdrop in the ANE. We show that the vine, its products, and symbolism were common in the world of the OT, and there was no speculation regarding what the vine metaphor meant. Proper understanding of this background will hopefully influence our interpretation of the metaphor in John.

CHAPTER 3

Viticulture and the Vine Metaphor
in the ANE and the OT

3.1 Introduction

The previous chapter demonstrated the need to research the background of the vine metaphor to its fullest extent to illuminate the metaphor in John. This chapter will show the important place of viticulture, the fruit of the vine, and the vine metaphor in the ANE and OT. This includes attention to the development of viticulture and the vine metaphor in Mesopotamia, Egypt, and Syria-Palestine.[1] These places are significant for understanding the development of ANE culture as a whole as well as within the Israelite life-history. ANE culture is the milieu for reading the references to the vine and its products in the Bible. Indeed the ANE religious system is the "most powerful reading scenario for the Bible."[2] It is difficult, if not impossible, to

---

1. In a thesis of this length it is not possible to explore the entirety of the ancient Near East in detail. Hence we have narrowed our focus to three areas that influenced the development of viticulture and the vine metaphor among the Israelites. While the influence of Hellenism on Palestinian Judaism in the late second temple has been established beyond doubt by Martin Hengel, *Judaism and Hellenism: Studies in Their Encounter in Palestine During the Early Hellenistic Period* (1st English ed.; 2 vols.; London: SCM Press, 1974), we have not included Greece since there is no clear evidence of the influence of Greek thought on the OT. Where reference is made to Greece and Greeks it is very limited. See Curtis, *Atlas*, 47-48.

2. Jagt, *Anthropological Approaches*, 21; also see Walter Beyerlin, ed., *Near Eastern Religious Texts Relating to the Old Testament* (OTL; London: SCM Press, 1978), xxi-xxii, for the importance of the ANE background for understanding the OT.

study the ANE religious system without finding metaphorical references to the vine or its products. The production of grape wine in this region made a significant contribution to the region's religious and ideological consciousness. This religious consciousness is interpreted through the symbolism of vines and wine.[3]

Poo gives five symbolic uses of the vine in ANE religious consciousness: 1) the death of the vine in winter and its dramatic rebirth and growth in spring became a symbol for the death and rebirth of the god and for the whole agricultural cycle; 2) the resilience of the products of the vine as they hold within them the secret of rebirth and strive beyond the autumnal and winter death of the parent vine took on symbolic and ritual significance; 3) the ability of wine to intoxicate and engender a sense of "other-worldliness" provided a means by which people could actually come into contact with the gods; 4) wine could represent the dichotomy between "good", when taken in small quantities, and "evil", when taken in excess; 5) due to wine's ability to break down reason and social customs, and its consequent role as a catalyst for human intercourse, its cycle was linked to human fertility.[4] These symbolic uses of the vine show its significance in ANE religion in general and will become clearer as we focus our study on Mesopotamia, Egypt, and Syria-Palestine.

3.1.1 Viticulture and the Vine Metaphor in Mesopotamia

Mesopotamia is important in the development of the vine and its metaphorical usage in ANE culture. It is likely that the *Vitis sylvestris,* which is the living progenitor of the domesticated vine species and its cultivars,[5] was first domesticated there.[6] Unwin suggests that even before the domestica-

---

3. Mu-Chou Poo, *Wine and Wine Offering in the Religion of Ancient Egypt* (London: KPI, 1995), 2.

4. Tim Unwin, *Wine and Vine: An Historical Geography of Viticulture and the Wine Trade* (London: Routledge, 1991), 60-61.

5. McGovern, *Ancient Wine,* 11, 20. Cf. Oded Borowski, *Agriculture in Iron Age Israel* (UMI, 1979), 155.

6. There is no scholarly consensus on the exact place and date for the domestication of the vine. Nikolai I. Vavilov, "Studies on the Origin of Cultivated Plants," *BAB* 16 (1926): 1-148, a Russian botanist, is the first to claim that the world's earliest wine culture

tion of the vine wine was made in Mesopotamia and the Caucasus from the grapes of the *Vitis sylvestris*.[7] The first wine was discovered by chance in this region between 10,000 B.C.E. and 8000 B.C.E. when someone drank the fermented juice of wild grapes that had been collected and stored.[8] Unwin associates the cultivation of vines and the origin of wine to the social, economic, and ideological structures that emerged in the Caucasus and northern Mesopotamia in prehistoric times.[9] He also suggests that there is clear evidence for the cultivation of vineyards at the start of the third millennium B.C.E. when the Sumerians established themselves in southern Mesopotamia.[10]

The domestication of the vine was important to enable the vintner to control the size, color, and ultimately the taste of the grapes. Once these were controlled, vintners could ensure the quality and marketability of their product. Domestication also allowed for experimentation with new and improved ways of viticulture. For example, Matthews suggests that "the best means of ensuring a consistent and marketable crop comes from

---

emerged in Transcaucasia, a region stretching between the Black Sea and the Caspian Sea. Vavilov's claim is further advanced by M. A. Negrul, "Evolution of cultivated forms of grapes," *CASUSSR* 18 (1938): 585-88, who suggests that "the hearth of the domestication of the grape vine was probably Asia Minor and Transcaucasia, where gradual selection of vines with small juicy fruits took place from 8000 BC." Unwin, 59, suggests that Mesopotamia and the Caucasus are the most likely places for the origin and development of the domesticated species of *vitis*. However, McGovern, *Ancient Wine*, 20, suggests the domestication of the wild grapevine cannot be attributed to one geographical area. It happened more than once and in more than one place. Therefore, it is safe to speak of multiple domestications.

7. Unwin, 59.

8. Unwin, 63. A full account of this story is recorded by William Younger, *Gods, Man and Wine* (London: TWFS, 1966), 27. The story is Persian and is about King Jemsheed, one of the culture-heroes of Persian mythology. A similar story is found in the Sumerian *Epic of Gilgamesh*. Also similar, though dating later is the biblical story of Noah's accidental discovery of wine. However, Unwin suggests that this can only be conjecture. Ronald Gorny, "Viticulture and Ancient Anatolia," in *The Origins and Ancient History of Wine* (eds. Patrick E. McGovern, Stuart J. Fleming, Solomon H. Katz; Amsterdam: GBP, 1996), 133 (hereafter called *Origins*), suggests that opinions such as these are as much legend as truth and may or may not have any basis real events. Nevertheless, there is enough evidence to prove that the first wine was made from the *vitis sylvestris*.

9. Unwin, 59.

10. Unwin, 64.

taking cuttings from proven producers and by grafting branches to new vines from those plants that have produced superior fruit."[11]

Despite the significant role of Mesopotamia in the development of viticulture, wine does not appear to have been common there.[12] The climatic conditions were not favorable for the expansion of viticulture there. Also, the high salinity in the soil in southern Mesopotamia favoured barley. Only the land nearer to the sources of the Tigris and Euphrates allowed for an extensive cultivation of vines. Thus the most common drink seems to have been beer made from barley and dates.

The short supply of wine in Mesopotamia contributed to the culture of sharing. The Assyrian sage Ahiqar remarks that persons who are the most pleasing to other people and the gods are those "who share their wine."[13] In Mesopotamia, at least from the third to the first millennium B.C.E., wine was a rare and expensive commodity[14] and remained the drink of the gods, kings, religious elites, and the rich few. For example, reliefs from Nineveh at the time of Ashurbanipal show "the king seated with his wife under a bower of vines, drinking what is almost certainly the wine of grapes."[15] In order to meet such demand, additional wine was imported from the Zagros range

---

11. Victor H. Matthews, "Treading the Winepress: Actual and Metaphorical Viticulture in the Ancient Near East," *Semeia* 86 (1999): 20.

12. Karen Rhea Nemet-Nejat, *Daily Life in Ancient Mesopotamia* (Westport: Greenwood, 1998), 158, reports that "wine could be made only once a year, when the grapes ripened." See also McGovern, *Ancient wine,* 151, who stresses that "the grapevine was certainly not at home in the harsh saline conditions of southern Iraq." Unwin, 67, suggests that "Southern Mesopotamia (Babylon and Ur) was never an important home for vines, and that much of the wine drunk there was date wine." Marvin A. Powell, "Wine and the Vine in Ancient Mesopotamia," in *Origins,* states that even as late as 2000 B.C.E. "there is no unequivocal evidence for wine in Babylonia itself, whether in the form of native production, of tribute, or of imports. However, it must be noted that later during the time of the Assyrian empire there is evidence for the cultivation vineyards in this area. Matthews, "Treading," 21, indicates that the Assyrian empire drew sufficient quantities of wine in tribute and taxes to be able to boast of its widespread use.

13. Matthews, "Treading," 21.

14. According to Powell, *Wine and the Vine,* 105, the price of a liter of raisins in the Ur III period (shortly before 2000 B.C.E.) ranged from about five to ten times the price of barley or dates. By the time of Nabonidus (1500 years later) wine by volume was thirteen times as expensive as barley, fifteen times as expensive as dates.

15. Unwin, 66, who also notes that by the first millennium B.C.E. Nineveh became renowned for its wines.

in western Iran where the winters were cooler and essential for the successful cultivation of vines. The Babylonians imported much wine from Syria, Iran, Armenia, and Elam. Nebuchadnezzar (605-562 B.C.E.), who offered to the gods mountain beer (pure wine) like the uncountable waters of a river, ordered his wine from northern Iraq, Turkey, and Syria.[16] This follows the already established fact that the best wines come from the mountain or from hilly situations. Other products of the vine in Mesopotamia included grape juice, vinegar, and raisins.

Apart from a drink for the priests and the ruling elites, the vine had a more important usage in Mesopotamia. First, its symbolic importance is reflected in the frequent pairing of *lal* (grape syrup) and *geštin* (grapes or some form of must, including wine) as the mark of good times and abundance in Sumerian literary texts.[17] Second, it was used in certain religious rites and ceremonies as a sacrifice to the gods and as a libation.[18] Third, it was used in sacraments as the means of imparting divine life.[19] Furthermore, it was associated with fertility and with specific divinities. For example, the Assyrians and the Babylonians had the vine goddess, Geshtin or Ama-geshtin (Geshtinanna or Ama-Geshtinna),[20] and the vine god Pa-Geshtin-Dug. This significance of the vine in religious rites and in worship is similar to what we later find in Egypt.

3.1.2 Viticulture and the Vine Metaphor in Egypt[21]

Like the Mesopotamians, the Egyptians did not grow vines in large quantities. The soil and climatic conditions were unfavourable and annual flooding

16. Powell, "Wine and the Vine," 102.

17. Powell, "Wine and the Vine," 103.

18. Unwin, 64. See also Goodenough, 12:108.

19. Goodenough, 5:112. Seltan, *Wine*, 21, gives details of how the divine life was perceived to be imparted into the partaker. When wine was discovered it was attributed to a god. The god was perceived to be in the wine, and the wine was his blood. As the partaker drank the wine the god entered into him or her so that for a time he or she partook of the godhead.

20. Scholars vary in their naming of this goddess: e.g. Goodenough, 5:113, Geshtin; McGovern, *Ancient Wine*, 154, 173, Geshtinanna, who also adds that the name derives from the Sumerian *geštin*, meaning "grape," "vineyard," or "wine."

21. Although geographically isolated from the rest of the ANE, Egypt is important for this research due to its access to and control over the land and sea routes along the

of the Nile River necessitated artificial elevation of their vineyards. As in Mesopotamia, beer was the main alcoholic beverage in ancient Egypt.[22] It was the most common drink available for the masses' daily consumption and for social and ritual occasions. From the end of the fourth millennium B.C.E. and the beginning of the third millennium B.C.E., however, it seems that wine was used as a luxury to be enjoyed by the kings and priests and officials who owned vineyards. The evidence of this is grape pips and large wine cellars found in association with the temples and tombs of First Dynasty kings.[23] The Genesis story of the dream of Pharaoh's cupbearer is consistent with the practice of viticulture by the Egyptian nobility (Gen 40:9-15). Alongside the wine from the vine Egyptians produced wine from fruits such as dates and pomegranates.

Despite the unfavorable soil and climatic conditions in Egypt, there is evidence that Egyptian viticulture later became widespread. For example, Unwin notes that during the reign of Ramses III (1197-1165 B.C.E.) numerous vineyards were constructed throughout the country.[24] Also, the *Papyrus Harris* dating from this period lists 513 vineyards which were then temple property.[25] Different types of vineyards and methods of wine making were employed to ensure steady supplies. Where the land lacked hills the Egyptians made artificially raised plots and supported their vines on trellises, which also provided pleasant shady walkways for their owners.[26]

Levantine coast for commercial and strategic reasons. Egypt also forms an important backdrop for the stories of the OT. See Curtis, *Atlas*, 38.

22. Matthews, "Treading," 21; Jack M. Sasson, "The Blood of Grapes: Viticulture and Intoxication in the Hebrew Bible," in *Drinking in Ancient Societies: History and Culture of Drinks in the Ancient Near East* (ed. Lucio Milano; Padova: Sargon srl, 1994), 399-400, who states that beer was a staple in Mesopotamian and Egyptian cultures.

23. Daniel Zohary, "The Domestication of the Grapevine Vitis Vinifera L. in the Near East," in *Origins*, 28; Poo, 5.

24. Unwin, 71; Poo, 11.

25. Anne Marrie Van Nest, "vine," *EGHD* 3:1338, suggests that King Ramses III donated 514 gardens or their sites to various temples. It is likely that these are the vineyards associated with the temple during his reign. Poo, 11, gives details of Ramses' donation: Theban temples, 433 vineyards, Heliopolitan temples, 64, Memphite temples, 5, and various small temples were endowed with 11 vineyards. Also see Younger, 36, who describes the great *Papyrus Harris* as giving "detailed information about the property of the temples of Egypt."

26. Unwin, 69.

According to Younger, Egyptians cultivated leisure-gardens whose vines had a triple purpose: decoration, shade, and grapes.[27] Pictorial records found in their tomb paintings and statues show details of Egyptian viniculture.[28]

The Nile Delta was one of the areas famous for wine production in the Pharaonic Period.[29] Wine-jar stamps and cylinder seals attest that there were vineyards located both in the Eastern and Western Nomes of the Delta,[30] which contained both royal and private vineyards. Private vineyard-owners also contributed wine to royalty.[31]

Even at this period, however, where it is clear that Egypt produced local wine, there is evidence of imported wine. In the Bronze Age and the Middle Bronze Age there was Egypto-Canaan trade and commerce evidenced by the discovery of the "Canaanite jar" in Egyptian tombs and paintings from the Middle Bronze Age. For example, the discovery of the "Canaanite jar" in Egyptian tombs and paintings of the Middle Bronze Age is sufficient basis for commerce with Canaan. At least three reasons necessitated the import of wine into Egypt: First, Egyptian wine was rarely of good quality. The salinity of the soil and the high temperatures affected the quality of the product. Younger is probably right to suggest that "fermentation in the hot Egyptian climate may often have been too rapid, and would have produced a difficult wine which could easily turn sick."[32] Second, according to Singleton much of the drinking water would make a person ill, but when

---

27. Younger, 37.

28. The Hieroglyph sign for a vineyard consists of a vine, from which bunches of grapes hang down, supported by two notched sticks, and this indicates the method by which Egyptian vines were most commonly trained. L. Lesko, *King Tut's Wine Cellar* (Berkeley: B. C. Scribe, 1977), 7, records that three dozen wine jars were found in the tomb of King Tutankhamen. H. Kees, *Ancient Egypt* (London: FF, 1961), 82, reports many wine jars found at the Ramesseum at Thebes and at the royal city of Amarna. Also see Poo, 5-112, for a detailed account of Egyptian viticulture.

29. Poo, 11, 12. See also Younger, *Gods, Man and Wine*, 34, who suggests that "Most of the wines of the first seven Dynasties came from the Nile Delta in Lower Egypt."

30. Poo, 6-8, suggests the presence of two important wine-presses in the Early Dynastic Period both in the East and the West of the Nile Delta: "wine-press of the Eastern Nome" and "wine-press of the Western Nome."

31. Poo, 15.

32. Younger, 47.

mixed with wine the water could be sanitized.[33] Laboratory experiments show that living typhoid and other dangerous microbes rapidly die when mixed with wine; wine was used to make contaminated water safe and potable. Third, the demand for wine was great because of its medicinal and embalming uses.[34] Wine was also supplied to soldiers as reward for military success.[35] There was, therefore, a need for importing good quality wine from Syria, Greece, and Phoenicia.[36]

The vine also served two other purposes in Egypt from the time of the kings of the first dynasty: social and religious. On a social level, wine, the fruit of the vine, was particularly popular in banquets and feasts of the upper classes where it became "the crowning glory."[37] In these banquets wine-jars were placed in all parts of the room fixed in stands and decorated with flowers. Each jar was carefully marked with the name of the vineyard and the year the vintage was put down.[38] The guests drank from cups which were carefully kept full by servants. Common people had easy access to much wine during the festivals. For example, the annual festival at Bubastis, which according to Herodotus was attended by seven hundred thousand people, had more wine drunk than in the whole year.[39] Here commoners could drink wine and celebrate uninhibitedly.

On a religious level, apart from its use in sacrifices and libations, in Egypt wine was associated with specific deities. For example, Osiris was called "Lord of wine," also interpreted to mean "possessor of wine."[40] Wine

---

33. Vernon L. Singleton, "An Enologist's Commentary on Ancient Wine," in *Origins*, 75.

34. Poo, 31. Here Poo, relying upon Joachim, *Papyrus Elbers* (1890), "prescriptions," includes a list of sicknesses that the Egyptians cured with wine.

35. Poo, 32.

36. See Marc Van De Mieroop, *A History of the Ancient Near East ca. 3000-323 B.C.E.* (Oxford: Blackwell, 2004), 133, 278 who suggests that Egypt imported wine and oil from the Aegean and Syria.

37. Unwin, 71.

38. Alan W. Shorter, *Everyday Life in Ancient Egypt* (London: SLMC, 1923), 51; Jeremy Geller, "Wine making," in *EAAE* (ed. Kathryn A. Bard; London: Routledge, 1999), 881, suggests that named vineyards, such as The Enclosure of the Beverage of the Body of Horus, and vintages are known from first Dynasty records.

39. See Poo, 29; Herodotus, *Historia* Book II: 60. It may be that the wine Herodotus mentions is actually beer.

40. Poo, 148-159, shows how different deities in Egypt were associated with wine or its

was perceived as the provision of the gods, a divine drink, endowed with divine essence. Its use in libations and sacrifices includes its ability to draw blessings from the deity, to foster a relationship with the deity and to actually unite the worshiper with the deity. Also, the vine was associated with the resurrection of Osiris and a new life-cycle.[41] This was shown in tomb paintings where the vine was not only decorative but also a symbol for resurrection. According to McGovern, in Egypt, where "wine's special benefits were traced back to the gods, wine served to invoke divine assistance and to bridge the chasm between this life and the next at many festivals."[42] Nevertheless, wine and the vine never achieved the prominent position of religious and social dominance in Egypt that it had in places such as Syria-Palestine and later, Greece and Italy.

3.1.3 Viticulture and the Vine Metaphor in Syria-Palestine[43]

> It was a good land, named Yaa.
> Figs were in it, and grapes.
> It had more wine than water.[44]

The Egyptian tale of Sinuhe, from the Middle Bronze Age, praises the land of Syria-Palestine for its extensive viticulture and abundance of wine. Along with olive and fig trees, the *Vitis vinifera* is one of the most characteristic plants of Palestine. Indeed "the domesticated grapevine, *Vitis vinifera*, had taken hold in Palestine and Transjordan by the Chalcolithic period, at least by 3500 BC."[45] McGovern cites a report made at the end of the third

---

festivals.

41. Poo, 150-151.

42. McGovern, *Ancient Wine*, 134.

43. Syria-Palestine is used here in a general sense and is synonymous with Canaan. John J. Bimson, Consulting ed., *Illustrated Encyclopedia of Bible Places* (Leicester: IVP, 1995), 80, describes Canaan as fundamentally indicating the land of the Syro-Palestinian coastland, especially Phoenicia proper or Syria-Palestine in general.

44. "The Story of Sinuhe," *ANET,* 19. Cf. Peter Damian Akpunonu, *The Vine, Israel and the Church* (New York: Peter Lang, 2004), 5.

45. McGovern, *Ancient Wine*, 213.

millennium concerning whole dried grapes (raisins) found at Jericho in the southern part of the valley. From this he concludes that the *Vitis vinifera* had already been cultivated there since the *Vitis sylvestris* could not have grown in this arid region.

The OT provides us with vast evidence for both the general distribution of viticulture within the lands neighboring Israel and Judah, and the symbolic significance of wine and the vine, much of which was later to be incorporated into the Christian religion.[46] Beginning with the account of Noah's vineyard, there are numerous references to the vine and wine throughout the OT. There is evidence that by the time the Israelites settled Canaan the Canaanites already had a fully developed system of viticulture. According to Akpunonu, "the vine was grown and produced large fruit in Canaan even before the Israelites settled there."[47] In Deuteronomy a case is made for the bounty of the Promised Land. Numbers records the return of the Israelite spies with a bunch of grapes to symbolize the paradisiacal character of Canaan. The children of Israel are promised the inheritance of a region that has already been tamed by its previous inhabitants: Cisterns have already been hewn from the soft limestone slopes of the hills, and vineyards and olive groves are already well established (Deut 6:11). The Egypto-Canaan trade, which included quality wine, and the story of the cluster of grapes brought by the twelve spies, support this view.

Clearly, viticulture became an important aspect of Israelite life in Palestine. Describing the weaving of viticulture into the daily life of the Israelites, Baron writes, "first in the valleys and then on the mountain slopes, entire clans of farmers built their houses, planted their orchards and vineyards, and cultivated their fields as closely as possible to the source of water."[48] He further refers to "vineyards, orchards, and truck gardens in the immediate vicinity of the dwellings,"[49] which may suggest the practice of subsistence viticulture. Elsewhere the Jew is described as a person who

---

46. Unwin, 82-83.

47. Akpunonu, *The Vine*, 6.

48. Salo Wittmayer Baron, *The Jewish Community: Its History and Structure to the American Revolution* (3 vols.; Westport: Greenwood, 1942), 1:32.

49. Baron, *Jewish Community*, 42.

concentrated all his thoughts upon three values: "his family, his faith, and his vineyard."[50] The conflict between Naboth and Jezebel over Naboth's vineyard is an example of an Israelite passion for the family vineyard (1 Kings 21:1-12).

The growing of vines in Syria-Palestine was made easy by climate and topography, which allowed for the maintenance of vineyards in nearly every village in the hill country. Its hills and mountains provided the cool winters and the long hot summers required by the vine.[51] Vines were grown on a small scale for daily personal use as well as on a larger scale for commercial purposes. In the small holdings "vineyards were planted near the farmer's house and were mixed with orchards and sometimes trained to climb up the trees."[52] Alongside this were also individual and family vineyards situated some distance from the villages, possibly in central locations that served all inhabitants.[53] On the slopes of the Judean hills, where over-grazing and deforestation had caused erosion, the vintners constructed retaining walls and transported new top soil from elsewhere to fill the terraces and ensure that the vines receive the requisite amount of moisture.[54]

The methods of extracting the juice varied. Examples include treading the grapes under foot or crushing them in wicker baskets above a catchment basin.[55] A detailed description of one of the processes of pressing is offered:

> the harvested grapes were first placed in a "treading trough" made of mud brick and sealed with a plaster surface. A group of men, holding on to a pole hung horizontally over the trough, then worked the grapes into a mash with their feet . . . a particular rhythm was encouraged by their cadence. A further pressing process then occurs when the crushed grapes are placed into a sack or closed wicker basket that is stretched

---

50. Younger, 70.

51. Unwin, 75.

52. Matthews, "Treading," 20.

53. Borowski, *Agriculture*, 103.

54. Matthews, "Treading," 25.

55. Matthews, "Treading," 20.

over wide-mouth jars and twisted by a team of three or more men.[56]

Certain regions of Syria-Palestine were favorable for viticulture in ancient times: Lebanon (Hos 14:8), the territory around Helbon (Ezek 27:18), the south and western portions of Judah (Gen 49:11; Jud 14:5), especially the district around Hebron (Num 13:23). Other places included the Philistine coastal plain (Jud 15:5), the plains of Sharon and Jezreel (1 Kings 21:1), the regions around Shechem (Jud 9:27), Shiloh (Jud 21:20), and Gibeon, where large areas were set aside for the production and storage of wine, and the oasis of Engedi (Cant 1:14) near the Dead Sea. Also, Sibmah, in the Transjordan, was known for its vineyards.[57] This popular participation in viticulture meant that in Palestine the products of the vine were enjoyed in abundance. Wine formed part of the daily meal[58] and became a substitute for water since surface water may have been tainted and large areas were patched and waterless. According to Seltan travellers carried a wine-skin while journeying.[59] The importance of wine as a beverage and aspect of everyday life is attested to by scripture.[60]

Wine was also important in temple worship. It was one of the first fruits and tithes which must be offered, and it was used with many other sacrifices in the temple. New wine, *tîrôš*, was to be brought to the altar of YHWH for a drink offering from each of the tribes of Israel year after year.[61] The Israelites were to pour this new wine on the altar of sacrifice with great rejoicing.[62] The vine's first fruits were reserved for God and the choicest *tîrôš* was handed over to the priests (Deut 18:4; Num 18:12). Wine was

---

56. Matthews, "Treading," 20. Cf. T. G. H. James, "The Earliest History of Wine and its Importance in Ancient Egypt," in *Origins*, 208.

57. Isa 16:8-10; Jer 48:32-33. Cf. Akpunonu, *The Vine*, 6-7.

58. Kirsten Nielsen, *There is Hope for a Tree: The Tree as Metaphor in Isaiah* (JSOTSup 65; Sheffield: SAP, 1989), 78.

59. Seltan, *Wine*, 18.

60. Ruth 2:14; Hos 2:7; Dan 10:3; John 2:1-11.

61. 11QT XIII. 12; 1 Sam 1:24; 10:3.

62. 11QT XLIII. 8. The annual celebration was called the "festival of wine."

referred to as the "blood of the grape" and was said to make a pleasing odor when poured at the foot of the altar.[63]

This abundance of wine in Israel contrasts with Mesopotamia and Egypt where wine was a luxury enjoyed only by kings and priests and the élite.[64] Unlike Mesopotamia and Egypt, where farmers depended on irrigation, Canaan's farmers benefit from seasonal rains which provide water for the production of a bountiful harvest (Deut 11:10-12). The *terra rossa*, a type of soil characteristic of Israel and other Mediterranean areas, favored the production of vines.[65] Its high iron, low humus, and slightly alkaline character is suitable for viticulture. The loamy soils with a mixture of clay with silt, sand, stones, and organic material are best for vines, figs, and olive trees because they encourage the roots to penetrate deep into the soils to reach the moister earth beneath.[66] The vine could survive the hot, dry summer months because of its ability to thrive on the nightly dew.[67] Too much moisture would cause mould to grow on the skin while a small precipitation would help the skin to expand and enhance fruitfulness.

The extensive practice of viticulture in Canaan gave birth to a powerful symbolism that reminded Israel of the richness of the Land of Promise and of YHWH's faithfulness. Thus "Wine was from early times a proverbial part of the richness of the Promised Land, and it naturally appears to have been an important aspect of the life of Jews at all periods after they came to Canaan."[68] As a living reminder, it was incorporated into the culture, daily life, worship, and total existence of Israel, the holy people of God.

---

63. Sir 50:15; Similarly found in Ugaritic literature: Poo, 152.

64. Unwin, 66, 68; Leonard Cottrell, *Life Under the Pharaohs* (London: EBL, 1955), 57-58.

65. Carey Ellen Walsh, *The Fruit of the Vine: Viticulture In Ancient Israel* (Eisenbraus: Winoma Lake, 2000), 31.

66. E. C. Semple, *The Geography of the Mediterranean: Its Relation to Ancient History* (NY: Henry Holt, 1931), 381.

67. Walsh, *Fruit*, 33. The importance of the nightly dew in association with the vine and wine is highlighted in several scriptures: Gen 27:28; Deut 33:28; Isa 18:4; Hos 14:5-6; Zech 8:12.

68. Goodenough, 5:129.

3.3 The Vine in Jewish Metaphorical Usage

Appreciation of Israel's background is vital for developing an understanding of the liveliness of the vine metaphor in Jewish usage within the late 2TP. The Jews had numerous metaphorical themes connected with the vine and its products. These themes took diverse forms within Jewish social, religious, economic, and political life. The Jews "never reduced the wine symbols to a single one: wine could be represented as the vine, the cluster of grapes, the cup, a wine jar, baskets of grapes, vintage scenes, and the wine press."[69] These powerful metaphors, some of which were used by Israel's poets and prophets, were inspired by the life cycle of the vine and the metamorphosis of its fruit.

First, the vine or the vineyard is a favorite metaphor for the nation of Israel in the OT.[70] Two factors are particularly emphasized here: 1) the corporate existence of Israel as YHWH's chosen people; 2) the covenant relationship between Israel and YHWH which embeds the holiness of Israel as people belonging to YHWH. This imagery is used particularly by some OT prophets[71] contrasting the ideal and obedient Israel, seen as a well-cultivated fruitful vine or vineyard, with the people who have disobeyed God, consequently represented as a fruitless degenerate vine or vineyard. It is to this imagery that the prophets turn when forging paradigms for the constantly fracturing relationship between YHWH and Israel. Often it is when the ideals of "corporateness" and "covenant" are compromised that Israel is portrayed as a fruitless vine.

Second, in Hebrew erotic imagery, the vine is a metaphor for the beloved (Cant 7:7-13). Her breasts are like clusters of the vine and her kisses are sweeter than wine. Here the metaphor functions hand-in-hand with the

---

69. Goodenough, 5:99.

70. See Isa 5:1-12; Jer 6:9; Ps 80:8-16; Ezek 15:1-8, 18:10-14; Hos 9:10; 10:1; Beasley-Murray, 272; C. H. Dodd, *The Interpretation of the Fourth Gospel* (Cambridge: Cambridge University Press, 1955), 411; Raymond Brown, *The Gospel According to John* (2 vols.; London: Geoffrey Chapman, 1970), 669-71; D. A. Carson, *The Gospel According to John* (GR: Eerdmans, 1991), 513; Keener, II: 991; Andreas J. Köstenberger, *Gospel of John* (GR: Baker Academic, 2004), 448-9; Leon Morris, *The Gospel According to John* (GR: Eerdmans, 1995), 593; Unwin, 82.

71. Isa 5:1-7; Hosea 10:1; Jer 2:21; 5:10; 6:9; 12:10; Ezek 15:1-8; 17:3-10; 19:10-14.

similar metaphor of bride and groom where Israel is pictured as YHWH's beloved bride.[72] However, in Israel's prophetic tradition she is portrayed as an unfaithful bride who has given herself to adulterous relationships. This negative use of the metaphor is akin to the prophets' usage of the vine metaphor where Israel is a contaminated vine bearing sour fruits or none at all.

Third, the vine, together with the fig, became a symbol of "the prosperity and above all the peace of the Promised Land."[73] Any period characterized by peace, prosperity, joy, and well-being was described as a time when all people sat under their own vines and fig trees.[74] A time when the covenant people of God, together as a community rather than individuals, enjoyed peace with God and one another. The abundance of vines and vineyards is an expression of God's favor. Borowski and Staley add that planting vineyards was a sign of stability and permanent settlement.[75] The prophets proclaim that forgiven Israel will be given vineyards (Hos 2:15-17), and that in the promised days of YHWH's visitation the treader of grapes shall overtake him who sows the seed (Amos 9:13; Isa 27:2-5; 25:6-8.). The contrast to this is being vine-less (Isa 24:7; Jer 8:13), which symbolized judgement, abandonment, and destruction. This was shown by scenes of wine drying up at the press, representing haunting images of futility and frustration (Jer 48:33; Mic 6:14-15).

Fourth, wine, the fruit of the vine, functioned symbolically as a drink, an expression of "hope for salvation and future life."[76] The vine was considered to be the "vine of life," a notion also applied to bread and fishes, and

---

72. E.g. Isa 54:5; Jer 2:2; Hos 2:16, 19, 20.

73. Akpunonu, *The Vine*, 11.

74. Borowski, *Agriculture*, 155; Nielsen, *Tree*, 78; 1 Kings 4:25; Mic 4:4; 1 Macc 14:12; *Jub*. 13:6; *1 En*. 10:19; 4QM 1:4-5. We will explain this rendering of the metaphor later due to its widespread usage in Israel.

75. Borowski, *Agriculture*, 155; Jeffrey L. Staley, "The Politics of Place and the Place of Politics in the Gospel of John," in *What is John? Vol. 2: Literary and Social Readings of the Fourth Gospel* (SBLSymS; Ed. Fernando F. Segovia; Atlanta: Scholars, 1998), 267, who sees vegetable gardening as a concrete way of saying "This is my home, this is where I have put down roots and will stay."

76. Goodenough, 6:173. See also Poo, 148, where the same imagery is found in Egyptian Pyramid texts and wine is portrayed as a divine drink.

wine-drinking was considered symbolic participation in the vine.[77] This accounts for the frequent use of the pitcher, jar, cup, branch, or the vase as funeral ornamentation, indicating the attachment of an eschatological implication to the drinking of wine.

3.4 The Vine as a Metaphor for Israel in the OT

The vine metaphor refers first and foremost to Israel, the holy covenant people of God, within the OT.[78] However, a debate is on-going regarding whether it refers to the whole nation of Israel or if it is restricted to the leadership. Chaney argues that the metaphor refers only to the ruling élites of Israel and Judah.[79] He suggests that those trapped into self-condemnation in the juridical parable (Isa 5:1-7) can only be the ruling elites of Judah and Israel since the peasant majorities of Israel and Judah were the victims of viticultural injury. But Yee[80] argues that this juridical parable is different from other similar parables in that the inhabitants of Jerusalem and the people of Judah, rather than the king, are requested to judge the vineyard. Following Yee, Kloppenborg Verbin and Williamson also argue against Chaney that the juridical parable concerns the whole of Israel and Judah rather than just the leadership.[81]

The vine metaphor is used in the OT either to refer to Israel as a whole or to groups or individuals within Israel. In Isa 5:7, for example, the writer states categorically that "the vineyard of the Lord is the house of Israel," suggesting that the vineyard song of Isa 5:1-7 including the polemic falls on the nation as a whole.[82] Here "vineyard" is a corporate symbol used for

---

77. Goodenough, 5:100.

78. Isa 5:7; Jer 6:9; Ezek 15:1-8; 18:10-14; Hos 9:10; 10:1; 14:8; Ps 80:8-18.

79. Chaney, "Whose Sour Grapes?," 105-122.

80. Gale A. Yee "A Form-Critical Study of Isaiah 5:1-7 as a Song and Juridical Parable," *CBQ* 43 (1981), 30-40.

81. John S. Kloppenborg Verbin, "Egyptian Viticultural Practices and the Citation of Isaiah 5:1-7 in Mark 12:1-9," *NovT* 44 (2002): 137; Williamson, *Isaiah 1-5*, 338-339.

82. Williamson, *Isaiah 1-5*, 342-343; Adrian Curtis, *Psalms* (EC; Peterborough: Epworth Press, 2004): 170.

the holy covenant people of YHWH. It is this people who are the Lord's vine/vineyard and it is their covenant infidelity or apostasy that is called to question. YHWH is the dedicated vinedresser-friend who has concentrated all his efforts on his vineyard, expecting it to yield choice vines. The question, "what more was there to do for my vineyard that I have not done in it?" (v. 4) spells the extent of YHWH's dedication to his vineyard: he "dug it up," "cleared it of stones," "planted it," "built a watchtower in it," and "cut out a vat" (v. 2). The dedicated work required of a vinedresser can be summarized:

> the vine requires much attention. It must be protected not only from external dangers (wild animals, thieves, enemies, etc.) (cf. Isa 5:2; 27:3), but the soil around it must be ploughed and cleared of stones; it must be supported by low walls (terraced cultivation), and the plants must be pruned, supported and staked if they are free-standing and not decumbent vines.[83]

That YHWH has done all that needs to be done by a vinedresser places the responsibility upon the vineyard; its fruitlessness can only be its fault. Indeed it is Israel's fault that she has been unfaithful to YHWH as a covenant partner. The fruit required by YHWH from Israel his vine is summarized in two words, justice and righteousness, and their antithesis is given respectively as bloodshed and an outcry. According to Akpunonu, "justice is the righting of wrongs, bloodshed is inflicting wounds. Righteousness is right living and right relationships, but cries and screams indicated wrong relationships and the anguish of oppression."[84] It is in the failure to produce justice and righteousness that Israel has become fruitless or has yielded stinking[85] grapes. That justice and righteousness are central to Isaiah's perception of the ideal society is clear in an earlier indictment: "How the faithful city has become

---

83. Nielsen, *Tree*, 77.

84. Akpunonu, *The Vine*, 41.

85. See Kloppenborg Verbin, "Egyptian," 142, who suggests "stinking grapes" as a proper translation of *běušîm* rather than the unlikely "wild grapes" on the grounds that no remains of the *vitis sylvestris* have been found in Canaan and that the passage suggests corruption of what had been planted rather than planting of foreign plants.

a whore! She that was full of justice, righteousness lodged in her—but now murderers" (Isa 1:21). This perception of an ideal society is shared among Isaiah's contemporaries. For example, Amos, a northern contemporary of Isaiah, made strong calls for justice and righteousness to roll like a river and to flow like a never failing stream (Amos 5:24). Micah suggests that God's requirements for justice, kindness, and humility are communicated clearly to Israel: "He has told you, O mortal, what is good; what does the Lord require of you but to do justice, and to love kindness, and to walk humbly with your God" (Micah 6:8). But how should these calls for justice and righteousness at the center of the vine metaphor be understood?

First, Israel's covenant relationship with YHWH is the main issue. Israel is related to the holy God as his holy covenant people. It is on account of this covenant relationship that Israel is called to righteousness and the fulfilment of covenant terms. While YHWH has remained righteous in fulfilling the terms of the covenant (Isa 5:16), Israel has been unfaithful and has gone in rebellion (1:2) and idolatry (2:18). Israel has spurned the Torah, the covenant charter, and no-longer walks in YHWH's path, and has thus ceased to be a beacon to the nations. Instead of walking with God in humility, Israel has become proud and lofty and arrogant. As long as this situation prevails Israel, the vine/vineyard of YHWH can only be a contaminated vine bearing stinking grapes.

Second, Israel's internal social relations are significant. The covenant relationship with YHWH must naturally be visible in the practice of proper social justice. Unfortunately, the conventional cry of the prophets is that this quality vanished from Israel. Social injustice is rampant and this is evident in the exploitation of the poor and the failure to defend widows and orphans, and the perversion of justice by taking bribes (Isa 1:23). Undoubtedly, this is the outcome of Israel's rejection of God, and, Brueggemann is right to say "where the creed is distorted, public life becomes skewed."[86] Thus the prophets could speak of the vine as stinking and degenerate. The ideal vine is a reversal of this and portrays the true people of God in community where justice, righteousness, and regard for

---

86. Walter Brueggemann, *A Commentary on Jeremiah: Exile and Homecoming* (GR: Eerdmans, 1998), 35.

the poor abound. It is clear that the polemic nature of the prophetic oracles regarding the vine centers primarily on the loss of righteousness, justice, kindness, humility, and regard for the poor. It is also clear that this is how the OT writers intended the vine metaphor to be read and interpreted.

Third, the concern for Israel's social relations led to the crafting of a formula, "sitting under the vine and fig tree,"[87] used to depict a messianic time of peace with God and with one another, when the leaders will no more oppress their subjects, and when the poor, the widow, the orphan, and the traveller will be cared for. This proverb embeds within it every detail of Israel's daily life: social, political, religious, and economic. Micah connects it with the beating of swords into plowshares and spears into pruning hooks, another reference to agricultural prosperity, equity, and tranquillity (Mic 4:3). The same notion is expressed in Isaiah where reference is made to ferocious beasts living peaceably with gentle animals (Isa 11:1-9; 65:25). This was a dream time when there was no war, no renegades and outlaws, and when Israel enjoyed victory over all her enemies. In 1 Kings 4:24-25 it is associated with Solomon's reign when Israel gained "peace on all sides," and everyone lived in safety "all of them under their vines and fig trees."

In Zech 3:1-10 this is entirely associated with religious restoration. Zechariah, who prophesied at the dawn of the 2TP, puts the vine metaphor in the context of the restoration and cleansing of the priesthood in a Heavenly Court scene.[88] He associates the metaphor with God's servant, the branch, and the stone, with the latter functioning as a cleansing agent and the resultant era characterized by neighbors inviting one another "under the vine and fig tree." According to Smith, the two metaphors of "branch" and "stone" refer to the coming messiah, who Zechariah saw both as priest and king.[89] As we shall show, this formula is known in 2TJ and to John's audience in late first century C.E.[90]

---

87. Mic 4:4; Zech 3:10; 1 Kings 4:25; 2 Kings 18:31; Isa 36:16.

88. Zech 3:1-10; Carol L. Meyers and Eric M. Meyers, *Haggai, Zechariah 1-8: A New Translation with Introduction and Commentary* (TAB; New York: Doubleday, 1987), 179; Ralph L. Smith, *Micah – Malachi* (*WBC* 32; Waco: WBP, 1984), 199.

89. Smith, *Micah – Malachi*, 201.

90. See 1 Macc 12:14; Also 4QM 1:3-5 where wine is symbolic of being shown the face of God: a time of blessing and peace when God opened his good treasure in heaven and a

3.5 Conclusion

From the data available in the ANE and in the OT, it is apparent that the symbolism of the vine, including its products, has a rich background. Throughout the ANE and the OT the vine and its products feature as important social and religious devices. Whether in Mesopotamia, where the fruit of the vine is scarce and restricted only to the sumptuous banquets of a rich élite, or in Syria-Palestine, where the vine is plentiful and available to all, the social and religious importance of the vine is clear.

Careful attention given to this background may cast significant light upon the rich nuances of the vine metaphor in John 15. Further consideration of the notion of "sitting under the vine and fig tree," which strengthens the metaphor's aspects of social justice and communal holiness, is needed. The most popular interpretation regards Israel as God's chosen vine, yet even that is seldom unpacked within the scholarly literature. It needs to be linked to God's call to Israel to practice righteousness and justice including all the implications for communal holiness. As YHWH's vine, Israel stands before God not as individuals but as a people; a community with salient duties to God and, most importantly, to each other. The communal holiness of God's people as they live in unity with YHWH and with each other, an important aspect of vine symbolism in the ANE and the OT, is the main concern of this research. There is evidence from the ANE and the OT that the vine metaphor concerns social or communal holiness. It is about belonging to God and belonging to each other.

Whether this background will be useful in interpreting the Johannine vine metaphor, however, depends on whether there is continuity or discontinuity in Jewish understanding of the metaphor. This will be tested in the next chapter which explores the vine metaphor in 2TP.

---

time characterized by fruit and wine and oil in plenty; John 1:48.

CHAPTER 4

The Vine Metaphor in
2ⁿᵈ Temple Jewish Literature

4.1 Introduction

The importance of 2TL for understanding early Christianity is highlighted in recent scholarship.[1] This chapter will show how the vine metaphor is used in the 2TP, particularly with reference to the covenant people of God. It investigates non-canonical Jewish literature in order to ascertain significance of the vine and its metaphorical usage in the period leading to the NT. Particularly helpful for understanding Jewish thought of this period is the Dead Sea community, "a Jewish movement nearly contemporary with NT communities."[2] As will become clear, a study of the literature of this community suggests that plant metaphors, including the vine, played an important role in the self-understanding of the community. The focus here

---

1. W. F. Albright, "Recent Discoveries in Palestine and the Gospel of St. John," in *The Background of the New Testament and its Eschatology* (ed. W. D. Davis and D. Daube; Cambridge: Cambridge University Press, 1956), 153-171; R. E. Brown, "The Qumran Scrolls and the Johannine Gospel and Epistles," in *The Scrolls and the New Testament* (ed. K. Stendahl; London: SCM, 1958), 183-207; Stephen Smalley, "New Light on the Fourth Gospel," *TynBul* 17 (1966): 39-40, who refers to "impressive points of contact between the literature of Qumran and John's Gospel"; Brooke, "The Dead Sea Scrolls and New Testament Ecclesiology," in *HENT*, 16-18; Brower, *Gospels*, 24; Dwight D. Swanson, "Holiness in the Dead Sea Scrolls: The Priorities of Faith," in *HENT*, 19; Smalley, *John*, 33-36.
2. Brooke, "Ecclesiology," in *HENT*, 17.

will be on literature dated prior to, or contemporaneous with, the GOJ.[3] Also of interest is determining if there is continuity or discontinuity with the OT in Jewish understanding of the vine metaphor in the 2TP. If there is continuity, the interpretation of John's vine metaphor based on OT and 2TP usage stands on solid ground.

This study includes a discussion of the "pleasant planting" motif which the 2TP writers use for the people of God in right relationship with God. In chapter 2 it was noted that the OT does not give a clear picture of what Israel should look like as YHWH's ideal vine other than in the polemic of the prophets. However, in 2TL the symbolic presentation of the people of God as a "pleasant planting" give clues regarding YHWH's ideal vine. These are embedded in the self-understanding of the Dead Sea community, which saw itself as the faithful remnant.[4] The "pleasant planting" motif embraces key themes that are central to the vine metaphor in the OT and NT such as holiness, covenant, temple or sanctuary, and living according to God's commands.

The "pleasant planting" motif and the vine metaphor are connected in 2TP literature. The writer of 4Q500, for example, juxtaposes the pleasant planting with the vine/vineyard and carefully weaves together the motifs of planting, Eden, and the sanctuary. This strengthens the plausibility of interpreting the pleasant planting with regard to the temple or God's holy space.[5] The writer of *1 En.* 10:16-19 also uses "pleasant trees" as a synonym for "vines", suggesting that they can be used interchangeably. The writer associates the pleasant planting motif with cleansing from injustice, oppression, sin, and iniquity.

The OT shows that early Jewish usage of the vine metaphor centered theologically upon describing Israel's covenant relationship with God and

---

3. The date of the GOJ remains subject to scholarly debate. For the purpose of this research we stick to the period favorable to most scholars at the end of the first century C.E.

4. See F. F. Bruce, *Second Thoughts on the Dead Sea Scrolls* (London: Paternoster, 1966), 110-122; Paul Swarup, *The Self-understanding of the Dead Sea Scrolls Community: An Eternal Planting, A House of Holiness* (LSTS 59; London: T&T Clark, 2006).

5. See George Brooke, *The Dead Sea Scrolls and the New Testament: Essays in Mutual Illumination* (London: SPCK, 2005), 235-261; Joseph M. Baumgarten, "4Q500 and the Ancient Conception of the Lord's Vineyard" *JJS* 40 (1989): 1-6; Swarup, 65-66.

socially in describing human-human relationships. Does the vine metaphor follow these trajectories in the 2TP? This theological and social use of the vine metaphor in relation to the new covenant people of God and the daily life of the covenant community will be explored. Vitally, the notion of "sitting under the vine and fig tree" is used in the OT with reference to peace with God and humankind. This concerns the whole welfare of the people of God: social, economical, religious, and political. The corporate picture of the people sitting under the vine and fig tree denotes peace on all dimensions, horizontal and vertical. Close examination of this notion as used in 1 Macc 14:12, and echoed in John 1:48, shows that a right relationship with God and humankind was an important theme for 2TP Jews as well as the writer of John.[6] This will be shown below in our discussion of the vine as metaphor for social justice, true worship, and blessing.

4.2 The Pleasant Planting

The "pleasant planting" or "righteous planting" motif found in 2TL cannot be separated from the metaphors used to describe the covenant people of God prior to, during, and after the 2TP.[7] To be planted means to be blessed and established securely in the land, and, conversely, to be uprooted means to be cursed and judged and removed from the land.[8] Other variations of the motif include "everlasting trees" (1QH XVI.4-8, 12), "trees of life" (*Pss. Sol.* 14:3), "plantation of fruit" (1QH XVI.19-20), and "plant of truth" (*1 En.* 92:2). The motif is covenantal and, as Bach[9] observes, stems from the theme of Israel's salvation-history, God's guidance to the Promised Land, as well as liturgical terminology concerning a blessing of the settled

---

6. Brueggemann, "Vine and Fig Tree," 188-204.

7. See Exod 15:17 and Num 24:6 in the Yahwistic source and 2 Sam 7:10 in the Deuteronomistic source; cf. Isa 5:7; Jer 2:21; 11:16-19; 12:2; 24:6; 31:41; 42:10; Ezek 17:10; Ps 44:3; 80:8-18.

8. Mark Adam Elliot, *The Survivors of Israel: A Reconsideration of the Pre-Christian Judaism* (GR: Eerdmans, 2000), 329.

9. Robert Bach, "Bauen und Pflanzen," in *Studien zur Theologie der alttestamentlichen Überlieferungen (Festschrift für Gerhard von Rad)* (ed. R. Rendtorff and K. Koch, Neukirchen, 1961), 7-32.

life in the land.[10] It embraces the eschatological hope for the restoration of the people of God (Isa 61:3). The plant is often presented as growing from insignificant and small beginnings to be like a fruitful plant growing into gigantic proportions and eventually having significant impact over the globe.[11]

This motif is associated with the righteousness of the covenant people of God and is used by Isaiah[12] in an eschatological promise for establishment and security to those restored from exile. In Isaiah the returnees are promised a time of prosperity when there will be no more misery caused by invasion. Fujita argues correctly that this motif and various other plant metaphors have a long standing usage in Judaism as metaphors for the righteous within Israel.[13] The motif also carries messianic implications, as shown in Isaiah, where the prophet puts it in the context of the Davidic messiah as "shoot" or "branch."[14] As we shall see, the motif is sometimes used in a sectarian way in Qumran literature to refer to the righteous within the author's community.[15]

In the *Hodayot,* where the planting motif is most explicit, it is used by the Teacher of Righteousness (TR)[16] to describe himself and the community for which he presents himself as responsible. The latter describes the righteous in terms of a privileged community, trees of life hidden among the trees of water, and a fruitful plant that continually bears the fruit of life. According to the TR, God has chosen the righteous from among the children of men, and they are like a green tree beside streams of water bringing forth its leaves and multiplying its branches. The TR uses the shoot, tree, branch, and fruit symbols to refer to himself and his followers (1QH XVI.4-7). He

---

10. S. Fujita, "The Metaphor of Plant in Jewish Literature of the Intertestamental Period," *JSJ* 7 (1976): 36-37.

11. Swarup, 21. Cf. Isa 27:6; 37:31-32.

12. Isa 60:21; 61:3. Cf. Isa 5:7.

13. Fujita, "Plant," 36-37. See also Brooke, *DSS*, 240; Swarup, 24.

14. See Isa 11:1; Jer 23:5; 33:15; Zech 3:8; 6:12.

15. E.g. 1QH XVI. 6, 19-20. Also CD 7:1 where the Qumran community is called the plant.

16. See Brooke, "Ecclesiology," *HENT*, 3-5, for a discussion of the identity of the TR and possible dating of his activity at Khirbet Qumran.

perceives himself and his followers as a fruitful plant that will eventually become the Eden of Glory and bear fruits of life. Those who are against the TR and his sect are called "wicked trees" (1QH XVI.19), and they will be destroyed. The modes of destruction, "the flame of the searing fire" (1QH XVI.12) and the "powerful waters" (1QH XVI.19), are allusions to the fires of Sodom and Gomorrah and the Genesis deluge.

The author of the Psalms of Solomon clearly identifies the planting motif with the righteous within Israel who truly love God, endure his discipline, and live in the righteousness of his commandments (*Pss. Sol.* 14:1-6). His reference to loving God and keeping the commandments allude to the *Shema* and properly encapsulates the monotheistic essence of Judaism (Deut 6:4-9). That the tree (planting) is metaphorical for Israel in a right relationship with YHWH is clear in this text. The reference to the eternal rooted-ness of those who live in the righteousness of God's commandments possibly echoes Psalm 1:1-3 where the righteous are described metaphorically as an evergreen tree planted by streams of water that bears fruit in due season. Echoed here is Isa 58:11 where the prophet addresses the restored people of God as a well-watered garden and a spring whose waters never fail (cf. Jer 32:41). The reference to the righteous as the Lord's Paradise and trees of life parallels that of the righteous as the Eden of glory, and both carry the nuance of a dwelling place free from trouble where the human and the divine are related.[17] Such relationship is expressed by the faithful adherence to the Law which as the covenant document contained the *Halakah*, the way of life.[18]

1 Enoch links the idea of the people of God as a righteous planting with the fall of the Watchers of Heaven and the subsequent flood and the new start of Noah and his family. According to the writer, when the injustice done by the Watchers and their children to humanity is destroyed, "every iniquitous deed will end, and the plant of righteousness and truth will

---

17. See Swarup, 29.

18. The important place of the Law is expressed by the Levite Taxo in his address to his sons: ". . . let us die rather than transgress the commandments of the Lord of lords, the God of our fathers" (*T. Mos* 9:4-7).

appear forever and will plant joy."[19] The plant of righteousness is ushered in as God's new beginning. The writer describes the newly created world as one that is cleansed from all injustice, defilement, oppression, sin, and iniquity.[20] It is a world that will be worked with righteousness, "all of her planted with trees . . . pleasant trees . . . vines."[21]

The Apocalypse of Weeks associates the righteous planting motif with Abraham and his posterity: "a man will be chosen as the plant of righteous judgement, and after him will go forth the plant of righteousness forever and ever."[22] That the "man" alludes to Abraham, and the "plant" to Israel, the chosen people of God, is strengthened by its recurrence in v. 8 where Abraham is regarded as the chosen seed from which a plant of righteousness is to grow and Israel "the whole race of the chosen root." Similarly to that of Noah, the writer puts the election of Abraham in the context of his evil generation so that his election as a seed and root of the plant of righteousness is placed against the prevailing unrighteousness of his generation. Thus Fujita's observation is probably right that "God raises up the righteous to oppose a prevailing evil power."[23]

Jubilees opens with a promise of restoration whereby the righteous ones are promised that they shall be transplanted as a righteous plant: "And with all my heart and with all my soul I shall transplant them as a righteous plant" (Jub. 1:16). Like 1 Enoch, who puts the motif in the context of the corruption of the Watchers, Jubilees puts it in the context of the persecution of the prophets, the captivity, and the loss of the cult. There is a sense in which the people of God are restored and are called to a new beginning. God calls them to himself so that as they repent they shall be transplanted as a righteous plant. The need for a proper response to God's call is made clear in this passage: "When they seek me with all their heart and with all their soul, I shall reveal to them an abundance of peace and

---

19. *1 Enoch* 10:16-17. *The Old Testament Pseudepigrapha: Apocalyptic Literature and the Testaments* (Trans. James H. Charlesworth; London: DLT, 1983), 18.

20. *1 Enoch* 10.16, 20. Trans. Charlesworth.

21. *1 Enoch* 10.18-19. Trans. Charlesworth.

22. *1 Enoch* 93: 5. *A Commentary on the Book of 1 Enoch Chapters 1-36; 81-108* (Trans. George W. Nickelsburg; Minneapolis: Fortress, 2001), 434.

23. Fujita, "Plant," 37.

righteousness."[24] The consequences of this response are great. Those who respond are not only planted as a righteous plant; they are also blessed and not cursed and are made the head and not the tail (*Jub.* 1:17). The language of blessing and cursing echoes Gen 3:1-24 and suggests a reversal of the Edenic curse. This reversal of the curse ties perfectly with God's building of his sanctuary among his people and abiding with them forever. Here the writer juxtaposes the motif of the pleasant planting with the sanctuary or temple motif. The backcloth of this is probably the self-understanding of the DSS community as a house of holiness and a holy of holies (1QH VIII.4-5) where God abides and atonement for the sins of Israel occurs.

The author of Jubilees uses the Hebrew patriarchs, Abraham, Isaac, Esau, and Jacob, to form a lineage of the plant of righteousness motif. For example, Isaac admonished his sons to "Remember . . . the Lord, the God of Abraham . . . that he might multiply you and increase your seed like the stars of heaven . . . and plant you on the earth as a righteous planting which will not be uprooted for all the eternal generations" (*Jub.* 36:6). The community is perceived as the true descendants of Abraham and, therefore, to participate in the blessings of Abraham. This places upon the community the same ethical demands placed upon Abraham.[25] Thus the motif is associated with remembering, worshipping, and serving the Lord in righteousness and joy. Following the righteous Abraham, Isaac, and Jacob, the community is to worship and serve God. All the righteous remnant of the righteous root are the true righteous plant: "the righteous remnant of the righteous forefather is the eschatological Israel to which the author of the book himself also belongs."[26]

In Jubilees we also learn that being planted has preconditions. In the Testament of Noah, for example, justice and righteousness are the preconditions for being planted and being honored before God.[27] Later Isaac advised his sons to love each other with compassion and righteousness because anyone who seeks evil against his brother will be "uprooted from

---

24. *Jub.* 1:15; Jer 29:13-14.
25. Swarup, 62.
26. Fujita, "Plant," 36.
27. *Jub.* 7:34; cf. Jer 11:17; Amos 9:15

the land" of the living and his seed will be destroyed from under heaven.[28] Those with no righteousness, justice, and love are cursed. For example, the Seed of the Philistines and the evil Seed of Canaan are to be uprooted and destroyed and removed from the earth.[29] The connection between the notion of the pleasant planting with justice and righteousness can be seen as an allusion to the biblical justice and righteousness, which the prophets link to the vine metaphor and other tree metaphors for the people of God (e.g. Isa 5:7).[30]

The perception of the righteous as a "plantation of fruit" (1QH XVI.19-20) anticipates the notion of fruit bearing (compare 15:1-8), which the writer interprets in various ways. The righteous are not only a plant but they are "a fruitful plant" and they bear "fruits of life." They are "a life-giving community."[31] The "fruits of life" must be understood in light of the TR's emphasis on holiness among members of the Dead Sea community. This emphasis is made clear by the consciousness of sin and the need for forgiveness and the reference to the members of the sect as those who "drink the waters of holiness" (1QH XVI.13). The consciousness of sin and need for forgiveness is so strong that the writer refers to himself as a "foundation of shame, source of impurity, oven of iniquity, building of sin, spirit of mistake . . ." (1QH IX.22). Despite this predicament, however, the writer makes it clear that by his Holy Spirit God has "purified [the erring spirit] of a multitude of sins" (1QH IX.31-32). Since the TR and his followers believe the fountain of life they now have the right to drink the waters of holiness (1QH XVI.14), commune with the angels of presence, and live forever in the very holiest place where atonement for sins is effected.[32] The connection between the notion of fruit-bearing and holy living is even clearer in the Community Rule when the writer refers to the "fruit of holiness" (1QS 10:22).

---

28. *Jub.* 36.9. For a detailed account on brotherly/sisterly love see the Testament of the Twelve Patriarchs, especially the Testament of Simeon.

29. *Jub.* 24.29-30; 25.9.

30. Swarup, 62.

31. Swarup, 58.

32. Swanson, "Holiness," *HENT*, 25. Swarup, 21.

When the righteous ones have drunk from the waters of holiness they do not only bear fruits of "life" but they also bear "the fruit of the lips" (1QH IX.28). According to the writer the "fruit of the lips" relates to God's creation of breath for the tongue which he established before the tongue could make any words. The writer ascribes to the creator the establishment of the fruit of the lips and through the lips the creator brings forth all sounds that they may tell of his glory and recount his wonderful works (1QH IX.30). Although the fruit of the lips may include the natural ability to speak, it is clear that the writer refers to speaking of God and declaring all the wonders achieved by his mercy. Elsewhere in 1QS the writer refers to the "fruit of praise" (1QS 10:8), strengthening the suggestion for speaking of God and his works. The fruit of the lips is the writer's way of describing the sharing of God's goodness and works of truth with all people so that they may know him and bless him forever.

The TR makes it clear that in order for the planting to blossom and thrive it must depend upon the gardener, God. The planting is the work of God and apart from God it remains wicked and hopeless. It has life and bears fruit only as it is dependant upon the presence of God. God uses his faithful servant, the TR, to care for his glorious garden. The TR says, ". . . but if I remove my hand it will be like the aca[cia in the desert,] its stump like nettles in salt flats, its furrows will make thorns and reeds grow, brambles and thistles . . . the trees of its banks will turn into sour vines" (1QH XVI.24-25). The reference to the trees turning into sour vines gives the impression that this is a vineyard. It is important to note that the vines turn sour when the TR, who represents God, removes his hand. That is, when the covenant relationship is strained the vines turn sour or wild. The sour vines may be an allusion to Isaiah 5:2 and are symbolic of covenant infidelity.[33]

Reference to the righteous as a pleasant planting is also clear in 4Q500 fr.1. In this fragment the writer describes God's people as delightful branches, a description possibly rooted in Isa 5:7 where Israel is described

---

33. The reference to the contaminated vine common in 2TL is found in the OT. See Deut 32: 31-32 where the writer speaks about grapes of poison, and Jer 2:21 where the prophet speaks of corrupt Israel as a wild vine.

as the planting of God's delights. In 4Q500 fr.1 the writer juxtaposes the planting with the vineyard and uses both motifs to describe the people of God as his holy sanctuary. He uses aspects of the vineyard such as the tower and the winepress to refer to the temple and altar respectively.[34] Also present here is an allusion to Eden which was considered to be "the holy of holies and the dwelling place of the Lord."[35] It is clear that the pleasant planting motif was, in Israel's exegetical tradition, associated with motifs of divine presence. The themes that are central to the pleasant planting motif, such as holy community, Eden, temple, or sanctuary, are important for understanding the vine metaphor in the NT. The connection between the pleasant planting motif and the vine/vineyard metaphor presents this motif as a plausible background for the vine metaphor in the periods subsequent to the 2TP. With this link between the planting and the vine established, we shall explore the negative use of the vine metaphor to describe the people of God in 2TL.

4.3 The Vine Metaphor as a Negative Portrait of God's Covenant People

Like most OT passages where the vine metaphor is used regarding the people of God, 2TL uses the vine metaphor in a negative sense to describe a contaminated relationship between God and his people Israel. While the "pleasant planting" describes Israel or some part of it in a right relationship with God, the absence of this planting or the corruption of its fruits show the antithesis. The writers stress the negative deliberately to show the unacceptability of the broken relationship between God and his covenant people. Under the broken covenant relationship 2TP Jews, following the OT, describe the corrupt practices of Israel's leaders and the general failure of the nation in walking according to the teaching of the Law in various ways. Frequently the failed relationship between God and his people is shown in the corrupt social practices of the people, especially when the

---

34. Swarup, 66; Brooke, *DSS*, 239; Baumgarten, *4Q500*, 3.
35. Swarup, 64.

leaders and the rich disregard poor widows and orphans. A period characterized by the evils of injustice and inequity was described negatively as a
time when there was "no seed of the vine" (*Jub.* 23:18, 21) or when the vine
turned into "the serpent's venom" (CD VIII.9; cf. Deut 32:33). Such times
invited the judgment of God, regularly symbolized by the uprooted plant
or the failed winepress.

4.3.1 The Serpent's Venom

The writer of the Damascus Document (CD) describes the ethical life of
the enemies of God as "wine turned to serpent's venom."[36] The writer's
commentary suggests that wine could be used as a metaphor for paths (CD
VIII.10-11). In biblical language paths can refer to ethical conduct.[37] If the
paths are straight the way of life is righteous and if the paths are crooked it
is unrighteous. If ethical conduct is upright the wine is good, and if ethical
conduct is polluted it means the wine is venomous. For the writer of the
CD, as is for the Deuteronomist (Deut 32:33) and the OT prophets, upright ethical conduct is associated with holiness, expressed in social justice
and caring for the oppressed, orphan, widow, poor, and marginalized of
society.[38]

The NT represents the serpent, whose venomous bite and cunning
deception woo its prey, as a type of Satan.[39] The serpent is associated with
divine judgement.[40] To describe the rulers and kings of the people as serpents sounds harsh but fitted the leaders of this time due to their injustices
and ill-treatment of the people. The period was characterized by exploitation and oppression of the poor by the rich élites, a similar scenario to that
of Sodom, in Israel. The people of God have rejected God, evidenced in
their complicity in far-reaching social injustice. As long as this prevailed, all
that could be expected was poisonous vines if not an empty field where "no

---

36. CD VIII. 9; Deut 32:33.

37. See for example, Ps 17:4-5; 23:3; 25:4; Prov 2:13, 20; 3:6, 17; 4:11; 7:25; 8:2, 20; Isa 2:3; 3:2; Matt 3:3; Mark 1:3; Luke 3:4; Heb 12:13.

38. CD VI. 15-20; Isa 5:8-23.

39. For a full description of the serpent and how it is presented in the Bible as a type of Satan, see L. McFall, "Serpent," *NDBT*: 773-75.

40. Acts 23:3-4; 1 Cor 10:9.

songs are sung, no shouts raised; no treader treads out wine in the presses" (Isa 16:10), or simply, "no seed of the vine" (*Jub.* 23:18, 21).

The writer of CD is clear that the problem is covenant unfaithfulness. Rather than ethics dictated by the covenant terms, the people of God have copied the faithless ethics of their enemies and literally "walked on the path of the wicked" (CD VIII.9). They have responded to God's faithfulness with wickedness, rebellion and insolence. While God remains "a faithful God who does no wrong" the people "have acted corruptly towards him" (Deut 32:4-5). The writer's interpretation of the serpents as the kings of the people suggests that a leadership irregularity has caused this degeneration. The association of this corruption with the civic and religious leadership of Israel and Judah is clearly stated by Bruegemann, who states: "Priests no longer provide serious leadership. Judges forget their central commitment to justice. Rulers forget that power is a trust from Yahweh. Prophets forget that God has summoned them."[41] Deut 32:32-33, the text in the background of CD VIII.8-12, suggests Sodom as the context and her leaders as the evil influence. That the degeneration refers to social issues is underscored by Ezekiel's polemic against Jerusalem: "This was the guilt of your sister Sodom: . . . pride, excess of food, prosperous ease, but did not aid the poor and needy" (Ezek 16:49-50).

4.3.2 "There will be no seed of the vine" (*Jub.* 23:18, 21)

> Behold, the land will be corrupted on account of all their deeds, and there will be *no seed of the vine*, and there will be no oil because their works are entirely faithless . . . and they will pronounce the great name but not in truth or righteousness. And they will pollute the holy of holies with their pollution and with the corruption of their contamination.[42]

In Jubilees the vine metaphor carries the concepts of righteousness and faith, or, negatively, unrighteousness and faithlessness. This can be inferred

---

41. Brueggemann, *Jeremiah*, 35.
42. *Jub.* 23:18, 21. Emphasis is mine.

from the author's eschatological description of the period of the absence of the seed[43] of the vine as the cause for the corruption of the land and the entire faithlessness of the future evil generation. Clearly, the author associates the absence of the seed of the vine with spells of doom, deficiency in faith, unrighteousness, and the reign of evil.

Ironically the absence of the seed of the vine does not equal the absence of religion or forms of worship. Rather, it equals the lack of truthfulness and sincerity in worship and the lack of ethical holiness, which was visible in the entirely faithless works and in the desolating sacrilege. With its characteristic misuse of wealth, cheating, stealing, mentioning of the divine name improperly, and defiling the holy of holies, the absence of the seed of the vine is utter rejection of the covenant.[44] The defilement of the holy of holies implies that the priests, including the high priest who alone enters there, are involved in the corruption.

The seed of the vine is a complete contrast to the vine of Sodom, the evil seed of Canaan, and the seed of the Philistines used elsewhere to describe an evil generation to be uprooted and removed from the earth.[45] Its absence implies a full reign of the vine of Sodom, the evil seed of Canaan, and the seed of the Philistines characterized by abominations of all kind including hypocrisy and pollution of the holy of holies. The seed of the vine and the evil seed of Canaan do not cohabit. According to *Enoch* the evil seed of the wicked will experience curse (*1 En.* 80:2-3), judgement[46] and obliteration[47] while the righteous seed is preserved for kingship and great glory (*1 En.* 65:12).

The juxtaposition of the absence of the seed of the vine with that of olive oil strengthens the anathema of the evil generation. The olive is a luxuriant and vigorous tree, and, as the fat of the time, its oil was essential for cooking, lighting, wound treatment, cosmetics, and as offering.[48] Due to the quality

---

43. See Elliot, *Survivors*, 314-328, for a thorough discussion of seed theology and its significance in Jewish thought.

44. James C. VanderKam, *The Book of Jubilees* (Sheffield: SAP, 2001), 58.

45. *Jub.* 24:29-30; 25:9.

46. *1 En.* 108:3. Also *Jub.* 16:7-9.

47. *1 En.* 80:2-3; 84:6. Also *Jub.* 16:7-9; 35:14.

48. Nielsen, *Tree*, 76.

of its fruit, the strength of its shoots from the roots, and the evergreen leaves, it is a suitable image for representing vitality.[49] Pairing these creates a double emphasis used by the author to connote the deficiency in justice and righteousness at the time of the evil generation.

4.4 The Vine as a Metaphor for Social Justice

The story of the Maccabaean struggle for independence under the leadership of Simon offers the best example of often recurring socio-political nuances of the vine metaphor in 2TL. Maccabees' author uses the metaphor in the context of liberation where a previously oppressed minority community overcomes the oppressor and gains a momentous victory. The text is a celebration of a new era characterized by a new distribution of freedom, power, and goods; an era marking the end of the threat of foreign taxes and exploitation.[50] For the vine is not only about the covenant people of God and their relationship with God; it also concerns the social welfare of the people of God in the land.[51] This includes both the leadership's sensitivity to and provision for the social needs of the people alongside a sound foreign policy.

The author describes the victory won by Simon and the subsequent political stability in this way: "He established peace in the land, and Israel rejoiced with great joy. All the people sat under their own vines and fig trees, and there was none to make them afraid. No one was left in the land to fight them, and the kings were crushed in those days."[52] Clearly, the metaphor is used here to describe a political turn, the reversal of a scenario

---

49. Ps 128:3; Jer 11:16; Hos 14:6-7. See Nielsen, *Tree*, for a detailed analysis of the olive juxtaposed with the vine and its overall significance in the OT.

50. Brueggemann, "Vine" 202.

51. See Davies, *The Gospel and the Land*, 24-35, 49-104, for a detailed analysis of the significance of the land. Davies uses the phrase "dogma of Judaism" to describe the emphasis on the land. Also Marcus Borg, *Conflict, Holiness and Politics in the Teachings of Jesus*, (rev. ed.; Harrisburg: Trinity, 1998), 75, who echoes Davies' words and stresses that "the land of Israel was Yahweh's land and thus holy. It was sacred space not to be profaned (Num 35:34).

52. 1 Macc 14: 11-13.

of powerlessness, oppression, and exploitation. According to Bartlett, it is "more concerned with politics than religion."[53] The constant threat and fear of being attacked by an enemy is now history. Thus the writer can speak of "peace in the land." The writer adopts the metaphor from the OT[54] to use it in his context in the 2TP. Three elements can be identified in his use of the metaphor: first, rest in the land, which comes with a leader who seeks the best for his/her people; second, peace in the land, which comes with a leader who protects and provides enough food supplies for his/her people; and third, regard for the poor and underprivileged of society. These all suggest an alternative social and economic practice and further anticipate a new distribution of freedom, power, and goods. With provision for these needs comes a scenario where everyone will sit under his/her own vine and fig tree. However, Simon's reform of the temple and its cult shows that social reform alone is not sufficient to bring peace.

4.5 The Vine Metaphor as an Appeal for True Worship

As noted, the Prophet Isaiah and his contemporaries use the vine metaphor to describe the serious social, moral and religious decay of 8th century Israel and Judah. On the religious level, the prophets decried the perversion of worship practices and rebuked religious leaders for earning wealth at the expense of pure religious practice.[55] They called for a reversal of the anomaly of professional prophets and priests of local shrines behaving more like merchants than servants of God.[56] They deprecated the deceptive outward practice of religion that did not spring from a true heart of worship and, therefore, did not translate to justice and regard for the poor.

---

53. John R. Bartlett, 1 *Maccabees* (Sheffield: SAP, 1998), 87. It is important to note that the cleansing of the temple recorded in 1 Macc 14:15 reflect that religion and worship are an integral part of Simon's reforms.

54. Zechariah differs in that it is entirely religious and has no mention of a political leader. Instead, the focus is on the priest who is an omen of what YHWH is doing or is about to do. YHWH will remove the guilt, sin and punishment of the land and consequently, "you shall invite each other to come under your vine and fig tree."

55. See for example, Mic 1:7; 3:5-7, 11; 5:11-13.

56. Ralph L. Smith, *Micah – Malachi* (WBC 32; Waco: WBP, 1984), 5.

Jewish literature shows that the vine metaphor functions in the same way in the 2TP and beyond. One of Simon's cherished achievements which characterize the messianic era of "sitting under the vine and fig tree" is the restoration of true worship. For Simon the enthronement of YHWH and the dethronement of all other deities is crucial if the people's living conditions are to improve. True peace is realized when YHWH's divine kingdom is in the midst of his people: ". . . the appearance of YHWH's reign on earth will inaugurate an imperial peace that transforms the conditions of life for nations and individuals."[57]

The Maccabaean writer says Simon ". . . made the sanctuary glorious, and added to the vessels of the sanctuary" (1 Macc 14:15). This action is a reversal of the wrongs done by Antiochus IV, who dishonored the temple and took away its glorious vessels.[58] The temple is the important symbol of God's dwelling in the midst of his people and, therefore, must be sanctified. Integral to this sanctification is the dethronement of foreign gods and the enthronement of the one true God. If God's house is not sanctified, and God is not enthroned, and if God's people are not walking according to God's Law, there is no sitting under the vine and the fig tree.

Simon's cleansing of the temple and enshrining of the Law is a true reflection of the religion of post-exilic Israel. The Torah and the temple were the two foundational institutions of Israel throughout the Maccabaean period and into the NT.[59] That Simon "sought out the Law and did away with all the renegades and outlaws" (1 Macc 14:14) recalls the polemical approach of Israel's prophets and has strong ethical implications. The importance is not in the performance of empty rituals but in living according

---

57. Mays, *Micah*, 93.

58. 1 Macc 2:8-13. This lament by Mattathias shows how strongly the Jews felt about the land. Occupation of the land by gentiles was the most sacrilegious act Jews could imagine. Further, nothing could be deemed worse than watching the beauty and splendor of the temple laid waste and profaned by the gentiles. Mattathias and his sons' response—tearing their garments, wearing of sackcloth, and mourning bitterly—are expressions of gross displeasure, shame, or discontentment. In the OT the public tearing of garments displayed despair (Gen 37:29), grief (Job 2:12; Ezra 9:13), mourning (2 Sam 1:11-12), and loss of status (Num 20:26).

59. Marcus Borg, *Conflict, Holiness and Politics in the Teachings of Jesus* (rev. ed. Harrisburg: TPI, 1998), 51. Borg also mentions the cardinal importance of holiness as the *imitatio Dei* in the interpretation of the Torah and function of the Temple.

to the Law which is the covenant charter. According to Vermes, "all Jews of the inter-testamental era, the Essenes as well as their rivals, agreed that true piety entails obedience to the law . . ."[60] The formula, "sitting under the vine and fig tree" is about seeking God first and following the demands of his righteousness as set forth in his word and instruction. Such instruction concerns the terms of the covenant including upholding communal holiness and rejecting oppression of the poor and helpless. The leaders, both civic and religious, must stop ripping the skin and eating the flesh the Lord's people.[61] The entire national life of Israel must be permeated by holiness, upholding daily the two institutions of Torah and temple.

4.6 The Vine as a Metaphor for Blessing and Prosperity

The vine metaphor functions as a symbol of blessing and prosperity in the 2TP. The reference to blessing and prosperity stems from the use of the metaphor to describe the riches and agrarian prosperity of the Promised Land. For example, in his sojourn at Bethel, Abram saw that "the land was wide and very good and everything was growing in it: vines and figs and pomegranate trees . . ." (*Jub.* 13:6). The vine is used metaphorically, describing the prosperity of the land and of the people of God in it.

In 2TL this is also depicted by the plant motif. The righteous are planted and they begin to grow, blossom, and bear fruit.[62] According to Jubilees, the transplanted people of God will become a blessing and not a curse, a head and not a tail, and God will build his sanctuary in their midst and dwell among them.[63] The themes of blessing and cursing are important in ANE literature and in the OT. In the ANE, for instance, where life

---

60. Geza Vermes, *DSS*, 38.

61. Mic 3:3. See Gary Stansell, *Micah and Isaiah: A Form and Tradition Historical Comparison* (Atlanta: Scholars, 1988), 106. "Ripping the skin and eating the flesh" is what the leaders are guilty of. The metaphor portrays harmful actions against one's neighbour. It is not a reference to cannibalism but is a metaphor used elsewhere for wicked actions against defenceless persons (cf. Ps 14:4; Pr 30:14; Hab 3:14).

62. See, for example, 1 QH XVI. 6, 20; *Pss. Sol.* 14:3-4.

63. *Jub.* 1.16, 17.

was dominated by the need to cope with the terrifying threat of curses and omens, there was a massive amount of rituals and incantations for the revoking or breaking of curses. According to Evans, the belief in the efficacy of blessings and curses was so strong that people could only live normally because there was a possibility of such revocation.[64] Thus the pronouncement of blessing on a person or group of people guaranteed freedom from the bondage of fear of curses or omens. Blessing was a sign of favor from the deity and it meant that the god was happy that his subjects kept his rules. The writer uses "head" metaphorically to mean chief, first, or top.

In the OT, however, blessing is part of the covenant between God and his people. It begins with participation in the covenant, which means being in a relationship with YHWH, and for the Qumran community, includes withdrawal to the desert. The subsequent blessing in material terms such as fertility, prosperity, peace, and victory come as the relationship is maintained. Deuteronomy states clearly that if the people of God uphold the covenant and remain faithful they shall be blessed.[65] This is probably why the writer of Jubilees ascribes the blessing to those who have been transplanted, that is, the covenant people of God. In the same way the curses of drought, famine, sickness, defeat, and general ignominy follow automatically when the covenant is rejected. The curse is the true essence of life lived outside a relationship with YHWH.[66]

The Book of Watchers associates the blessing and prosperity of the righteous with God's preservation of his elect and the shining of God's light

---

64. M. J. Evans, "Blessing/curse," *NDBT*, 398. Also John G. Gager, *Curse Tablets and Binding Spells from the Ancient World* (NY: Oxford University Press, 1992), 107, who records that "the Geniza preserved numerous charms, spells, and amulets . . ." and that "The materials from the Geniza reveal how widespread such beliefs were in Jewish communities of the ancient world and how broadly this material circulated, crossing linguistic, chronological, cultural, and religious boundaries." Similar traditions exist throughout Africa where casting a spell on someone can secure his or her affections or bind him or her from any success in life. Breaking such spells and curses is done by prayers of certain gifted prophets or by incantations of traditional doctors.

65. Deut 27-28. See also Alex Deasley, *The Shape of Qumran Theology* (Carlisle: Paternoster, 2000), 140, for a concise description of the covenant and its terms as set out in the OT. Deasley rightly states that this covenant, which was significant both as a political and religious instrument, persisted into the Hellenistic period and served as the foundation of the Qumran Community's basic beliefs.

66. Evans, *NDBT*, 398.

upon them: "And to all the righteous he will grant peace. He will preserve the elect, and kindness shall be upon them. They shall all belong to God and they shall prosper and be blessed; and the light of God shall shine upon them" (*1 En.* 1:8). Again we note that blessing is covenantal. It is a promise for the elect; those belonging to God are in relationship with him. The blessing of peace is promised to them all together in community regardless of social status.

A similar tone is found in 4QM where the Sons of light are themselves a blessing and are shown the face of God (1:3), and the time of blessing and peace is considered a time when God has opened his good treasure in heaven.[67] The metaphor of the face of God refers to the character of God, especially his favor towards his people. When God turns his face to his people he looks at them with favor and offers them his grace and help.[68] At this time God showers his elect with blessings, dew, rain in its time, and fruit in plenty. The opening of treasure in heaven recalls the blessing of Malachi (3:10) which the prophet links to financial faithfulness. The antithesis is when God turns his face against his people and withholds his favor and blessing.[69]

4.7 Conclusion

Several facets of the vine metaphor in the OT and the ANE are observable in the 2TP. These are important for understanding the richness of the vine metaphor and for its exegesis in the NT.

First, it is conspicuous that Israel (or some precursor of it) is the vine and the tree of God's planting. Reference to them as the vine or vineyard suggests a covenant relationship with God. Usage of plant metaphors to portray the covenant people of God and their relationship with God and with each other is characteristic of the Jews of the OT and 2TP. Where

---

67. 4QM 1.4, 5.

68. Num 6:24-26 where the face of God is a sign of blessing; cf. Ps 4:6; 31:16; 67:1; 80:19; 105:4; 119:135; Ezek 39:29.

69. See Ps 44:24; 13:1; 88:14.

the relationship is broken the plants are rotten or fruitless. Thus the vine metaphor also became a device to scrutinize and to critique, first, the relationship with God and, second, the social life of the people of God. It is a device for the polemic of the prophets against the religious and political leaders, while not sparing the whole people of God, who have spurned the covenant and its terms. As a theological device it represents divine-human relations and as a social device it represents human-human relations. Thus both sets of relations are embedded in the vine metaphor with the latter focusing primarily on the critique of leader-people relations.

Second, it is also clear that 2TP Judaism includes a heavy signification of the vine and its products, especially wine as a libation and sacrifice. This indicates a strong belief in the efficacy of the vine and its products enhancing divine-human experience. The extensive use of wine and *tîrôš* in 11QT in table fellowship and in community worship is sufficient evidence of that.[70] Thus we can affirm that in the mind of the Jews of the 2TP, as in those of the period prior to it, the vine and its products persist as powerful theological devices used to foster a relationship of the divine and the human.

Third, the notion of "sitting under the vine and fig tree" is important for understanding the vine metaphor in the OT and 2TP. This formula concerns the restoration of shared peace and tranquillity and is richly corporate in character. Its emphasis on relationship, both divine-human and human-human, is a concern for covenant fidelity and communal holiness and thus a cry for the recreation of the holy people of God. It is an expression of the intrinsic desire to return to the status of an ideal vine where righteousness, justice, solidarity, and concern for the poor are embraced as foundational pillars of the community.

The next chapter will show how the qualities of the ideal vine are met in John's portrait of Jesus as the true vine. It seems clear that John's audience identified Jesus with the ideal vine against Israel's failure to be that. We shall

---

70. See 11QT XIII.12 where *tîrôš* is brought to the altar of YHWH year after year from the tribes of Israel as a drink offering; cf. 11QT XLIII. 8, where the writer describes the annual festival of wine whereby the children of Israel were to pour *tîrôš* on the altar of sacrifice with great rejoicing.

show how Jesus surpasses Israel by fulfilling God's requirements for fidelity, righteousness, justice, obedience, corporateness, and communal holiness.

CHAPTER 5

The Vine Metaphor in the Gospel of John

5.1 Introduction

5.1.1 John 15:1-17 in Context

The examination of the historical background of the vine and its meta-phorical usage in the ANE, OT, and 2TP in the two preceding chapters has demonstrated its significance for understanding the vine metaphor in 15:1-17. NT scholars have a near consensus concerning its OT background. Hence, Bultmann's suggestion of a Mandaean background for the vine metaphor is rightly questioned.[1] Carson[2] suggests two factors in favor of an OT background: 1) the frequency of John's appeals to the OT, both in allusions and in quotations; 2) the dominance in the GOJ of the "replacement" motif. The latter remains a matter of scholarly debate. Dennis, for example, argues that the Johannine community "would not have understood its belief in Jesus the Messiah of Israel as a 'leaving behind' of 'Judaism' but

---

1. See *Ginza* 59:39-60:2; 301:11-14. Bultmann, on the basis of Mandaean texts, suggests that the background for the metaphor is the Gnostic idea of the vine as the tree of life. This is unlikely since there is no evidence that Mandaeanism predates the GOJ: see Craig A. Evans, *Word and Glory: On the Exegetical and Theological Background of John's Prologue* (Sheffield: SAP, 1993), 13.

2. Carson, *John*, 513.

rather as the true realization of all that the Jewish prophets, Scriptures and expectations pointed to."[3]

John's appeal to the OT is evident in how he leads his readers through key themes and motifs of the OT, carefully showing how these are fulfilled in Jesus.[4] Some themes include the presentation of Jesus as Jacob's ladder, the true descending-ascending revealer of God (1:18, 51); the portrayal of Jesus as the true Mosaic prophet[5] and Messiah (1:41; 4:25-26); the portrayal of Jesus as the true temple (2:19-22), true bread (manna), and the embodiment of the Law (6:25-51); the presentation of Jesus as the Holy One of God (6:69); the designation of Jesus as shepherd and his followers as sheep (10:1-19); and the portrayal of Jesus as the true embodiment of Israel, the covenant people of God, which is central to the vine metaphor.

An OT/2TP motif that underlies our interpretation of 15:1-17 is the Jewish notion of "sitting under the vine and fig tree."[6] The use of this motif early in the Gospel when Jesus sees Nathanael "under the fig tree" shows that it is known to John's audience.[7] For John, the one who sits "under the fig tree" is "truly an Israelite in whom is no deceit!" (1:47), indicating "religious and moral integrity."[8] Indeed, it is "an Israelite in whom there is no Jacob."[9] The link with Jacob suggests lessons concerning communal holiness. Also pertinent are OT passages where the "vine and fig tree" are used with reference to peace with God and humankind.[10] It is not clear why

---

3. John A. Dennis, *Jesus' Death and the Gathering of True Israel: The Johannine Appropriation of Restoration Theology in the Light of John 11.47-52* (Tübingen: Mohr Siebeck, 2006), 46. Dennis clearly rejects Carson's view.

4. See Barnabas Lindars, *The Gospel of John* (TNCBC; GR: Eerdmans, 1972), 36-38, for more information on the Jewishness of the GOJ; Smalley, *John*, 68-70, for helpful information on John's use of the OT. Smalley argues persuasively that John's use of the OT demonstrates a profound understanding of its thematic contents.

5. Deut 18:15-19; 1 Macc 4:46; 1QS 9:9-11; John 1:17-18; 7:40-41.

6. See chapter 3.

7. See Koester, *Symbolism*, 40, for the connection between John 1:48 and Zech 3:8 and other OT passages regarding the Davidic Messiah.

8. Lindars, *John*, 118.

9. Craig L. Blomberg, *The Historical Reliability of John's Gospel: Issues and Commentary* (Leicester: IVP, 2001), 83.

10. See Morris, *John*, 67, and Blomberg, *Historical Reliability*, 83, for possible link with the OT texts that use the formula.

Johannine scholars have not seen the importance of this for understanding the Johannine vine metaphor. We, therefore, suggest that the peace with God and humankind that underlie the OT passages where the formula is used establishes an important milieu for reading 15:1-17.

A message of peace[11] suits the social context of the Gospel writer. We will refer, for example, to two major problems John's community faced at the time of his writing. First, an internal problem where the disciples were excommunicated from the synagogue is stated clearly in the Gospel (9:22; 12:42; 16:2). This suggests a late first century context when normative rabbinic Judaism was taking measures to exclude various expressions of heterodoxy, which had become regarded as heresy, including belief in Jesus as Messiah.[12] The severity of this is described by Rensberger whereby believers faced being "cut off from much that had given identity and structure to their lives . . . social ostracism and thus the loss of relationship with family and friends, and perhaps economic dislocation as well."[13] Second, the persecution of believers by some emperors for refusing to worship other deities, including the emperor, must also be considered for understanding John's vine metaphor.[14] It is also clear that the disciples will continue to

---

11. See chapter 4.

12. Dunn, "Let John Be John," 304.

13. See David Rensberger, *Johannine Faith and Liberating Community* (Philadelphia: Westminster, 1988), 26-27, who also suggests that "it is surely correct to give this experience a central role in understanding the background of the Fourth Gospel"; F. F. Bruce, *The Gospel of John: Introduction, Exposition and Notes* (GR: Eerdmans, 1983), 13, who suggests the exclusion of Christians from the synagogue as plausible background for reading the GOJ. A close example would be a scenario where a Muslim converts to another faith where social ostracism, even to the point of honor killing, would be excusable punishment.

14. See Koester, "Saviour," 666; Reed, "Rethinking John's Social Setting," 95-6; Kierspel, *The Jews*, 181-212; Hans-Joseph Klauk, *The Religious Context of Early Christianity: A Guide to Graeco-Roman Religions* (Minneapolis: Fortress, 2003), 250-330; Sjef Van Tilborg, *Reading John in Ephesus* (NovTSup 83; Leiden: Brill, 1996), 174-212; S. R. F. Price, *Rituals and Power: The Roman Imperial Cult in Asia Minor* (Cambridge: Cambridge University Press, 1984); Stephen S. Smalley, *Thunder and Love: John's Revelation and John's Community* (Milton Keynes: Word Publishing, 1994), 41; Steven J. Friesen, *Imperial Cults and the Apocalypse of John: Reading Revelation in the Ruins* (Oxford: Oxford University Press, 2001), 5-131; Paul Trebilco, *The Early Christians in Ephesus from Paul to Ignatius* (WUNT 166; Tübingen: Mohr Siebeck, 2004), 11-52; Adolf Deissmann, *Light From the Ancient East: The New Testament Illustrated by Recently Discovered Texts of The Graeco-Roman World* (4th ed.; NY: GHDC, 1927), 364; Paul N. Anderson, *The Fourth Gospel*

experience persecution in future (15:18-16:4), Peter going so far as to be martyred (21:18-19). The impact of these problems upon the social and religious lives of the believers must not be minimized. It is this context that is reflected in the Gospel and must be taken seriously if the words of John are to mean anything to its readers.

Much has been said in the last two chapters concerning the rich background from which NT vine metaphorical speech is drawn. Now two questions are raised regarding the vine metaphor in John: What is the meaning of 15:1-17 in its context and how might it have been understood by its first audience? Addressing these questions is the task of this chapter. In doing so, we will draw from the conclusions of previous discussions about metaphorical usage of the vine in the OT and 2TP. Reading the metaphor in conversation with the whole farewell discourse, we examine each of the images that make up John's vine metaphor in relation to how John uses them to describe vertical and horizontal relationships. In order to put the vine metaphor in its proper context we begin with a brief discussion of the relationship between the Gospel and the other Johannine writings and the nature of the farewell discourse.

5.1.2 The Gospel's Relation to the Other Johannine Writings

"Discussion of Johannine Christianity is dependent on the recognition of a discrete collection of distinctive Johannine writings, the Gospel, three Epistles, and the Apocalypse."[15] As this quote suggests, the GOJ belongs to a group of literature traditionally attributed to the authorship of John, the beloved disciple and Apostle: the Gospel, 1, 2, 3 John, and Revelation.[16]

---

and the Quest for Jesus: Modern Foundations Reconsidered (New York: T&T Clark, 2007), 34, 63; Even more important is the consideration that at about the same time that the GOJ was written the emperor Domitian (81-96 C.E.), like others before and after him (Tiberius (14-37 C.E.), Caligula (37-41 C.E.), Trajan (98-117 C.E.) and others), declared himself as *Dominus et Deus* (master and god) and demanded his worship.

15. John Painter, *The Quest for the Messiah: The History, Literature and Theology of the Johannine Community* (Edinburgh: T&T Clark, 2nd ed., 2001), 33. Cf. David E. Aune, *Revelation 1-5* (WBC 52; Dallas: Word Books, Publisher, 1997), liv.

16. There is no scholarly consensus on the authorship of the Johannine literature. Debates on the authorship and/or redaction which led to the final work traditionally attributed

However, current scholarship often rejects this tradition.[17] Many scholars argue that the GOJ and the Epistles were written by different authors while many others argue that the Gospel and Revelation were written by different authors.[18] Although there is no scholarly consensus regarding the authorship of these writings, there has been no serious challenge to the suggestion that they derive from the same community.

A plausible approach focuses on the common features and similarities in these writings, strengthening a suggestion for coherence. Among other scholars, Smalley argues persuasively that these Johannine writings are a coherent corpus suitable for narrative criticism.[19] According to Smalley, subsequent research into the linkages within the Johannine corpus "has brought into focus the existence and nature of a community behind this collection of literature: a church with a life and problems of its own, struggling not only with the persecution from outside, but also with growing doctrinal (. . .) tensions from within the circle."[20] If Smalley is right, as we posit, the Johannine writings belong together and, therefore, must be studied together.

The Gospel's closest links are with the Epistles.[21] The style and language of the Johannine Jesus are closer to those of the epistles.[22] Clear similarities between the Gospel and the Epistles include use of same major motifs such as abiding, light, life, death, love, truth, and testimony. Also clear among

---

to John fall outside the scope of this research. This thesis works with the final form of the GOJ (see chapter 1).

17. See W. G. Kümmel, *Introduction to the New Testament* (trans. H. C. Kee; NY: Abingdon, 1975), 442, for a review of scholarship rejecting this tradition. Kümmel, 445, however, argues that the grounds for attributing 1 John to another author are not strong. Cf. Keener, I:126-139.

18. See Fernando F. Segovia, *Love Relationships in the Johannine Tradition: Agapē/Agapan in 1 John and the Fourth Gospel* (SBLDS 58; Chico: Scholars Press, 1982), 14-24, for a history of scholarship on the relationship between the Johannine writings, particularly the Gospel and 1 John.

19. Stephen S. Smalley, "The Johannine Literature: A Sample of Recent Studies in English," *Theology* 103 (2000): 13-28.

20. Smalley, "The Johannine Literature," 13. Cf. Smalley, *John*, 145-148.

21. Smalley, *Thunder and Love*, 57.

22. See C. H. Dodd, "The First Epistle of John and the Fourth Gospel" *BJRL* 21 (1937): 129-156.

the similarities is the use of ethical dualism where the world is seen as the sphere of unbelief and as hating believers. In his discussion of the relations between 1 John and the GOJ, Bultmann suggests: "The relationship between 1 John and the Gospel rests on the fact that the author of 1 John had the Gospel before him and was decisively influenced by its language and ideas."[23] While differences also exist between these writings,[24] we concur with current scholarship that these similarities show that "1 John is very close indeed to the mind and spirit of the Gospel."[25] The Gospel and the Epistles, particularly 1 John, are similar in theological standpoint, terminology, and style.

The relationship between the Apocalypse and the other parts of the Johannine corpus is subject to much dispute. "A great gulf appears to be fixed between"[26] them. Differences in style and content have convinced most Johannine scholars that the John of Revelation is not the writer of the Gospel. The quality of his Greek is much inferior and the way he uses the OT diverges from that of the Gospel. His eschatology, which is characterized by future expectation, differs markedly from the so-called realized eschatology of the Gospel. However, despite the differences, the Gospel and the Apocalypse do have similarities. They have some themes in common, such as the ethical dualism in which the world's political powers are hostile to people of God; the motifs of witness and martyrdom; negative references to the synagogue; use of "I Am" sayings; portrayal of Jesus as word, shepherd, and lamb. It is in accounting for these similarities that the links between the Apocalypse and the other Johannine writings is forged. Links can be traced to the existence of the Johannine community, a church whose history "can be traced from Revelation, through the Gospel, to the Johannine letters."[27]

---

23. Rudolf Bultmann, *The Johannine Epistles: A Commentary on the Johannine Epistles* (Hermeneia; ed. Robert W. Funk; Philadelphia: Fortress, 1973), 1.

24. E.g. Different uses of shared themes: some concepts (such as abiding) associated with Jesus in the Gospel are associated with God in the Epistles; the absence in the Gospel of key motifs such as antichrist, glory, anointing, fellowship, seek, etc.

25. Whitacre, *Johannine Polemic*, 5.

26. Smalley, *Thunder and Love*, 57.

27. Smalley, *Thunder and Love*, 69.

5.1.3 The Nature of the Farewell Discourse

The farewell discourse is set in the context of a community meal where Jesus, knowing that his hour had come to depart from this world, washes his disciples' feet and dines with them before giving his last words (13:1-30). The farewell discourse consists of three units: 1) the first farewell speech (13:31-14:31); 2) the second farewell speech (15:1-16:33); 3) the third farewell speech or prayer (17:1-26).[28] All these farewell speeches "turn upon one central theme—what it means to be united with Christ."[29] They underline the theme of Jesus' continued presence with his people through the Holy Spirit.[30]

The second farewell speech (15:1-16:33), to which the vine metaphor (15:1-17) belongs, can be divided into three sub-units: 1) Jesus, source of life in the community (15:1-17); 2) tension between the disciples and the world (15:18-16:15); 3) sorrow in suffering and future joy (16:16-33).[31] The farewell discourse is a unique monologue addressing the disciples in private. The themes developed in the farewell discourse are introduced in the Book of Signs[32] but never fully developed there. For example, the mutual abiding motif is introduced in 1:33 with the reference to the Spirit remaining on Jesus but developed fully in 15:1-17 in the imagery of the vine and the branches.[33]

In the farewell discourse, Jesus speaks to the disciples concerning their relationship with him, the Father, and with one another. As Jesus approaches the end of his ministry, he gathers his disciples and speaks to them about his imminent departure, giving them comfort and assurance. Jesus' departure will cause them to be sorrowful (14:1-3, 28-29) and they will experience persecution and suffering for their allegiance to Jesus (15:18-16:15). They will be hated by the world, put out of the synagogue, and be

28. See Akpunonu, *The Vine*, 125-126;

29. Dodd, *Interpretation*, 418.

30. Keener, II:898.

31. Akpunonu, *The Vine*, 126. Cf. Talbert, *Reading John*, 211.

32. The GOJ can be outlined into four major divisions: I. Prologue (1:1-18); II. The Book of Signs (1:19-12:50); III. The Book of Glory (13:1-20:31); IV. Epilogue (21:1-25). See Köstenberger, *John*, 19.

33. See Dodd, *Interpretation*, 396-397, for more examples.

killed. Nevertheless, by metaphor as well as plain speech, Jesus invites his disciples to face the bleak future in unity, mutuality, and solidarity with one another, the Father, Son, and Spirit. The vine metaphor, including all its characteristic images, stands at the center of the farewell discourse and illustrates the key elements of Jesus' last teaching to his disciples.

5.2 A Reading of the Metaphor (15:1-8)

Reading 15:1-8 confronts us with the writer's fascination with imagery. The writer's use of images from daily life to illuminate a significant reality for believing in God is conspicuous in the vine and its characteristic images. The writer weaves together at least seven inter-related images in order to illustrate the richness of the relationship the disciples have with Jesus and with one another. Each of these images functions on two levels: within the earthly reality of viticulture as well as theologically. This serves to illustrate reality either in divine-divine, divine-human, or human-human relationships. As noted in chapter one, the concern here is what happens to the reader as he/she reads each of these images with care and sensitivity. How does each of these images sound when read with intimate participation by a reader who allows him/herself to become vulnerable to its influence? An intra/intertextual examination of these images will show how they may have been understood by their first audience and how they might possibly be contextualized for the people of God in the twenty-first century.

5.2.1 The Image of the Vine (v. 1, 5)

The image of the vine is familiar to John's audience since the vine and its products were common in Palestine and the Mediterranean world. It is an accurate reflection of "the everyday reality of vines and vinekeeping."[34] Popular interpretations[35] of the vine metaphor in John 15 point primarily

---

34. Francis J. Moloney, *Glory not Dishonor: Reading John 13-21* (Minneapolis: Fortress, 1998), 60.

35. C. K. Barrett, *The Gospel According to John: An Introduction With Commentary And Notes On The Greek Text* (London: SPCK, 2nd ed, 1978), 393; Beasley-Murray, *John*, 272; Carson, *John*, 513; Morris, *John*, 593; Keener, II:991; Köstenberger, *John*, 449.

to the use of the metaphor for Israel or some precursor of it in the OT[36] and the 2TP. Typically they stress that Jesus embodies Israel as the people of God. In this case Jesus is the faithful people of God in view of Israel's failure in that vocation. Scholars who emphasize the importance of the covenant community and the renewed people of God in understanding the vine metaphor rightly stress the need to see the metaphor in light of the strong sense of community in early Judaism and Christianity.[37]

This thesis does not deviate from this scholarly consensus. However, this consensus has some gaps which we must fill. It is necessary to ask questions concerning the failed vocation of Israel which meets perfect fulfilment in Jesus and the implications for being the renewed people of God. What was it that Israel, the vine of God, failed in, which Jesus, the true vine, claims to fulfil? How does the true vine contrast with the vine of Israel?

When read in light of the background of the vine/vineyard as the covenant people of God in the OT, John's image of the vine is a case for a new covenant community, moreover, a community that shares a strong monotheistic relationship with God amidst the religious pluralism of the late first century C.E. It can be read as a challenge to anyone or any community that worships self-made deities and a repudiation of any form of deity which elevates itself above the one true God. It speaks to the religious pluralism of the late first century[38] as well as that of all ages and functions as a polemic against the gods with which the nations of the world have replaced the only true God. The Johannine presentation of Jesus as the true vine is a declaration of loyalty to one God. It is in effect to say "I have one

---

36. Ps 80:8-18; Isa 5:1-7; 27: 2-6; Jer 2:21; Ezek 15:1-8; 19:10-14; Hos 10:1.

37. See John F. O'Grady, "Shepherd and the Vine and the Branches" *BTB* 8 (1978), 86-89; John G. Gager, *Kingdom and Community: The Social World of Early Christianity* (Englewood Cliffs: Prentice-Hall, 1975), 131-2; Donald Guthrie, *New Testament Theology* (Leicester: IVP, 1981), 722; Beasley-Murray, *John*, 272; Keener, II:993; Koester, *Symbolism*, 247; Kanagaraj, *Mysticism*, 264.

38. The worship of Dionysus among other gods and his association with wine as a vine god may also be in view here. Such deities may be vines but for the Johannine community they are not the true vine. See Trebilco, *Early Christians*, 19, who lists 9 deities worshipped in Ephesus alone, above whom stood Artemis who was considered the most powerful deity of the city; Also Kierspel, *The Jews*, 200-203, places certain Johannine trajectories against these mystery cults and interprets the signs as implicit polemic against other gods and emperors.

God, and I shall bow to no other" and portrays the Johannine community as one that deliberately shuns the worship of Caesar or any other gods of the Greco-Roman world. Also, in view of Johannine Christology, it is more than to say "I have one God" but it is to say "I am that only one God."[39]

To understand the creation of a new covenant community the background of the Jewish notion of the "pleasant planting"[40] must be considered. As demonstrated in chapter 4, in the OT and 2TP the pleasant planting is a metaphor for the covenant people of God. John 15 recalls the OT and 2TP texts where God is portrayed as a Gardener and the people of God a pleasant or righteous planting. The prophet Isaiah, for instance, states categorically that Israel is God's pleasant planting and uses this notion synonymously with the vineyard of the Lord (Isa 5:7). In John 15 the Father is growing a vine that he clears and prunes so that it will bear fruits. That is, he is raising a new people for himself and at the center of his new people is Jesus. In John this image is covenantal and is similar to the new birth image where God is birthing for himself children and this happens in and through his Son (3:3-10).[41]

"I am the true vine" suggests that Jesus represents the holy people of God *par excellence*, the true pleasant planting outside of which the existence of the people of God is not possible. It is a proclamation of a new era and a turning point in the history of the people of God. All other means of connecting with God are rendered invalid and a new way is opened. What unbelieving Israel failed to attain in her vocation as the people of God is fully attained in Jesus. Thus, in the image of the vine, John is articulating a new way of becoming the holy people of God. Judaism, Caesar worship, and any other forms of worship are disproved and the only true way to God, inculcated and modelled in Jesus, is articulated. The efficacy of Jesus

39. See Richard Bauckham, "Monotheism and Christology in the Gospel of John," in *Contours of Christology in the New Testament* (ed. Richard N. Longenecker; GR: Eerdmans, 2005), 148; John 1:1; 10:30; 14:7, 9-11.

40. Isa 5:7; 60:21; 61:3 1 QH XVI. 4-8, 12; *Pss. Sol.* 14:3; 1 QH XVI. 19-20; *1 En.* 92:2.

41. See Sharon H. Ring, *Wisdom's Friends: Community and Christology in the Fourth Gospel* (Louisville: WJK, 1999), 62, who suggests that "those who accepted the Logos became the new community of 'children' (1:12) or 'friends' (15:12-17) of God." Compare 3:3-9 and Paul's metaphor of the new creation (2 Cor 5:17).

in this vocation is certain since Jesus is in union with God and has the full experience of what it means to be in the Father (10:30; 14:10). In fact he is the Word who was in the beginning with God and is indeed God (1:1).

In view of the prophets' polemic regarding the contaminated vine (Isa 5:2; Jer 2:21) and/or the absence of the fruit of the vine (*Jub.* 23:18, 21), a right divine-human (covenant faithfulness) and human-human (communal holiness) relationship is central to the vine metaphor.[42] In the GOJ Jesus stands at the center of these relationships and as the God-man and reconciler makes possible a proper relationship with God and with people. In him God's requirements for justice and righteousness are met. He is the true vine of peace and savior of the world who offers what the *pax Romana* and *Ara Pacis* could not offer.[43] John presents him as the giver of peace to the new people of God (14:27). The peace that he gives transcends the *pax Romana* since it dispels all fear. There is a parallel here to the "peace on all sides" and the "no one to attack them" themes carried in the notion of the vine and fig tree in the OT and 2TP. Jesus grants the disciples his peace and in turn requires them to model it to the world. In him God's plan to save the world initially embedded in the vocation of Israel comes to total fruition.

As chapter 4 demonstrated, the failed vocation of Israel focuses almost entirely on two important qualities: righteousness and justice. Jesus' claim to be the true vine suggests that these two qualities are abundant in him. Whilst Israel replaced YHWH with false idols, Jesus maintains a right relationship with the Father. The relationship between the Father and Jesus in John is deeper and includes a bond that makes them one. In fact a mystical union exists between the Father and Jesus so that the two indwell each other,[44] as introduced in the Prologue, where John states clearly that Jesus, as the pre-existent Word, is himself God. It runs through the Gospel and

---

42. See our discussion of "The vine as a metaphor for Israel in the OT" in chapter 3.

43. The *pax Romana* (Roman peace) was secured and maintained by the military might of Augustus (30 B.C.E.-14 C.E.), the first Roman emperor. The *Ara Pacis* (altar of peace) was erected by Augustus to celebrate his inauguration of the *pax Romana*. See Köstenberger, *John*, 443-44; Also Beasley-Murray, *John*, 262, who further remarks that the *Ara Pacis* still stands in Rome as a testimony to the world's empty messianic pretensions.

44. 10:30; 14:10, 11, 20.

climaxes in the farewell discourse where it includes the participation of the children of God. Unlike Israel, in matters of justice Jesus rules with fairness, defends the cause of the poor and marginalized, gives deliverance to the oppressed, and crushes the oppressor (9:1-41; 12:1-8; 13:29).[45]

The polemic against injustice in the contaminated vine of the OT concerns Israel's oppression of and disregard for the poor.[46] This concern is also the focus of Micah who decried the injustice of his time and yearned for the reign of justice when everyone will sit under the vine and fig tree (Mic 4:1-4). Later, when the Maccabaean Simon restored peace and compassion for the poor everyone sat under the vine and fig tree (1 Macc 14:12). When the Johannine vine metaphor is read in the light of this background, it critiques the growing gap between the rich and poor including all the underlying injustices in the late first century. Since the vine metaphor served its OT users as a social critique, and its subsequent 2TP users in the same way, it is at least possible that it plays a similar role in John's usage in the late first century.

Beasley-Murray's suggestion that the metaphor "contains no polemic"[47] must, therefore, be questioned. The polemic is likely in the warning to fruitless branches (15:2a). The fruitless branch must be interpreted, in light of the background of fruitless Israel (Isa 5:1-7), as a selfish disciple who does not care for the needs of others. If bearing fruit is understood as holiness, peace, and outward-looking love, as we shall show later, it is plausible to suggest a polemic here. The metaphor can be treated as the Johannine Jesus' declaration of his position regarding matters of communal holiness: rejecting any form of discrimination and embracing peace, justice, hospitality, and mutuality. It can be read as a public declaration of identification with the weak, poor, and marginalized, which is in keeping with his practical ministry throughout the first twelve chapters of the Gospel.[48]

---

45. See Joachim Jeremias, *The Eucharistic Words of Jesus* (London: SCM, 1966), 54; Robert J. Karris, *Jesus and the Marginalised in St. John's Gospel* (Collegeville: Liturgical, 1990), 9-12; Leslie J. Hoppe, *There Shall Be No Poor Among You: Poverty in the Bible* (Nashville: Abingdon, 2004), 157-158.

46. Isa 3:14-15; 5:7; Jer 2:21, 34.

47. Beasley-Murray, *John*, 288-9.

48. 2:1-11; 4:4- 26; 5:1-8; 8:1-11; 11:1-46.

Jesus' identification with the marginalized can also be read as a polemic against a system that has disenfranchised them and continues to subject them to fear and threat. Treated in this way, the metaphor retains its power "to summon its readers to a new world and a new social reality."[49]

5.2.2 The Image of the Gardener (v. 1)

The word "gardener" is a general word for "one who tills the soil" or a farmer. It can also describe a farmer who owns a vineyard. Gardener is used here to parallel the word "Father," which appears about 120 times in the GOJ and depicts authority.[50] It describes the authority and monopoly that the vinedresser exercises over his vine. According to Charlesworth, "in the ancient Near East the deity was the gardener."[51] Embedded in this idea is the thought that the deity brings rain and is responsible for the fruitfulness of the land. Such depiction of God as gardener is also deeply entrenched in Jewish scriptures. Its usage in connection with vines recalls the role ascribed to God in Isaiah 5:1-7 and Psalm 80:8-18. Its function in this passage is to underscore at least two ideas: first, that God is the creator and sustainer of life; as sustainer the Father functions as the refuge of those who are persecuted, especially those persecuted by unbelievers;[52] second, that Jesus has a close filial relationship with God as his Father.[53]

The picture of God as gardener recalls the description of the Lord's people in plant metaphors. John 15 follows this trend and presents a picture of the God who owns a vineyard and is fully responsible for its life and vitality.

---

49. Gail R. O'Day, "Toward a Narrative-Critical Study of John," *Interpretation* 4 (1995): 344.

50. See Tan Yak-Hwee, *Re-senting The Johannine Community: A Postcolonial Perspective* (SBL 107; NY: Peter Lang, 2008), 126, who states that "the vinedresser is authoritative and powerful."

51. James H. Charlesworth, "Jesus as 'Son' and the Righteous Teacher as 'Gardener'," in *Jesus and the Dead Sea Scrolls* (ed. James H. Charlesworth; London: Doubleday, 1992), 148.

52. See Mary Rose D'Angelo, "Abba and 'Father': Imperial Theology and the Jesus Traditions," *JBL* 4 (1992): 611-630, for an analysis of the functions of "Father" in first century Judaism.

53. 10:30; 14:10 and 17:11, 22 describe the filial relationship between Jesus and God such that it is difficult to distinguish between the Father and the Son because they are one. However, the subordination of Jesus is made clear by this vine-vinedresser relationship.

The precedent is in Psalm 80:9 where YHWH is said to have "cleared the ground" for his vine and Isaiah 5:1-7 where the work of the vinedresser includes "digging the vineyard up", "clearing it of stones", "building a watchtower", and "cutting out a winepress". Vineyards were also hedged and guarded against animals and thieves. The importance of this for John is underscored by the strong emphasis on the Son's dependence on the Father,[54] a model for the disciples' dependence on Jesus (15:5, 10). The work is entirely of the Father, as throughout the Gospel he is ultimately responsible for what Jesus does and says. If God's people in Jesus are his vine or vineyard, God is the owner and vinedresser. If the vine metaphor is about the peace of the Lord's people, as we suggest, God is the author and finisher of this peace.

It is clear here that "God the Father is cultivating a vineyard in which only one life-giving vine grows."[55] Jesus is the true vine and from him God causes branches and fruits to grow.[56] From the onset the metaphor presents a corporate reality, it is hard to imagine a vine without branches in an agrarian culture such as first century Palestine's. The vintner's problem is excess rather than shortage of branches. Branches are integral to the vine and to refer to Jesus as the true vine implies true branches as well. That the metaphor deals with a fully grown vine where the dresser concentrates on the pruning and removal of branches shows that Jesus is not a vine in isolation from his disciples. Rather, he is the vine in union with the disciples.

The unnecessary dichotomy created by Segovia between Jesus and the church (disciples) regarding Jesus' supplanting of the vine of Israel must be questioned. His suggestion that Jesus rather than the church supplants Israel can be misleading.[57] Rather, the disciples in Jesus embody Israel as the new people of God. In other words, Jesus together with his disciples

---

54. 4:34; 5:19; 12:49, 50; 14:24, 31.

55. Burge, "Territorial Religion," 394.

56. The Gospel writer is clear that Jesus' followers are drawn by and given from the Father (6: 37, 39, 44; 10:29).

57. F. F. Segovia, *The Farewell of the Word: The Johannine Call to Abide* (Minneapolis: Fortress, 1991), 136. "Supplant" is a strong word for research that is not anti-Semitic. It is significant that "salvation is from the Jews" and that "Jesus and his disciples are Jews and he is "King of the Jews." For a full account of the Semitic character of the GOJ see Kierspel, *The Jews*.

(mutually indwelling each other) are the new covenant people of God and the fruit-bearing vine of God. "The community of the disciples designated in the metaphor as the fruitful branches (vv. 3-5) abiding in Jesus, the true vine, becomes the new vineyard of Yahweh."[58] This strengthens the view of the disciples as a holy community and a people belonging to God. They are the workmanship of a holy God, and they mutually indwell the holy one of Israel. The union between the vine and the branches is so close that it is almost impossible to separate one from the other, each is nothing without the other, and that each is wholly and only for the other. Jesus can only represent the true people of God.[59] To speak of Jesus without his disciples as the new people of God compromises the union suggested by the metaphor.

The image of the farmer is also important for John's emphasis on corporateness. It suggests that God's people are one family, one community, and one plantation under the workmanship of one Lord. Like the metaphor of the Shepherd and the sheep (10:1-21), the picture of one vine planted and tended by one vine-dresser suggests union and solidarity; belongingness to God and to each other. This has implications for holiness among members of the community, especially sharing one another's joys and sorrows. Also present here is a polemic against contemporary faith communities, especially those who excluded the Johannine community from the synagogue or those who venerated Caesar and other Greco-Roman gods. Since God has planted only one vine, all other plants are not from the creator and source of life.[60]

When read against the veneration of the Emperor, who himself was regarded as the "father" of the nation and savior of the world, the title suggests that the Johannine community knows and subscribes to a source of life, peace, and protection other than Caesar. But for them honor, status, and power must be attributed to the Father of Jesus and not to any earthly figure. It is neither Caesar nor Dionysius who is the source, keeper, and

---

58. Chennattu, *Discipleship*, 114.

59. See Dodd, *Interpretation*, 246, who sees Jesus as the "inclusive representative." Pryor, *John*, 126, suggests that "Jesus is Israel, both individually and corporately."

60. See Matt 15:13 where "every plant that my heavenly father has not planted will be pulled up by the roots."

sustainer of life. Life is given from God, and he alone is worthy of worship. The title may be read as a deliberate snub of the fatherhood of the Emperor.

For John it is important to have the right "father" since this determines ethical conduct.[61] The role of the Father as farmer, therefore, suggests nurture, nourishment, and production of character. The Father's diligent pruning and cutting off of the branches show that he is not just in the background of the metaphor as some scholars suggest.[62] The farmer exercises full autonomy and has in his hands the life and vitality of his vine. In Palestine "the state of a tree's fruit was said to attest how well its farmer had cared for it (Sir 27:6)."[63] The success of the vineyard is dependent upon the farmer and his diligent care. The Father's unrelenting focus on the branches demands an investigation of the meaning of John's image of the branches.

5.2.3 The Image of the Branches (vv. 2, 5, 6)

The image of the branches is the writer's expression for the mystical union and interdependence between the Son and the disciples. The emphasis on the impossibility of the branches' life apart from the vine is crucial, pointing to solidarity. In the OT, where the vine is a metaphor for Israel, the prophets speak of the barren vine rather than barren branches. Vine language assumes the inclusion of the branches. For example, if a vine does not reproduce, it is the vine and not the branches that do not bear fruit. The vine is unlike other trees where one may distinguish clearly between the trunk and the branches. John makes it clear that by the branches Jesus refers to his disciples. The image of the branches stresses two important trajectories.

First, it is clear that the disciples are in union with Jesus and that there is a mutual indwelling. The image emphasizes the completeness of the union so that without branches the vine is not just incomplete but unthinkable, and without the vine the branches are dead. The vine consists of its branches and both flow together into one. This is the unique aspect of

---

61. 8:38, 44; Rom 11:16; Matt 12:33.
62. Rudolf Schnackenburg, *The Gospel According to St. John* (3 Vols.; eds. J. Massyngbaerde Ford and Kevin Symth; Kent: Burns and Oates, 1982), 3:100, rightly suggests that the Father does not play a secondary part in John 15.
63. Keener, II: 994.

John's ecclesiology: the disciples and Jesus indwell each other. Throughout the Gospel John uses various verbs and metaphors to refer to the notion of being in Jesus.[64] This idea underscores the descending movement of the transcendent God to the human realm and to the community of disciples in particular. In essence the disciples participate in the Word made flesh, the holy one of God (6:69), and thus share his holiness. They are holy, not only because they belong to God but also because they share the life of God's only Son. The image is similar to the figure of Christ as a body that includes the church.[65] The difficulty of imagining a vine without branches parallels that of imagining a head without a body where Jesus is the head and the church his body.

Second, it is also clear that the vine and the branches mutually depend upon each other for fulfilling the Father's mission of fruit-bearing. So active is the vine in the work of fruit-bearing that the end product, wine, is called "the fruit of the vine" rather than "the fruit of the branches." No less indispensable than the vine to the branch is the branch to the vine. Since fruits are produced on branches, clearly, without the branches the vine cannot fulfil the Father's mission. A vine without branches can bear no fruit. Yet branch life and fruitfulness is conditioned by its remaining intact to the vine. The daily inflowing of the life-sap of the vine is its only power to live and bring forth fruit. Thus Jesus says, "apart from me you can do nothing" (15:5).

5.2.4 The Image of Removing Branches that Do Not Bear Fruit (vv. 2, 6)

In v. 2 the writer states that branches that do not bear fruits are removed from the vine. This is mentioned as the first of the vinedresser's activities, and demonstrates the desire for fruits as the end for which he/she grows

---

64. The most common verb John uses, "to believe", appears ninety-eight times in the Gospel, by far the most in any NT book. In chapter 1:14, 51 the incarnation is central to the descent of God to indwell the disciples. An important OT notion here is the tabernacle, which became the dwelling place of God in the midst of his people: See C. R. Koester, *The Dwelling Place of God: The Tabernacle in the Old Testament, Intertestamental Jewish Literature, and the New Testament* (CBQMS 22; Washington D.C.: CBAA, 1989), 6-22.

65. 1 Cor 12:12-27; Col 1:18, 2:19; Eph 1:22-23.

the vineyard. Anything that might hinder that purpose is cleared away. Later, fruitless branches are interpreted as anyone who does not abide in the vine and their destiny is defined: they are removed, thrown away, wilt, are gathered, and burnt (v. 2, 6). This is a practical picture from viticulture.[66] But what exactly does John mean by this symbol? The verb "cut off" literally means "take away, remove" and in this context must be understood as "clear away."[67] The branches in view are "in me" but since they are not participating in the mission of the farmer they are removed. The reason for their barrenness is stated as failure to abide in the vine. They are cut off because they pose a threat to intact fruit-bearing branches. They compete for nutrients from the stem yet fail to transform it into fruits. They use the nourishing sap only to bear leaves and thus provoke the wrath of the gardener.

There is no consensus among Johannine scholars regarding how the image must be interpreted. Some suggest an allusion to Judas Iscariot.[68] Others see the final judgment of Gehenna.[69] The argument for the former should probably be supported on the ground that the fruitless branches are also "in me" and receive the same proportion of the vintner's care. As a disciple, Judas Iscariot partook of all Jesus' miraculous signs and teachings but could not bear the desired fruits. In 6:60-71 he is an example of those who do not believe and are offended by the teaching of Jesus.[70] They object to the idea of chewing the flesh and drinking the blood of Jesus. In sharp contrast to these is the group represented by Peter which believes and confesses that Jesus is the Holy One of God. In 12:4-6 the writer shows Judas' attitude towards money and the poor. He was unconcerned about the poor and habitually stole from the treasury. Clearly, these actions describe a lack of

---

66. See Bruce, *Gospel*, 309, for the uselessness of the wood of a dead vine; Ezek 15:2-8.

67. See Beasley-Murray, *John*, 268, for the details of the interplay between "remove" and "cleanse." Also Keener, II:1000-1, for the unlikelihood of the opinion that this refers to fallen branches that are "lifted up" rather than "cast away."

68. Samuel M. Ngewa, "John," in *Africa Bible Commentary: A One Volume Commentary Written by 70 African Scholars* (ed. Tokunboh Adeyemo; Nairobi: WordAlive, 2006), 1285; Keener, II:1001; Milne, *Message*, 221; for an antithesis to this see Schnackenburg, *John*, 98.

69. E.g. Keener, II:1002.

70. William R. Domeris, "The Confession of Peter According to John 6:69," *TynBul* 44 (1993): 167, suggests that Judas represents "the schismatics of the community."

concern for communal holiness. The word used to describe Judas' attitude to the poor is the same word used to describe the hired shepherds who do not care for the sheep in 10:13.[71] In the light of John's concern for communal holiness Judas might be seen as a prime example of those who are selfish and unconcerned with the unity and solidarity of the community.

The punishment with fire must not be treated as an allusion to the judgment of Gehenna.[72] The statement is general and describes the peril of condemnation and separation from the source of life and vitality.[73] Fire is symbolic of divine judgement in Jewish thinking[74] but this must be understood within the context of the GOJ. For John judgement links to the incarnation and is the consequence of choosing darkness and rejecting the Light from above.[75] In John's dualistic theology there are no grey areas and "no middle course."[76] Any faith that is not worth dying for falls short by Johannine standards and its bearer is under judgment. Therefore, in John judgement is a present reality in the life of those who refuse the offer of new life in Jesus (3:17-19).

Malina and Rohrbaugh's suggestion that the metaphor is individualistic cannot be right.[77] John's words, "whoever does not abide in me", (v. 6), do not suggest individualism. Rather, the words are a corporate reference to the disciples' community. As Kanagaraj states, "The sense is inclusive, denoting the many branches that are attached to the vine."[78] In fact, there is a strong polemic here against any individualistic behavior that might divide the community. The words suggest that sin is not a private affair. Anything that affects an individual believer also affects the whole community. The

71. Keener, II:864.

72. Beasley-Murray, *John*, 273.

73. See Ezek 15:1-8 where this notion is explained in detail with emphasis placed upon God "giving up the inhabitants of Jerusalem" like the wood of the vine among the trees of the forest.

74. Lang, *TDNT* 6:934-47; Carson, *John*, 1991, 517.

75. 3:19, 36; 9:39; 12:31. Also Bultmann, *John*, 157.

76. Lindars, *John*, 24.

77. Bruce J. Malina and Richard L. Rohrbaugh, *Social-Science Commentary on the Gospel of John* (Minneapolis: Fortress, 1998), 234. As demonstrated earlier, this research totally rejects an individualistic approach to the GOJ.

78. Kanagaraj, *John*, 498.

focus of the metaphor is more on disciples as a corporate body and holy community than on an individual believer. As we have seen where the GOJ deals with an individual believer as in the case of Nicodemus, he/she is representative of a certain constituency. The metaphor deals initially with the covenant relationship between God and Israel (Ezek 15:1-8), and John adopts it to use it for the new covenant people of God in Jesus. Collectively, the disciples are the branches of one vine just as they are one flock under one shepherd in John 10:1-18. Any attempt to divide the community in the GOJ, either by excluding oneself or another from the community, is met with the writer's harsh judgement.

5.2.5 The Image of Pruning Branches that Bear Fruit (vv. 2-3)

A second vine-dressing activity that enhances fruit-bearing is pruning productive branches. Fruit-bearing branches are pruned in order that they may bear more fruit. Like the clearing away of unproductive branches the image of pruning reflects everyday reality of vines and vine-keeping. Pruning is the vinedresser's way of ensuring that he gets the best out of his vine/vineyard. When the vine/vineyard is properly pruned it can fulfil its purpose to its maximum capacity. The OT makes numerous references to the practice, which shows that pruning had been known in Israel.[79] For the vinedresser "pruning is not just a chore. It's something that keeps the vine in balance."[80] In John's context balance suggests stability and steady growth in the community's relationship with God and one another. In view of the religious pluralism of the time it was necessary constantly to re-focus the disciples upon Jesus since "it is on him that God the Father has set the seal" (6:27). John's concern for the disciples' unwavering focus upon Jesus can be explained by his use of the "I am" formula that runs through the Gospel. The metaphor of the Good Shepherd, for example, stresses the disciples'

---

79. Lev 25:3-4; Cant 2:12; Isa 2:4; 5:6; 18:5; Joel 3:10; Mic 4:3.

80. Michael James, "Pruning Vines," n.p. [cited 30 January 2008]. Online: http://www. squidoo.com/pruning-grapes-vines. Note, an unpruned vine uses all its energy in its early stage and fails to reserve stamina for ripening its massive fruits. The outcome is sour grapes that are not useful to the vine-grower.

ability to distinguish Jesus' voice from that of a stranger (10:4-5). Constant pruning enabled disciples to remain focused upon Jesus.

Scholarly consensus relating to pruning suggests that the savage act of cutting back refers to God's chastisement.[81] In this case, God's actions in sending his people to exile and other means of disciplining rebellious Israel could be relevant. Keener, for example, suggests that pruning could involve judgement or difficulty and makes reference to *1 En.* 106:17 where the flood is described as a cleansing of the earth.[82] The corrective character of hardships, particularly the exile, was widely recognized in Israel.[83]

However, despite the consensus on the savagery of pruning, scholars have neglected an important aspect of this image. Pruning is not punitive. It is highly unlikely that it would mean God's chastisement when the writer's audience was facing persecution from the synagogue. The image focuses on the positive work of God in the community. Pruning is a life-enhancing activity that re-invigorates the branches. The image concerns the Father's commitment to the security and welfare of those whom the Father draws to Jesus (6:37, 39; 10:29). In the pruning image is embedded every care that the Father gives to his new covenant people including forgiveness, cleansing, assuring, blessing, sanctification, and the joy of answered prayer. The mode of pruning, the word, should help our understanding here. John's use of "cleansing" for pruning shows that he intends that pruning be read together with cleansing, carried out through the word of Jesus. Traditions concerning the "word" and its function in a covenant relationship should help bring clarity to our interpretation (e.g. Ps 119:50, 105). Pruning

---

81. Justin Martyr, *Tryph,* 110, suggests that pruning illustrates God's painful discipline for his true servants; Bultmann, *John,* 532, describes "remove" and "prune" collectively as "judgmental statements"; Carson, *John,* 514, describes pruning as a painful procedure and refers to Heb 12:4-11 where the Lord disciplines his own as a father disciplines his children; Beasley-Murray, *John,* 268, states that "pruning" can be used in the sense of clearing the earth of weeds; Keener, II:996, argues from 2TP literature that pruning could involve judgement or difficulty; Ngewa, "John," 1285, focuses his comments on the image entirely on the disciples' unpleasant experiences.

82. Keener, II:997.

83. Cf. *Pss. Sol.* 17:30 where the Messiah purges Israel to restore it in holiness; 2 Macc 6:12, 16, where those who are disciplined with calamities are assured that God does not withdraw his mercy at such times.

involves all God's work to qualify his holy covenant people for holiness. Moreover, it is non-pruning that is punitive in Israel's tradition (Isa 5:6).

John's use of "cleanse" to describe the pruning process is infused with Johannine theology since "it is not the most common expression from viticulture."[84] This offers clues for the spiritual reality intended by the pruning image. The words "he prunes" in other contexts mean "he cleanses." According to Barrett "cleanse" can be used to refer to "cleansing corn by winnowing and clearing weeds from the ground before planting" and "purifying a cup for libation."[85] John uses the language of cleansing in 13:10 and 15:3 to refer to the cleansing of the disciples. In both places he describes the disciples as those who are already clean. The mode of cleansing is described as "the word that I have spoken to you" (v. 3). Early in the Gospel John portrays the Jewish means of cleansing as empty (2:6). The use of cleanse here harks back to 2:6 and suggests a shift in the means of cleansing for the new covenant people of God.[86] The word of God replaces Jewish rituals of cleansing so that the new people of God are cleansed by no other means than by Jesus and his word. In this we must stress the emptiness of all ceremonial cleansing that is devoid of the word of Jesus.[87]

But how should the word lexeme be understood? The cleansing word is the whole message that Jesus delivers to the disciples.[88] In 6:63 the words that Jesus speaks are synonymous with Spirit and life. The Spirit is the agent of revelation during Jesus' baptism and appears descending and abiding upon Jesus. The Spirit who vivifies Jesus' flesh and blood is the same Spirit who is present in the words of Jesus, making them Spirit and life. The cleansing power in Jesus' words is the power of the Spirit since Jesus' words are imbued by the Spirit. As we shall show later, the word is also the

---

84. Keener, II:996; Morris, *John*, 669; Barrett, *John*, 473; Brown, *John*, II:660.

85. Barrett, *John*, 473.

86. For John not only the means but also the place (Temple) of cleansing is replaced. For it is "neither on this mountain nor in Jerusalem" that the Father will be worshipped (4:21).

87. Various African religious sects understand and administer purification in various ways. The Jericho Church, for example, uses the blood of a white goat or chicken for the ritualistic cleansing of family members thirty days after the death of a family member.

88. Phillips, *Prologue*, 74–95 for an intertextual analysis of word and how it is used in the GOJ.

sanctifier (17:17) and is synonymous with truth. When we understand that in John the truth[89] is Jesus, we grasp the depth of the mutual indwelling message of the vine metaphor. It is the indwelling Jesus who cleanses and consecrates his new covenant people. It is abiding disciples who are pruned.

5.2.6 The Image of Fruit Bearing (vv. 2, 4-5, 7-8)

Fruit bearing is the primary purpose of growing a vineyard. Other benefits such as the provision of shade, though also significant for meditation on the Torah (1:48, 50), should be considered secondary. John's haste in introducing the concept in 15:2 shows that the vinedresser's focus is upon the production of fruits. The savage treatment God gives to fruitless branches also shows that he will not settle for anything less than fruits. The vinedresser's painstaking pruning of fruit bearing branches shows his desire for much fruits. As noted, it was the desire to control the color, size, and quality of the fruit that resulted in the domestication of the vine in the ANE. Farmers would go so far as to take cuttings from proven producers and graft them to new vines to produce superior fruit.[90] In the OT YHWH would remove the hedge, break down the wall, make waste, not prune, and command the clouds that there be no rain upon the fruitless vine or the vineyard producing stinking grapes.[91] God's expectation of his holy people is embedded in the prophets' message that "Israel shall blossom and put forth shoots, and fill the whole world with fruit" (Isa 27:6; cf. Hos 14:4-8).

It is vital here to realize that fruit bearing is a communal effort involving the vinedresser, the vine, and the branches. It is also completely dependent upon the branches' remaining intact with the vine and cooperating with the vine-dresser's pruning. This is but one example of John's portrayal of the relationship of the Father, Son, and disciples. It shows the drawing together of the efforts of the three working together-as-one that culminates in much

---

89. 14:6. Cf. 1:17; 4:24; 5:33; 8:44; 17:17; 1 Pet 1:22 where obedience to the truth purifies the soul and begets mutual love, deep love.

90. See Matthews, "Treading the Winepress," 20.

91. Isa 5:5-6. Keener, II:998, suggests that "the image may develop the biblical picture of God requiring fruit from Israel," which could be an allusion to Isa 5:1-7 and other OT passages where Israel is portrayed a God's vine/vineyard.

fruit. Such fruit is the natural outcome of the mutual indwelling of the
Father, Son, and disciple.[92]

The question of the fruit's meaning is not new among Johannine scholars. Bultmann's answer is summary and amenable: "every demonstration of
vitality of faith, to which, according to vv. 9-17, reciprocal love belongs."[93]
For Beasley-Murray, it relates to "effective mission in bringing to Christ
men and women in repentance and faith."[94] The reciprocation of love is
probably most important for the vine metaphor, considering its position
in the farewell discourse. At the fore is how the disciples will live and relate
to each other as branches of the true vine. They are to reflect the life that
flows to them from Jesus the vine of life. Schnackenburg describes this
image as "all the fruits of a Christian life lived in close union with Christ
and especially of a fruitful community life which bears witness to itself in
faith and love."[95] The fruit-bearing branch is concerned with community
life, meeting the needs of the poor and marginalized, promoting unity,
hospitality, and mutuality.

2TL provides a clue to the intended fruit here. The word "fruit" is used
in three different ways in 1QS. First, it refers to music or speech as the
"fruit of praise."[96] Second, it refers to produce as "the tasty fruit of the
earth" (1QS 10.15). Third, it refers to holy living as the "fruit of holiness" (1QS 10.22). The last clearly corresponds with the reference to the
Qumran sect as those who "drink the waters of holiness" (1QH XVI.13).
It is natural for the plantation that drinks the waters of holiness to bear the
fruit of holiness. Later the Odes of Solomon also associated the notion of

---

92. See Barrett, *John*, 473.

93. Rudolf Bultmann, *The Gospel of John: A Commentary* (Philadelphia: Westminster,
1971), 523-33.

94. Beasley-Murray, *John*, 273. Cf. Bruce Milne, *The Message of John* (TBST; Leicester:
IVP, 1993), 220.

95. Schnackenburg, *John*, 100. Also Brown, *John*, II:675, who suggests good works and a
virtuous way of life as meaning for the Johannine fruit.

96. 1QS 10.8; also 1QH IX.28 where it is presented as "the fruit of the lips" and is
clearly associated with the telling of God's glory and recounting his wonderful works
(1QH IX.30) or declaring to the sons of man all the wonders achieved by the mercies
of God (1QH IX.33-34). In *Pss. Sol.* 15:3 it is rendered as "the tuned instrument of the
tongue." Cf. Hosea 14:2; Hebrews 13:15.

fruit-bearing with holiness (*Odes Sol.* 8:2), peace (*Odes Sol.* 10:2), and grace (*Odes Sol.* 11:1). Although probably written a century later, it is useful in showing that even after John was written Jewish Christians continued to associate fruit-bearing with holiness.[97] The fruit of peace in view here is when everyone sits under his/her vine and fig tree and entails a proper relationship with God and with community members regardless of social or economic status. John's fruit, therefore, must be understood in terms of the outcome of a union with Jesus as communal holiness and mission. The fruit of communal holiness here emphasizes practical acts of kindness and mercy in meeting the needs of the poor and underprivileged of society. This relates to the calls to social justice in association with the vine metaphor in the prophetic tradition.

The significance of mission[98] as the fruit of the vine has consensus among Johannine scholars,[99] Milne[100] going so far as to see it as the primary focus of the whole discourse (15:1-16:33). Mission is an integral part of the vine metaphor from its inception in the OT. The people of God are called to be outward-looking. As God's vine, Israel was to model the character of God to the nations. The moment the vine of Israel turned inward-looking it became fruitless and produced sour vines.[101] As the true vine, Jesus sees himself as sent by God (5:38), and establishes the new covenant people of God to join him in the mission of God in the world. Proclaiming God's wondrous deeds is part of being the holy people of God (Psalm 154:4-11). For John, the scope of God's mission goes beyond the boundaries of the

---

97. Charlesworth, *Pseudepigrapha*, 2:727, dates the Odes around 100 C.E. and suggests that they are from the same community/region in which the GOJ was composed. See also R. A. Culpepper, "The Odes of Solomon and the Gospel of John," *CBQ* 35 (1973): 298-322, who cautions against assuming that the Odes are dependent on John or visa versa and urges that the possibility of a shared community be considered.

98. Mission is used in this research to refer to witness to the incarnation, life, death, and resurrection of Jesus as God's plan to lead humankind to faith. The witness motif runs through the Gospel from its inception in the prologue with John the Baptist.

99. Lindars, *John*, 492; Pryor, *John*, 64; Schnackenburg, *John*, 100; Carson, *John*, 517; Köstenberger, *John*, 454.

100. Milne, *Message*, 218-224.

101. See the section on "the vine as a negative portrayal of the covenant people of God" in chapter 3 for an extensive coverage of Israel's fruitlessness.

Jewish nation. It is the world.[102] This is demonstrated clearly in Jesus' encounter with the Samaritan woman and the Greeks.[103] In both of these encounters John uses the notion of fruit-bearing to describe the propagation of the gospel (4:36; 12:24). The fruit of witness to the world and the fruit of communal holiness are a product of abiding in the vine. For John, it is only the branch that abides in the vine that will bear much fruit. Our next section will unpack the image of abiding.

5.2.7 The Image of Mutual Abiding (vv. 4-10)[104]

The mutual abiding image dominates vv. 4-10 of John's vine metaphor. The repeated emphasis on abiding suggests that it is the metaphor's theme. This should not be surprising due to the extensive discussion of the mutual abiding theme in the GOJ, particularly chapter 14, where it is Trinitarian and connected to the eschatological temple theme. In 14:2, for example, reference is made to the Father's house with many rooms a motif used elsewhere with reference to the temple (2:16). In 14:10-11 John makes reference to the mutual indwelling of the Father and the Son, suggesting union and solidarity between the two. John 14:20 shows how the disciple participates in this union by mutually indwelling the Son. In 14:16 the writer introduces the Spirit as one who dwells with the disciples whilst in 14:23 it is Jesus and the Father who jointly come and make their dwelling with the disciples. The picture is of a sanctuary where the people of God gather together in the presence of the Father, Son, and Spirit.

The use of the mutual abiding image in connection with the eschatological temple theme in John is not unique to the farewell discourse. Like other important themes in John it is introduced in the prologue and developed throughout the Gospel (1:14, 51; 2:19-22; 4:20-24). This will be shown in

---

102. 1:12, 29; 3:16; 4:42; 6:33. Cf. Craig R. Koester, "The Saviour of the World," *JBL* 4 (1990): 665-680.

103. 4:4-38; 12:20-22. See Koester, *Symbolism*, 42-44, for a discussion of the interconnections between particularity and universality in Jesus' identity as shown by the encounter with the Samaritan woman.

104. The image of abiding will be discussed in full in the next chapter since we consider it to be the main theme of John's vine metaphor in connection with the Temple theme in the GOJ.

the next chapter where the meaning of the mutual abiding motif in John's context will be discussed in relation to its inter/intratexts. John deliberately juxtaposes the vine metaphor with the image of "abiding" in order to underscore his portrait of the new people of God as God's sanctuary.

But what connection does John make between mutual abiding and the vine metaphor? First, branches only bear fruit as they abide in the vine. In order to be fruitful the disciples must abide in Jesus "just as" the branches abide in the vine (v. 4). The disciple who does not abide is thrown away "like a branch" (v. 6). "Abiding" is the only means for fruitful living. What is important for John at this point is what the metaphor best illustrates: the dependence of the branches on the vine for life and vitality that is comparable to the dependence of the disciples upon Jesus for the life of God. "Abiding" is the one thing without which the gardener's purpose for his vine, fruit bearing, is not possible. Due to its link with fruit bearing, its failure invites a similar judgement as the failure to produce fruit: being thrown away like a branch, withering, being gathered, thrown into the fire, and burned (vv. 2, 6). The two notions of mutual abiding and fruit bearing are tied together so that "to remain in Christ is to become fruitful."[105]

Second, 15:1-17 is a climax for the theme of abiding the writer uses throughout the Gospel to underscore the unity and intimacy of the divine persons with each other and with God's holy people (e.g. 1:14, 33; 6:56; 14:20). However, here mutual abiding includes another aspect which relates to the ethical holiness of those who abide in God. John refers to this as abiding in love or loving one another (vv. 9-17). Hence John's command to abide has a double focus: 1) abiding in Jesus (15:4-8) and, 2) abiding in Jesus' love (15:9-17). Both of these places of abode are modelled by Jesus' place of abode in the Father and in the Father's commands (15:10). The first regards the organic union with Jesus and the second the practical ethical expression of that union in keeping the commandments, specifically the command to love one another.[106] Thus John's interpretation of the vine metaphor in 15:9-17 may be summarized as abiding in Jesus' love shown

105. Beasley-Murray, *John*, 273.

106. Lindars, *John*, 490, who suggests that "love is shown by the voluntary keeping of the Master's commandments."

by obedience to Jesus' commandments, especially sacrificial love for one another. As the next chapter will show, the mutual abiding image captures the corporateness that is at the center of the vine metaphor, especially when used with reference to the covenant people of God.

5.3 Conclusion

The above discussion of John's vine metaphor shows that at least three trajectories are important if it is interpreted in consideration of its background in 2TP and context in the late first century.

First, the vine metaphor concerns God's creation of a new covenant people centered in Jesus the Son of God and covenant Lord. The new people of God are a monotheistic community under the care of one vine-dresser, God, who is dedicated to see the community blossom in holiness. Holiness to them has two dimensions: vertical and horizontal. They are holy as a people belonging to and cleansed by God and their holiness is expressed in the corporateness and solidarity of the community. Not only do they belong to God, but in Jesus they also belong to one another. That is, the holiness that comes from their right relationship with Jesus must be expressed horizontally in their treatment of others. The call in the metaphor is for the new people of God to keep in step with their new identity in Christ.

Second, the Father, who is a Gardener, is committed to the care of his new covenant people. The Father is not presented as a ruthless judge who cannot help but wait to rain fire on fruitless branches. In John he is a working God (5:17), ensuring life and abundant fruiting for his vine. Cutting fruitless branches is not his only work; he also prunes fruit-bearing branches. He has not left the disciples to toil alone in the discipleship journey. The metaphor may have strengthened the believers in the writer's community and encouraged them to remain in the Lord.

Third, unlike Israel, this new covenant community is abiding and fruit-bearing. The covenant relationship has been strengthened to a mutual indwelling, an abiding "in" rather than an abiding "with" or "amongst." That is, in the new covenant the Lord dwells in the temple of his people rather than a man-made temple among his people. It is this participation of the people of God in the mutual abiding relationship of the Father and the Son that the disciples are admonished to share with one another. The next chapter will explore the notion of abiding in relationship to the sharing of life among the new covenant people of God.

CHAPTER 6

Mutual Abiding and Shared Life in John 15:1-17

6.1 Introduction

This chapter will analyse how John uses the mutual abiding motif along with parallel motifs to create a sense of community identity and to encourage shared life within the new covenant community. We suggest that mutual abiding[1] is John's unique way of describing shared life, which he presents on three levels: first, the shared life of the Father with the Son, which functions as the prototype; second, the shared life of God with his holy people through the Son of God; third, the shared life of God's holy covenant people with one another, often nuanced by the disciples' selfless love for one another. These levels in which mutual abiding occur in the GOJ, will be discussed, including a survey of John's use of the mutual abiding motif in 1 John.[2] The intra/intertextuality of abiding will be explored

---

1. The terms mutual abiding, mutual indwelling, interpenetration, and coinherence are used interchangeably in this research to mean the same thing—see the definition for mutual abiding. See J. Abelson, *Jewish Mysticism* (London: G. Bell and Sons, 1913), 1-15, and Jey J. Kanagaraj, *"Mysticism" in the Gospel of John:* An Inquiry into its Background (JSNTS 158; Sheffield: SAP, 1998), 271-2, for John's possible sources for the mutual abiding idea.

2. See Smalley, *Thunder and Love*, 19-20, for the close relationship between the GOJ and the Letters of John. 1 John carries almost all the uses of the abiding motif outside the GOJ. Reference will also be made to 2 John 2, the only occurrence of the motif outside 1 John and the Gospel.

to see the implications for its use in 15:1-17 and how that illumines the communal life of the new covenant people of God. Beginning with a review of Kanagaraj's work, the passages where the abiding motif is used will be examined. In each of the passages, sustained attention is given to how mutual abiding in each category effects the unity of the holy community. The conclusion is drawn that the mutual abiding motif is John's chosen way of describing a right relationship between God and his holy people and that it is integral to John's purpose that this relationship be reflected in the ethics of the holy people of God.

6.2 The GOJ and the Mutual Abiding Motif

"Mutually indwelling the life of God is the heart and soul of John's understanding of salvation."[3] For John any relationship with God that does not encompass a divine-human mutual abiding falls short. To believe in God is to abide in God and vice versa. The domination of the mutual abiding motif in 15:1-17 shows that the key point of the Johannine vine metaphor is to underscore the essence of Johannine faith: a divine-human union described in terms of a mutual abiding relationship between a holy people and a holy God through the holy one of God. Jesus and his words abide in the disciples (vv. 4, 7). The disciples are commanded to abide in Jesus (vv. 4-7) and his love (vv. 9-10) and to show that by sacrificial love and obedience to Jesus' commands (vv. 12-17). Placing mutual abiding at the center of 15:1-17, Brodie suggests that "the essential purpose of the parable (15:1-17) is to portray how God works to bring people more fully into divine union, into their full potential of fruition and joy."[4]

---

3. Crump, "Johannine Trinity," 400.

4. Thomas L. Brodie, *The Gospel According to John* (Oxford: Oxford University Press, 1993), 475.

6.3 Kanagaraj and the Mutual Abiding Idea

A significant contribution to research on the mutual abiding motif is the work of Kanagaraj.[5] Kanagaraj considers mutual abiding to be central to 15:1-17 which he reads as a description of "mutual unity;" a unity that "emphasizes first its communal aspect, though the individual abiding is not missing, and then the life shared by that community."[6] He carefully shows that such unity does not mean deification or an absorption into the divine, as in Philo's mysticism. In his words, mutual abiding "speaks of a community, which absorbs divine life from Christ and which, as a result, can intimately relate with God."[7] For him the imagery of the vine and the branches portrays a tripartite union of the Father, the Son, and the disciple. The disciples are united with God by being united with Jesus.

Following Hauck, Kanagaraj suggests that John uses mutual abiding with a distinctive theological meaning to refer to the lasting immanence between God and Christ or believers and Christ, emphasizing the sense of permanence.[8] However, his suggestion for "permanence" is questionable in reference to the divine-human aspect of mutual abiding. With the example of Judas, the possibility of being cut-off[9] exists, which makes Johannine mutual abiding contingent upon fruit-bearing and keeping the commands. Kanagaraj argues that the union in John is a gift of God rather than the work of humans; it contrasts sharply with the union described by the *Hermetica* (CH 11.4b, 18-20; 12.13b). John's use of the word "already" in connection to the disciples' purification (15:3) before introducing the verb abide in 15:4 suggests that union with Jesus is already granted by God. "What the disciples are exhorted to do is to hold on loyally and continually to that givenness."[10]

---

5. Kanagaraj, *Mysticism*, 264-81.

6. Kanagaraj, *Mysticism*, 264.

7. Kanagaraj, *Mysticism*, 268.

8. Kanagaraj, *Mysticism*, 264; Hauck, *TDNT*, 574-81.

9. See the section on "the image of removing branches that do not bear fruit" in chapter 5 for the ongoing debate on the meaning of the cutting off of fruitless branches.

10. Kanagaraj, *Mysticism*, 265.

Kanagaraj also suggests, based upon John's use of house/home (14:2, 23), that the union is eschatological since it is described in terms of a heavenly journey, a journey already begun. Following McCaffrey, Kanagaraj says, "this journey is initiated in the union of the Father and the Son in the believer here and now."[11] He states, however, that the union is conditioned by the believer's love and obedience to Jesus (14:23a), which contradicts his emphasis on permanence.

6.4 Beyond Kanagaraj

Kanagaraj's discussion of mutual abiding is significant for this research. His view that the vine metaphor is about unity and community, intimacy with God, and the absorption of divine life from Christ is particularly important. The question that remains is whether it is possible to go beyond Kanagaraj. Answers lie in two areas that Kanagaraj omits: 1) intratextual connection between mutual abiding and the new temple motif in John; 2) the implications for communal holiness arising from the divine-human union. This will be developed in relationship to the levels of mutual abiding in John with careful attention to the implications for communal holiness arising from the divine-human union. Emphasis will be placed on the archetypal unity of the Father and the Son from which we shall develop the unity of the new community.

6.4.1 Implications for Communal Holiness

First, it is surprising that Kanagaraj leaves out the implications for communal holiness arising from the mutual abiding motif, especially its link to the hospitality language of John. Without this connection, the motif lacks the ability to call readers to task and invite response as initially intended by the Johannine Jesus. The mutuality and reciprocity suggested by the verb in context is not only vertical, divine-human, but it is also horizontal, human-human. For example, in 4:40 abiding is used twice with reference to either a

---

11. Kanagaraj, *Mysticism*, 266.

stranger's acceptance of or continuation in the context of hospitality.[12] The mutual abiding motif permeates the Johannine communal lexemes such as "one another" or "each other," which are embodied in Jesus' humble service (13:2-5). Mutual abiding, as Strecker suggests, "is concretized in the ethical acts of "brotherly love'."[13] It underlies the believers' fellowship which is seen as obedience to the commandments, especially the commandment to love.

6.4.2 The New Temple

Kanagaraj does not connect mutual abiding with the eschatological temple theme either. His discussion of "house/home" and his reference to the eschatological promise (14:2, 23) should have led him in that direction but does not.[14]

That the Johannine Jesus is the new temple is clear in the prologue and throughout the Gospel, especially in the passages where worship is concerned. The new temple motif is already implicit in 1:14 where the verb "dwelt" evokes the noun "tent", commonly used for the tabernacle in the LXX. In 1:14 Jesus is presented as the sanctuary of the Word made flesh that, while assuming the weakness and transitory nature of the human condition, contains the fullness of God's grace and truth. He is the temple of the definitive revelation of God just as the desert-sanctuary was to Israel in the OT. As one who has moved from the realm of God to the realm of humankind, Jesus is the meeting place between God and humankind.

The most explicit text on the temple theme is 2:19, 21, where Jesus' body is the temple and its destruction and rebuilding alludes to Jesus' death and resurrection. The reference to Jesus' body as the temple and true center of God's revelation renders the Jerusalem temple and its cult obsolete. Jesus made this clear in his conversation with the Samaritan woman regarding

---

12. Andrew E. Arterbury, *Entertaining Angels: Early Christian Hospitality in its Mediterranean Setting* (Sheffield: SPP, 2005), 131. Mutual abiding as hospitality is the theme of chapter 6.

13. Georg Strecker, *Theology of the New Testament* (Berlin: Walter de Gruyter, 1996), 440.

14. James McCaffrey, *The House with Many Rooms: The Temple Theme in John 14:2-3* (NovTSup 114; Roma: EPIB, 1988), 32-5, 176-185, 222-237; also Alan R. Kerr, *The Temple of Jesus' Body: The Temple Theme in the Gospel of John* (JSNTSup 220; Sheffield: SAP, 2002), 299-313; Steven M. Bryan, "The Eschatological Temple in John 14," *BBR* 15 (2005): 187-198.

the true place of worship (4:20-24). Here "Jesus broadly negates all fixed places of worship."[15] In Burge's words, "Jesus is the new holy space where God can be discovered."[16] Instead of the Jerusalem temple, focus will now be upon Jesus as the locus of God's revelation and one without which it is not possible to relate to the Father. "Jesus' body, as the temple, is the dwelling place of God and the assurance of God's presence among his people."[17] Dennis iterates, "in Jesus, the divine presence has returned to Israel (1:14) and the eschatological temple is in the midst of the people (2:19-22)."[18]

On another level, the temple theme in John centers on the new people of God as the true temple. In 15:1-11 the reciprocation and mutuality of abiding shows that the disciples are also the dwelling place of Christ. Chapter 14:23 states that believing disciples are the dwelling place of Christ and the Father. The new people of God are thus the living sanctuary, the means by which God dwells among humankind (Exod 15:17; 25:8; Ezek 37:26-28). As 4:21 shows, the presence of God in the world is no longer signalled by the holy place in the holy city. Rather, the new covenant people of God are called to be God's holy temple, a walking temple, indwelled by God wherever they go. In them the promises of God to dwell among his holy people Israel are fulfilled (1 Kings 6:13). They are the temple that God desires, a temple not made with human hands (Acts 7:48; 17:24; Heb 9:24). As becomes clear later, this has great implications for holy living.

6.5 Aspects of Mutual Abiding in John

We have described above how Johannine mutual abiding occurs at different levels: God and Jesus (Father-Son), Jesus and the disciples (Son-disciples), and the disciples' community (disciple-disciple). We have also explained how the mutual abiding between God and Jesus works as a prototype of the

---

15. Jerome H. Neyrey, "Worship in the Fourth Gospel: A Cultural Interpretation of John 14-17," *BTB* 36 (2006): 108.

16. Burge, "Territorial Religion," 388.

17. Margaret Pamment, "Path and Residence Metaphors in the Fourth Gospel," *Theology* 88 (1985): 121. Ps 11:4; 29:9; 138:2; Tob 1:4.

18. Dennis, *Jesus' Death*, 164.

human-human mutual abiding. We now focus on the texts that bear these examples of mutual abiding.

6.5.1 Mutual Abiding: Father-Son

6.5.1.1 I and the Father are One (10:30)

Jesus' claim for the Son's union with the Father is profound. That the Son pre-existed in union with the Father in eternity is a vital theme in John's Prologue and is here used by the author to show the security of believers. The Father and the Son are one with respect to the protecting care they give to the people of God, who are described with a communal metaphor as the sheep. The claim of 10:30 builds from 10:28, 29 where Jesus speaks of his and his father's love for the sheep. The sheep are in the Son's hand as well as in the Father's hand, and no one will snatch them out of either hand.

But how is the Father and the Son's oneness to be understood? The key to understanding this unity is the neuter gender of the word "one," suggesting "unity of purpose rather than identity of person."[19] The unity in view is, as Beasley-Murray says, "a functional unity."[20] It echoes Jesus' claims that his words and actions are the words and actions of the Father and that he says and does nothing by himself (14:10). 10:30 ties together all the scriptures which speak of God at work and shows that the Father and the Son are one in outward operation (5:17, 19; 7:28-9; 9:4). They are in agreement with regard to the execution of the Father's mission in the world. In view of the *missio Dei* thrust of the relationship, it must be conceived as dynamic rather than static, consisting in an activity originating with the Father and manifested in the Son. The Son carries out the Father's will in love and obedience. Barrett is probably right to suggest an expression of this unity in moral terms, stressing the complete obedience of the Son to the Father's will.[21] The union consists in Jesus working together with the Father (5:17, 19), Jesus' agreement with the Father (5:30; 8:16, 18), and Jesus' obedience of the Father's will and direction (6:38; 8:26, 28; 10:18).

---

19. Keener, I:826.
20. Beasley-Murray, *John*, 174.
21. Barrett, *John*, 318. Cf. 8:16, 28-9; 16:32.

The unity described in 10:30 is, however, also external. It constitutes oneness of essence and a deep sharing of one life. The writer's language suggests that Jesus and God are one in essence rather than in person. Morris is probably right to suggest that the "one" of this statement refers to "one thing" rather than "one person."[22] For Schnackenburg the unity includes "the metaphysical depths contained in the relationship between Jesus and the Father."[23] Likewise, Carson observes that "some kind of metaphysical unity is presupposed, even if not articulated."[24] The likelihood of this suggestion is supported by the response of the Jews, who immediately concluded that this was a claim to deity.

"I and the Father are one" also echoes the *Shema*, the fundamental confession of Judaism, "Hear O Israel: The Lord our God, the Lord is one" (Deut 6:4), and, like the *Shema*, serves to underscore the unity of God.[25] Jesus' claim to deity does not contradict Jewish (and Christian) monotheism. John's prologue is clear (1:1-5) that Jesus is already included within the unique divine identity as understood in Jewish monotheism.[26] To say that he is one with the Father suggests, not that Jesus is a rival god, but that he and the Father are "one God." Jesus and the Father mutually indwell each other: to see Jesus is virtually to see God (14:9).

In 1:32-3 the writer uses the mutual abiding motif to show that the Spirit too shares in this unity of the Godhead. He uses mutual abiding to describe the descent and abode of the Spirit upon Christ. The remaining of the Spirit upon Jesus suggests the idea of "a building in which the Spirit dwells."[27] This descent of the eternal Spirit to abide upon the eternal word suggests that John's use of abide follows a Trinitarian rather than a

---

22. Morris, *Gospel*, 465.

23. Schnackenburg, *John*, II:308.

24. Carson, *Gospel*, 395.

25. Bauckham, "Monotheism," 163.

26. Bauckham, "Monotheism," 149. Bauckham offers a helpful link between Jewish monotheism and the Johannine Jesus. His reconciliation of Genesis 1:1-4 with John 1:1-5, together with his interpretation of Jesus' divine prerogatives in the light of Deuteronomy 32:29, is informative.

27. Pamment, "Path and Residence," 121.

binitarian model, contrary to Crump.[28] The Spirit does not only dwell in Jesus but he also dwells with and in the disciples (14:17). Keener rightly makes the connection between the use of abiding here and in other texts to denote "mutual indwelling and continuous habitation."[29] As the next chapter demonstrates, the mutual indwelling modeled by the perichoretic interpenetration of the Trinity is at the center of Johannine soteriology and has profound implications for the communal holiness of the new covenant people of God.

6.5.1.2 ". . . the Father is in me and I in the Father" (10:38; cf. 14:11)

Jesus' claim to mutually indwelling the Father in 10:38 builds upon the functional unity already described in 10:30. The unity of the Father and the Son is expressed in the *missio Dei* as the people are called upon to view the works of the Father, through the Son, as evidence for a unity with God. The works refer to the whole outward manifestation of Christ's activity, both natural and supernatural. Here we find the oneness of the Father and the Son expressed through John's reciprocal formula. The intercommunion of the Father and the Son is an example of creating space and giving room for another, which is an archetype of the life of the new covenant people of God. In 14:11 appeal is made again to believe that Jesus and the Father mutually indwell each other or to believe the works. Köstenberger's suggestion that "Jesus' shift from his own person to his works is in keeping with the principle that a tree is judged by the quality of its fruit, and a prophet by his deeds (Matt 7:15-20)"[30] is accurate. As mentioned earlier, such allusion to plant metaphors properly identifies Jesus with the righteous planting motif. The connection between faith and works is important for our purpose.

---

28. Crump, "Johannine Trinity," 395-412. For a broader perspective on Johannine Pneumatology see Keener, I:460-461. Keener notes three uses of the title "Holy Spirit" in 1:32, 14:26 and 20:22 and treats the first and the third as inclusios for Johannine Pneumatology. The first introduces the Spirit as one who descends to the world on account of Jesus, the second emphasizes continuity between Jesus' revelation and that of the Spirit, with the third emphasizing Jesus' sending of the Spirit.

29. Keener, I:460.

30. Köstenberger, *John*, 317.

But what is the connection between faith and works and mutual abiding? First, the works evoke faith in the one whom God has sent. For example, after Jesus' sign in Cana, where he supplied the needs of wedding guests (2:11, 23), the disciples believed. For the Johannine Jesus good works are a greater witness to his divine provenance and they flow out of the Father's love for the Son (5:20, 36; 10:26). God does his works through the Son because he loves the Son and has sent him to the world.[31] Not only does God do his works through the Son but he also witnesses on his behalf (8:18).

The witness motif is one of John's important themes and begins with the work of John the Baptist in the prologue (1:6-8) and runs through the Gospel. Interestingly, the writer compares the works' witness to the witness of John the Baptist and concludes that the works are a greater witness. For the Johannine Jesus relationship with God does not depend upon a merely spoken claim;[32] it rests upon the acts which demonstrate that God is working through him. This is why it is imperative and urgent that the Son must complete the works of God before it is too late (9:4). The Father, who has sent the Son, is in the Son doing his works and the Son works only what he sees the Father working.[33]

Second, believing in the one whom God has sent is doing the work of God (6:29). Faith must be understood not just as a single decisive act but as a continuous state of faith. It is the one work which God requires of all people and in this one work all other good works are included.[34] Mutually abiding in Jesus cannot be divorced from bearing fruits, especially sacrificial love, and walking in the light (15:12-17; 1 John 2:6-12; 3:17-24). The juxtaposition of faith and works is uniquely Johannine. John does not make the apparent dichotomy that is made by Paul and James between faith and works (Gal 2:16; 3:2; James 2:14, 17-26). For John the two motifs are

---

31. See Bruce, *Gospel*, 236, for the coinherence of love, which includes the mutual love of Jesus and the people of God.

32. We do not minimise the importance of the spoken word. The Johannine Jesus oscillates between the words and the works since both are given from the Father (8:28; 14:10).

33. See Bruce, *Gospel*, 235-6, for the Son's carrying out of the Father's initiative and for the link between the mutual knowledge (10:14, 15) and mutual indwelling.

34. Carson, *John*, 285.

blended together so that believing is working. The inseparability of faith
and works in John's thought is well stated by Dodd:

> His thought has two inseparable strains. On the one hand we
> have the language of γνῶσις Θεοῦ [knowing God], of vision, of
> the indwelling man in God and of God in man. On the other
> hand we have the insistence on the deed, the fruit. Both these
> strains must be taken seriously. They do not lie side by side
> unassimilated. They are so fused that both acquire definition
> and fullness of meaning through their combination . . . it is his
> special characteristic that he combines these two aspects of the
> religious life in so remarkable a way. The idea in which they
> meet is that of the divine ἀγάπη [love].[35]

Brodie too suggests that "believing is working, indeed a high form of working—particularly because it opens the way for the working of God."[36]

A parallel statement is found in 1 John where the commandment is
juxtaposed with the practical working-out of that commandment in love.
Here the commandment includes both believing and mutual love: "And
this is his commandment, that we should believe in the name of his Son
Jesus Christ and love one another, just as he has commanded us" (1 John
3:23). Bruce emphasizes: "For believing in Christ and keeping his commandments are two things which cannot be separated; there is no true faith
without obedience, no true obedience without faith."[37] Thus the work of
God includes both believing and the practical outworking of that belief
in communal holiness. Believing is the work of God in the sense that it is
what God requires of his people. Within the context of John 6 believing is
working for the bread that lasts for eternal life. This is in accordance with
the object of the GOJ that people believe and have eternal life (20:31).

Third, in John works can also describe ethical behavior. John speaks of
either good works or evil works. Good works are associated with light and

---

35. Dodd, *Interpretation*, 198-199. Translation in parenthesis mine.

36. Brodie, *John*, 281; Rensberger, *Johannine Faith*, 127.

37. Bruce, *Gospel*, 160.

truth while evil works are associated with darkness and falsehood. In 3:19 those who reject the light and love darkness do so because their works are evil. They repel the light for fear that their evil works will be exposed. Also, in 7:7 Jesus declares that his polemic against the world focuses upon its works, which he describes as evil. His brothers, who don't believe, are in the same category as the world—thus the world will not hate them since it loves only its own (15:18).

On the contrary, those who do what is true come to the light so that it may be clearly seen that their works are done in God (3:21). This suggests a dwelling place for the believers in God. The description of believers as those who are in God (through Jesus) is characteristic of the GOJ. It distinguishes believers from non-believers who are perceived as the world and of the world.[38] It also describes the deep relationship that the new people of God have with God where they mutually indwell God. In the GOJ the verb "work", while referring to physical labor, may also refer to moral effort.[39] In 3 John 5 it is used in connection with doing good for brothers and strangers—charity. An even stronger reference to communal holiness is found in the intratext of 1 John 3:18 where the writer uses "works" in connection with the expression of love in practice, not in word or tongue.

Fourth, the one who believes shall do the works that Jesus is doing. He or she shall do even greater works than Jesus (14:12). Here is what the mutually indwelling tripartite family of the Father, Son, and disciple do in common: they all work the works of the Father. They are obsessed with the works culture of the Father. In 5:17 Jesus makes it clear that the Father is working and that in his works Jesus does what the Father is doing. At this time Jesus also mentions that the Father will show him greater works (5:20). Thus, there is a sense in which much work still remains. In 9:4 Jesus must do the works of the Father urgently before night when no one can work. According to Miranda, "Christ's mission is "not related to" good

---

38. See Kierspel, *The Jews*, for a discussion of the world in the GOJ; Ernst Bammel, "The Farewell Discourse of the Evangelist John and its Jewish Heritage," *TynBul* 44 (1993): 109; Jose Miranda, *Being and the Messiah: The Message of St. John* (Trans. by John Eagleson; NY: Orbis Books, 1977), 100-102. Cf. John 15:19; 17:14, 16 where Jesus and his disciples are hated by the world because they are not of the world.

39. Brodie, *John*, 280. Cf. Acts 10:35; Rom 2:10; 13:10; Gal 6:10.

works; rather it consists in good works."[40] It is the Father's works culture that Jesus passes on to the disciples and the new people of God.

Scholars interpret the greater works with the missionary success of the early church.[41] This is probably true in the light of the future tense of 14:12-14. However, focus is overly placed upon the gathering of converts as greater works with no consideration of the communal holiness of the gathered disciples. We argue that the greater works include, more importantly, meeting the social needs of the gathered people of God. It includes feeding the hungry, dressing the naked, receiving the stranger, caring for the widow and the orphan, and addressing issues of xenophobia, racial discrimination, and economic imbalances such as the early church faced in Acts 6:1. It is more than the gathering of converts. It includes every acts in which the power and character of God are made known. In John knowledge and the power of God are communicated through compassionate practice (9:3, 4; 10:38) and through the disciples' unity and love for one another (13:35; 17:23).

A crucial part of the greater works, often overlooked, is the communal holiness of the people of God such as described in Acts 4:32-37. This is a replica of the acts of mercy and kindness shown by Jesus throughout the GOJ, all of which reveal the power and character of God. A simple, yet profound perception of the works culture of the Son is underscored by Miranda's comments on 7:7:

> The world did not believe in Jesus Christ because it hates him, and it hates him because he testifies that its actions are antithetical to giving food to the hungry, drink to the thirsty, clothes to the naked, a home to the homeless. Most of us find it more comfortable to attribute the world's rejection of Christ to "irreligiosity," "worldliness," "sin," "immorality"—all taken in the broadest, vaguest, and most undetermined sense. But

---

40. Miranda, *Being*, 99.
41. Barrett, *Gospel*, 460; Bruce, *John*, 300; Köstenberger, *John*, 433.

good works and evil works are technical terms with a highly exact meaning.[42]

6.5.1.3 "We will come to them and make our home with them." (14:23)

How does the works culture of the Father come to permeate both the Son and the believer? The answer lies in 14:23. The plural "we" refers to the Father and the Son. This is no surprise since the Father and the Son mutually indwell each other. The believer is a dwelling place and a hospitable home of the Father and the Son. This is tantamount to where the believer is in regards to the Holy Spirit: "You know him, because he abides with you, and he will be in you" (14:17). Thus the believer is presented as a house or temple of the God. This, together with its implications for holiness, is well stated by Paul[43] to the Corinthians: "Do you not know that you are God's temple and that God's Spirit dwells in you? If anyone destroys God's temple, God will destroy that person. For God's temple is holy, and you are that temple" (1 Cor 3:16-17). Nothing could give the disciples greater ground for hope and confidence than knowing that the Father, Son, and Spirit abide in them. The conditions are stated clearly: loving the Son and keeping his words. Loving the Son brings the love of his Father to the believer. Again we see here how love shows itself by obedience to the commands.

The use of the plural "we" is a claim of divinity and suggests equality with the Father. It recalls 10:30 where Jesus declares that he and the Father are one. The coming of the Father and the Son to occupy space in the believer where the Spirit already abides must not be understood as the resurrection appearances or the coming of Jesus on the last day (although this is not entirely absent[44]). Rather, it parallels Revelation 3:20 and is the coming

---

42. Miranda, *Being*, 99; also Rensberger, *Johannine Faith,* 126-30.

43. Stephen Smalley, "The Christ-Christian Relationship in Paul and John," in *Pauline Studies: Essays presented to Professor F. F. Bruce on his 70ᵗʰ Birthday* (ed. Donald A. Hagner and Murray J. Harris; Exeter: Paternoster, 1980), 95-105, explores the relationship between the writings of Paul and John.

44. See Richard Bauckham, "Synoptic Parousia Parables and the Apocalypse," *NTS* 23 (1977): 162-176.

of Jesus upon which John's interest is concentrated, which is realized and explained through the mystical abiding.[45] For John, intimate communion with God is inaugurated in this world and overlaps into eternity. John 14 teaches that it is not only the Son but the Triune God who comes and makes his abode in believing humankind.

6.5.2 Mutual Abiding: Son-disciples (6:56; 14:20; 15:4-5)

As noted, Johannine mutual abiding does not only occur at the level of Jesus and God as Father-Son but also at the level of Jesus and his disciples as divine-human or, as John 15 shows, vine-branches. Through their indwelling of Christ, the people of God also indwell the Father who responds with love and mutual indwelling to anyone who loves the Son. This tripartite union of the Father, Son, and disciple remains a unique feature of the fourth Gospel. Seven texts in the GOJ refer to the abiding motif at the divine-human level: three of these (6:56; 14:20; 15:4-5) describe the full equation of mutual indwelling between Jesus and the disciples while the other four (14:18, 23; 17:23, 26) state that the disciple indwells Jesus.[46] Our focus will be on the texts that describe the full equation while the rest will serve as important support texts.

"Remain in me, and I will remain in you" (v. 4) is an imperative that looks back to earlier use of the abiding motif in the GOJ. The reciprocal union of the Son and disciple first occurs in 6:56 where the conditions of eating Jesus' flesh and drinking Jesus' blood are stated and is reiterated in 14:20 where it is the subject of future revelation. The latter doubtless refers to illumination by the Spirit of the truth concerning the abiding of Christ. However, nuances of the motif occur as early as 1:14. The vine-branch analogy shows that the relationship already existing between Christ and the disciples consists in mutual abiding which the disciple must continue by adhering to the conditions (6:56; 15:10).

---

45. G. K. Beale, *The Book of Revelation* (NIGTC; GR: Eerdmans, 1999), 308, makes a connection between Revelation 3:20 and Canticles 5:2 and suggests that Revelation 3:20 be understood within the context of an existing covenant relationship with God.

46. Crump, *Johannine Trinity*, 401.

But how should the mutual abiding of Christ and believers be under-stood? There are three ways of reading this motif: new identity, mutual temple, and sharing Christ's holiness. First, being mutually in Christ is about the people of God's new identity. What Rensberger says of John's high Christology can be said of John's mutual abiding motif: it "reinforces the community's social identity . . . its deprivation of identity and forma-tion of new identity."[47] Most important for understanding the believer's new identity here is the mutual abiding of the Father and the Son. For John the eternal union of the Father and the Son which existed in the begin-ning suggests a connection between the Genesis creation story and God's purposes to create for himself a new holy covenant people.[48] Thus in the incarnation the Son-Logos is creator of a new community, a community not defined by geographical or ethnic boundaries.[49] This finds support in the OT themes echoed throughout the GOJ regarding the covenant people of God.

The allusion to Genesis (in 1:1-4) indicates that the Word of God is the one without whom nothing comes to existence; in John, he is the one through whom the renewal of human existence is promised.[50] All who be-lieve in the Word of God[51] and accept him as a true revelation of God or "as the envoy of the Father,"[52] regardless of social status or ethnic origin, receive a new beginning and a new identity. The significance of believing and the irrelevance of descent is the subject of John 8 where physical descent from Abraham is irrelevant without producing Abraham's faith. Believing the Son then is the threshold to this new family, and all who believe become the

---

47. Rensberger, *Johannine Faith*, 119. Also Meeks, "The Man from Heaven," 70; Kierspel, *The Jews*, 180.

48. See Westcott, *John*, 2; Brown, *John* I:4; Morris, *John*, 72; Keener, I:365, for a connection between the Genesis story and John 1-3.

49. For the universal nature of the message of John's prologue, see Barrett, *Gospel*, 149; Brown, *John*, I:4-6; Keener, I:365.

50. Howard Clark Kee, *Who Are the People of God? Early Christian Models of Community* (New Haven; London: Yale University Press, 1995), 159.

51. Also described as believing in his name. So, Carson, *John*, 125: "The name is more than a label; it is the character of the person, or even the person himself."

52. Barrett, *John*, 163.

new covenant people of God and are called by various communal names and metaphors in John.

One of the names John uses for the people of God is "children of God" (1:12). As children of God they belong to an ethnically inclusive family where they participate in a new mode of communal life.[53] This inclusiveness is intended in the writer's use of "as many as" (1:12) and is exemplified elsewhere in John's portrayal of Jesus' transcendence of all boundaries.[54] It is also used in relation to the scope of God's mission in sending his only Son. They become children of God by believing in the Word of God. Later John adds that it is by new birth or birth from above (3:3-7), which suggests an interpretation with regard to a new beginning. This implies that even though the indwelling is mutual the initiative lies entirely with the divine side. There is no equality between the indwelling Jesus and the indwelling disciple. Other corporate names for the new people of God are discussed later in this thesis.

Second, and significant for the mutual abiding motif, is the tabernacle theme which is introduced in the Prologue and used to refer to the extension of the fellowship of the Father and the Son to humankind. In extending such fellowship, the Word pitches his tent in the realm of humankind and participates in humankind's creaturely weakness.[55] Here the divine Word moves from the sphere of the divine to the sphere of the human and thereby inaugurates the divine-human mutual sharing of life.[56] The allusion to the "tent of meeting" must not be missed here (Exod 33:7-34:5).[57] The Son has become the new place of divine revelation. The people are to look nowhere else for the presence of the divine. They must receive God's

---

53. Kee, *Community*, 159.

54. Jesus transcended all dividing walls between humankind. He associated himself with the weak, poor, lame, despised, and all marginalized people of God. His associations included Jews (respected and not respected), Samaritans, Greeks, women, and others (3:1-21; 4:4-42; 5:1-18; 8:1-11; 12:20).

55. Beasley-Murray, *John*, 14.

56. See Keener, I:406, expands on ideas on the impassiveness of Hellenistic deities.

57. See Carson, *Gospel*, 126-7.

alternative for the destroyed Jerusalem temple. God makes his tabernacle among them through Jesus.[58]

The temple imagery[59] in 2:13-21, together with the tabernacle imagery in 1:14, clearly portray Jesus as the new dwelling place of God.[60] Jesus' prediction of the destruction of the physical temple in Jerusalem and his erection of a new temple in three days is interpreted by John as referring to the temple of Jesus' body. The body in view is that by which the Word became flesh and abode among humankind (1:14). That the new temple of Jesus' body is superior is clear from the Greek vocabulary for temple. In 2:14, 15, where the Jerusalem temple is in view, John used the Greek noun which describes the temple without particular reference to the sacred edifice or holy of holies. However, in 2:19, 20, 21, where the new temple of Jesus' body is concerned, the writer uses the Greek noun which is used "only for the sacred edifice" and derives from the root meaning to dwell or inhabit.[61] John's careful selection of vocabulary portrays Jesus as the new holy of holies and a center of revelation in the midst of the people of God. As temple, the Johannine Jesus is the place where a unique manifestation of God takes place; the only legitimate center of true worship.[62] He is the new locus and focus of God's dwelling; the very presence of God in the midst of God's people.

In Jesus, God has also generously invited humankind to participate in the divine mutual indwelling. As 1:14 shows, the people of God also become Jesus' house. For John it is this participation in the divine that sets the people of God apart as God's walking temple in the world. This view of the people of God greatly influences John's perception of worship. In 4:23-24 the Johannine Jesus states that true worship is no longer confined

---

58. See Edwyn Clement Hoskyns, *The Fourth Gospel* (2nd rev. ed.; edited and completed by Francis Noel Davey; London: FF, 1947), 148; Lloyd Gaston, *No Stone on Another: Studies on the significance of the Fall of Jerusalem in the Synoptic Gospels* (NovTSup 23; Leiden: Brill, 1970), 209.

59. Brooke, *DSS*, 235-260, links the temple/altar and the vine/vineyard metaphor.

60. Peter Walker, *Jesus and the Holy City: New Testament Perspectives on Jerusalem* (GR: Eerdmans, 1996), 164.

61. O Michel, ναός, *TDNT* 4, 880. Michel, 882. Cf. Barrett, *Gospel*, 166; Carson, *John*, 181.

62. Barrett, *John*, 201. Cf. John 4:23-24.

to the Jerusalem temple or any manmade physical structure. The statement on the "hour" gives insight into John's realized eschatology without ruling out the future. In the present "hour" worship will take place wherever the holy people of God are and in spirit and in truth. The connection between worship and mutual indwelling harks back to the call for true worship that is pertinent to the polemic of the prophets' use of the vine metaphor.

Third, mutually indwelling Christ means sharing his holiness. Earlier in this research holiness was defined in terms of a right relationship with God. Here, we pursue our suggestion that mutual abiding is John's chosen motif for expressing this right relationship. Since in John Jesus is portrayed as the Holy One of God (6:69), a relationship with him is a relationship with the holy. John leaves no room for any doubt that a strong relationship of faith exists between Jesus and the disciples. The disciples have been cleansed by the words of Jesus (15:3), have kept God's word (17:6), and have believed that Jesus is from God (17:8). It is this faith in the Son and the keeping of God's word that cleanses the disciples (15:3). To have the cleansing words of the Son abide in them implies continued cleansing. This corresponds with the function of the word in 17:17 where it is truth and sanctifier. Therefore, in having the word abide them, the disciples actually have the sanctifier abide in them; just as in having the Son abide in them they have the Holy One of God sharing their life. Thus this mutual abiding relationship of the Son and the disciples is a sanctifying relationship.

6.5.3 Mutual Abiding: The Unity of the New People of God (17:11)

The key intratext for the mutual abiding of the holy people of God may be found in Jesus' prayer for his followers (17:11) where "the idea of unity by mutual indwelling receives classical expression in the prayer of Christ in ch. xvii."[63] As shown previously, the unity and mutuality of the Father and the Son anticipate the unity and mutuality of the holy people of God. The latter is the focus of the passages where the people of God are invited to abide in divine expressions, such as love.

---

63. Dodd, *Interpretation*, 196.

The statement, "as we are one" harks back to the mutual abiding of the Father and the Son previously discussed (10:30). It determines that the unity of the believers is not the product of human conjecture and endeavor. The believers' oneness originates entirely from God and its lifeline remains the work of God. It is an outworking of the unity of the Father and the Son with the disciple. It is not possible without the disciples' participation in the mutual unity of the Father and the Son, since "apart from me you can do nothing" (15:5). This is why Jesus prays that the disciples be kept in the Father's name (17:12), so that they abide and thereby experience the archetypal unity.

This prayer for archetypal unity appears four times in 17:1-25. Initially it appears in v. 11 with regard to the disciples, where it is linked with God's protection; then in v. 21 with regard to the disciples and those who will believe their word, where it results in the world's belief that God has sent Jesus; in v. 22 it is the outcome of the glory that Jesus has given to the disciples; in v. 23 with the result that the world will know that God has sent Jesus and loved the disciples as the Son.

This repeated emphasis on oneness must be viewed in light of the ultimate goal of the good shepherd that there be one flock and one shepherd (10:16). It is also echoed in Caiaphas' prophecy that the death of one man will "gather into one the dispersed children of God" (11:52). The same notion is carried in the view that believers are branches of the same vine tended by one ultimate vinedresser. Unlike the oneness of the Qumran covenanters, the oneness described in John is rooted in the being of God and revealed in the redemptive action of Christ,[64] and, therefore, outward looking. This outward looking character of the new union is in line with the universality of the prayer—"all who will believe their word" (17:20). It echoes the passages throughout the Gospel where the world is at the center of God's purposes for sending the Son."[65]

However, the union of mutual indwelling does not suggest that the new people of God will find the lowest common theological denominator.[66]

64. Beasley-Murray, *John*, 302.

65. 1:29; 3:16-17; 4:42; 6:33, 51; 8:12; 9:5; 12:46; 17:21, 23.

66. Carson, *Gospel*, 568.

Rather, it suggests oneness of purpose, love, and action. It is oneness of solidarity in seeking the Father's purposes for the community, loving God and each other selflessly, and together joining Christ in doing the mission of God in the world. It is a unity patterned after the unity of the Father and the Son, who remain one in purpose, love, and action.

6.6 Aspects of Mutual Abiding in 1 John

6.6.1 Introduction

There are at least three categories of mutual abiding in 1 John. However, there is a slight deviation from the pattern followed in the Gospel, with the conspicuous absence of emphasis on the coinherence of the Father with the Son. This is because the writer is concerned with the ethical implications of union with God for the community rather than debating the union itself. Certainly the writer of 1 John considers his audience to already have some degree of knowledge (1 John 2:21), presumably including the mutual abiding of the Father and the Son.

The first category of mutual abiding in 1 John occurs between the community of believers and the Son of God.[67] John indicates that the claim to abide in Christ was already common among some members of his community, including his opponents. To these he urged that this claim be accompanied by walking as Christ walked, adding a strong ethical side to mutual abiding.

Second, there is the mutual abiding of believers and God (1 John 2:24; 4:16; 5:20). Here the writer often speaks of believers abiding in God without referring to the Son's mediation. This must not be perceived as displacing the Son or suggesting that the disciples can detour around the Son and have fellowship with God. It is a clear reflection of the writer's conviction of the unity and solidarity of the Father with the Son. For example, for John to deny the Son is to deny the Father also (1 John 2:22) and to acknowledge the Son is to acknowledge the Father (1 John 2:23). Since the Father and

---

67. 1 John 2:6, 10, 23, 27, 28; 3:6, 24; 5:20; 2 John 1:9.

the Son are mutually abiding in each other, to be in the Father is to be in the Son. In John's thinking the believers' relationship is necessarily mediated by and inseparable from their relationship to Jesus.[68] To be in God is synonymous with being in his Son (1 John 2:23; 5:20; 2 John 1:9).

Third, there is the mutual abiding of believers and expressions of divine life.[69] For John the expressions of love, life, truth, and commandment(s) mutually abide in the children of God.[70] The abiding of these expressions also points to the abiding of God (1 John 1:5; 4:8; 5:20). For instance, in 1 John 3:17 the writer speaks of God's love abiding in believers when in 1 John 4:8, 16 he states that "God is love." Thus John uses these expressions of divine life to refer to God or his Son, so that abiding in these expressions is tantamount to abiding in God and vice versa. For example, in 2 John 2 he speaks of "the truth that dwells in us . . ." when elsewhere in John he makes it clear that "truth" is another name for Jesus (14:6). Because of this overlap these expressions are seen as further expansions and practical applications of the mutual abiding of Jesus/God and believers.

These expressions of divine life function in 1 John in almost the same way 15:12-17 functions in the Gospel, linking mutual abiding to communal holiness. The emphasis is on compassionate behavior towards fellow believers as proof of love's true abode. The abiding of God or God's love in one's life is evident in the practical sharing of the goods with fellow community members. To ignore the social needs of a fellow believer is a manifestation of failure to live out the mutual abiding life to which believers are called.

6.6.2 1 John 1:1-3

Here John points clearly to a mutual abiding of the Son with the Father in eternity, which, at the incarnation of the Son of God, made possible

---

68. Malatesta, *Interiority*, 273.

69. Rudolph Schnackenburg, *The Johannine Epistles: Introduction and Commentary* (NY: Crossroad, 1992), 101, refers to these expressions as formulas of reciprocity.

70. God's word, 1 John 2:14; life, 1 John 3:17; truth, 2 John 2; anointing, 1 John 2:27; doctrine, 1 John 2:9; light, 1 John 2:10. Also shared by Paul: 2 Cor 11:10 with regard to truth; Eph 2:10, 24 with regard to love and good works; Col 3:16 with regard to the word of Christ.

a mutual abiding of God and the Son with the holy people of God. The revelation of the pre-existent Son underscores the incarnation and parallels 1:14 where "the Word became flesh and lived among us, and we have seen his glory. . . ." What is now revealed is what eternally pre-existed with the Father. In the same way 1 John begins with a reference to the incarnated pre-existent Son of God, stressing what the community has heard, seen, and even touched of the Word of life (1 John 1:1).

The significance of the incarnation for this research is the abiding of the Son of God in the realm of humankind and its implications for holy community. Amidst docetic claims that Jesus had not come in the flesh, 1 John speaks strongly about the reality of the incarnation. He states categorically that in his humanity Jesus identified with humankind so that he could be seen and heard and touched. In Johannine terms seeing has a deeper meaning. Here it is synonymous with fellowship, something that the Johannine community already has with regard to God and his Son Jesus Christ (1 John 1:3). For John fellowship with God/Jesus is identical with mutually abiding in him and must be paralleled by fellowship with other members of the new covenant community.

6.6.3 1 John 3:24; 5:20

Mutual abiding is an important criterion for distinguishing the Johannine community—they are "in him who is true, in his Son Jesus Christ" (1 John 5:20). Not only are they abiding in Jesus but Jesus abides in them: "And by this we know that he abides in us, by the Spirit that he has given us" (1 John 3:24). Although this is the first time the Spirit[71] is mentioned in the epistle, it is clear that he has an important role in the mutual abiding of God/Christ with the believers. He is the source of the believers' knowledge of the Lord's abiding. And, knowledge here is not mere logic or theory; it is "a believing perception, a becoming aware, an apprehending and being apprehended."[72] There is a strong intertextual link between the function of the Spirit here and in Rom 8:1-16 where the indwelling Spirit bears

---

71. The Spirit appears again as the Spirit of truth in 4:2, 13 and as the Spirit of witness in 5:7.

72. Schnackenburg, *Epistles*, 221.

witness with the believers' spirit that they are children of God. Paul, too, stresses that it is those who are led by the Spirit who are the true children of God. For John, as for Paul, the role of the Spirit is important in the mutual indwelling of Christ and the believers.

6.6.4 1 John 2:2-11

The abiding of believers in the divine expression of light (1 John 2:9) must be treated as referring to the believers' abode in Christ. Three synonymous claims are found in this passage: "I have come to know him" (v. 4), "I abide in him" (v. 6), and "I am in the light" (v. 9). The conditions are also synonymous: obeying his commands, walking as he walked (*imitatio Christi*), and loving a brother or sister. The strong dualism of light and darkness is probably reminiscent of the community at Qumran.[73] John uses light with a distinct Christological purpose as another name for Christ both in the Gospel and the epistles.[74] The Johannine Jesus is "the light of the world" (8:12) and all his followers are children of light (12:36). However, being in the light is strongly determined by "obedience to the law of love."[75] Hatred has no place in the community of the new people of God (v. 11). Light is used with a soteriological connotation when linked to "walking" after Christ and having the light of life. Association with Christ must affect how people live especially with regard to others. The light of life refers to life modelled after Christ who is the Light of the world.

6.6.5 1 John 3:17

Here emphasis is given to the practical implications of mutually abiding in Jesus' love. The message is clear: anyone who has material possessions, notices a needy person, and deliberately refuses to offer any help, does not abide in love. The phrase, which the NRSV translates "refuses help," and the NIV, "has no pity on him," literally emphasizes the interiority of

---

73. See 1QS 1:9-11 for reference to the Qumran community as sons of light and their opponents as sons of darkness. The light is associated with life, truth, knowledge, and eternal life while the darkness is associated with death, falsehood, ignorance, and extinction. Cf. 1QM 1:1.

74. 1:7-9; 8:12; 9:5; 12:35, 36, 46; 1 John 1:5, 7.

75. Stephen S. Smalley, *1, 2, 3 John*, (WBC 51; Waco: WBP, revised ed., 2007), 58.

compassion in the life of the holy community. It is a polemic against the unholy practice of ignoring a poverty-stricken person by someone who is wealthy. Furthermore, it is deeper than "compassionate ministry" because it goes to the very level of self-giving, emphasizing mutuality. There is a very permeable boundary between people in the community, which means that the resources one "has" are not just for the individual but, on the basis of mutuality and love, are for the needy brother and sister. Mutual abiding has as its core purpose the manifestation of shared living or communal holiness. It has as its intended outcome the willingness to lay down one's life for another. There could not be a better message from Jesus as he bade farewell to the new people of God than to command them to be compassionate towards one another.

6.6.6 Conclusion

Finally, three things are clear concerning mutual abiding in 1 John. First, believers mutually abide in God and his Son Jesus Christ. Second, abiding in God and his Son Jesus Christ implies a life of fellowship with one another. Third, being in God and Jesus cannot be divorced from practical acts of kindness and hospitality towards fellow community members. That is, love, expressing itself in communal holiness, is the ultimate sign of mutually abiding in God and his Son Jesus Christ.

6.7 The Means of Abiding

But how are the people of God to obey the command of Jesus? The GOJ suggests two responses: 1) it is the one who chews Jesus' flesh and drinks Jesus' blood who mutually indwells Jesus (6:56); 2) abiding in Jesus' love (15:9, 10; cf. 1 John 3:16; 4:16). How should these symbols be understood?

6.7.1 Chewing Jesus' Flesh (6:56)

Chewing Jesus' flesh can be read in at least four ways: First, it must be understood in light of the "bread of life" motif which dominates 6:5-58, since John juxtaposes the two.[76] In 6:51b Jesus equates his flesh with the bread that he will give for the life of the world. The invitation to chew his flesh is not outrageous when we consider that his flesh is the life-giving bread. The symbolism of "flesh" must be read against the background of "manna" in the Mosaic traditions. Like manna, Jesus is the gift of God and nourishment of the world. He is the living bread that came from heaven, and, as the bread of life he mediates the life that he is. Important here for the vine metaphor is the theme of "enduring" and "perishing." The contrast is between the perishable manna and the enduring food of Jesus' flesh and blood (6:27), inviting Jesus' interlocutors not just to believe but to endure. Also, in view of Jewish traditions associated with manna, the bread of life motif suggests Jesus' perfection of the Torah[77] which was the revelation of God to Israel. Jesus is, therefore, portrayed as the true bread from heaven which the new covenant people of God eat and do not die.

Second, chewing Jesus' flesh and drinking his blood "suggests a sacrificial meaning."[78] Guthrie identifies this imagery with the sayings that view the passion as a sacrifice[79] and suggests that where flesh and blood are separated death is implied. He agrees with Dodd who recognizes "the idea of death, indeed violent death"[80] in the terminology of 6:51-59. Guthrie's interpretation must be supported in view of John's portrayal of Jesus' sacrificial death as in accordance with God's will and plan. The Johannine Jesus speaks plainly about his death and sees his life and ministry in terms of "the

---

76. An unresolved debate on whether this is an allusion to the Eucharist or symbolic is ongoing in Johannine scholarship. The weakness of the Eucharistic approach, however, is that it fails to acknowledge a pre-Johannine existence of the idea of chewing "flesh and blood" (Ps 27:2; 56:4; Isa 9:20; 49:26; Jer 19:9; Ezek 39:17, 18; Hos 8:13; Mic 3:3). For instance, there is evidence that in Jewish tradition "flesh and blood" was a way of speaking of the whole person and of describing the earthly character of human life. See Brown, *John*, I:282; Brodie, *Gospel*, 285; Lindars, *Gospel*, 268; Matt 16:17.

77. See Moloney, *John*, 214-15, 221. The idea that Jesus perfects the Law is embedded in John's presentation of Jesus as the nourishing gift of God from heaven. That the Law was perceived in this way is clear in Jewish writing (Isa 55:10-11; *m. Sanh.* 10:1).

78. Donald Guthrie, *New Testament Theology* (Leicester: IVP, 1981), 452.

79. 1:29, 35; cf. 11:50-53; Isa 53:3-7.

80. C. H. Dodd, *The Interpretation of the Fourth Gospel* (Cambridge: Cambridge University Press, 1968), 338. However, Guthrie disagrees with Dodd's sacramental interpretation of this imagery.

hour."[81] Thus the invitation to chew his flesh and drink his blood possibly echoes Isa 53:7 and is, in effect, a call to view Jesus as the paschal lamb in accordance with 1:29, 36.

Third, the motif also alludes to the incarnation (1:14)[82] and, therefore, nuances the extension of fellowship to humankind. In the light of this, we suggest that chewing Jesus' flesh indicates full participation in the life he offers, including both suffering and blessing, as demonstrated in his earthly ministry. It does not suggest an individual spiritual experience but a corporate sharing in the life of obedience and a readiness to join in the mission of God to the world, including laying down life for the new people of God. This is the main thrust of John's interpretation of the vine metaphor (15:12-17). As a condition for mutual abiding, chewing Jesus' flesh parallels keeping the commandments, especially the commandment to love (15:10; 1 John 3:24). It is about participating in the whole person of Christ—including his whole character.

Fourth, the motif of chewing human flesh has strong social justice overtones in early Judaism.[83] It is used in 2 Kings in a context of hunger to describe the gruesome results of the Samaritan siege where desperate women chewed the flesh of their babies. In the prophetic tradition it serves as a critique for the antisocial practices of the leadership of Israel and Judah. For example, in a strong polemic, Micah describes the unjust rulers of Israel as those "who tear the skin off my people, and flesh off their bones, who eat the flesh of my people" (Mic 3: 2-3). Likewise Josephus[84] uses this cannibalistic imagery to describe the severity of the Jewish revolt, describing factional leaders as "bestial monsters (non-Jews, even non-humans) who eat the raw flesh and gulp down the warm blood of the very fellow citizens they claim to protect."[85]

---

81. 2:4; 7:6, 8, 30; 8:20; 12:23, 27; 17:1.

82. Francis J. Moloney, *The Gospel of John* (SP 4; Collegeville: Liturgical, 1998), 221.

83. 2 Kings 6:28, 29; Mic 3:1-3, 9-10; Flavius Josephus, *J. W.*, Books IV-VII (London: Harvard University Press, 1928), 208-211, 362-363.

84. Josephus. *J. W.* 5.27-28, 526.

85. J. Albert Harrill, "Cannibalistic Language in the Fourth Gospel and Greco-Roman Polemics of Factionalism (John 6:52-66)," *JBL* 127 (2008), 145.

Why does John use this imagery in a positive sense when in Micah it is singularly negative? The answer to this question emerges in understanding John's subversive speech and anti-language. This cannibalistic imagery is identified with "the Fourth Gospel's regular subversion and reinterpretation of familiar symbolism."[86] Harrill, who argues that John's cannibalistic imagery must be read in the light of Greco-Roman polemics of factionalism, suggests that "the Johannine author revaluated the cultural taboo of cannibalism in positive terms as a means of self-definition for his community."[87] The Gospel writer uses this imagery in accordance with Greco-Roman and Jewish tradition as a polemic against factionalism and its resultant social injury, with a view to encouraging solidarity and compassionate love in the community.

Waetjen suggests that since Jesus is addressing ruling authorities in this passage, it is plausible that his use of the motif has a socio-political import.[88] This should not be lightly dismissed. The violent reaction of the Jewish authorities following Jesus' Sabbath healing initiates a process of gruesome suffering that will eventually lead to his death under the hands of Roman authorities (5:16-18). In 6:15 an attempt is made by the crowds to crown Jesus as king, a politically charged title emphasized in John's trial narratives.[89] If Rensberger's argument that "Jewish and Christian theology and politics could seldom be totally separated" in the late first century C.E. is to be considered, it is proper to interpret the chewing of flesh in the light of Jewish prophetic polemic (Mic 3:1-3, 9). Abiding in Jesus includes social responsibility and commitment to communal holiness.

---

86. Harrill, "Cannibalistic Language," 135. John introduces motifs familiar from Jewish tradition and deliberately subverts them and applies them to Jesus in accordance with his pattern of irony, subversion and polemic. E.g., the paschal lamb (1:29, 36); Jacob's ladder and ascent (1:51; 3:13; 6:62; living water (4:10; 7:37-39; the manna from heaven (6:31-42).

87. Harrill, "Cannibalistic Language," 136, 140. Harrill also shows that cannibalism is also used in Jewish culture as an idiom for factionalism.

88. Herman C. Waetjen, *The Gospel of the Beloved Disciple: A Work in Two Editions* (NY; London: T & T Clark, 2005), 214.

89. See Rensberger, *Johannine Faith*, 89, who states that "Christology and politics were not unrelated for the Fourth Evangelist," and that "the political nature of the charges against Jesus is given far more emphasis in the Fourth Gospel than elsewhere in the New Testament."

6.7.2 Drinking Jesus' Blood (6:56)

First, drinking Jesus' blood should probably be understood in light of the OT texts attributing life to blood.[90] The contrast, however, is that these texts forbid the drinking of blood whereas Jesus encourages the drinking of his own blood. Nevertheless, when read together with the chewing of flesh as John's subversive speech and interpreted in the light of Greco-Roman polemics of factionalism, it creates little or no difficulty. What is it that vivifies Jesus' flesh and blood so that they communicate eternal life? In 6:63 the answer lies with the Spirit: "It is the Spirit that gives life." The Spirit, who is the essence of life, dwells in Jesus' flesh and blood. Malina is probably right to treat the motifs as anti-language "synonymous with welcoming, accepting, receiving, believing in, and the like."[91] These motifs suggest a full commitment that involves the total person in following Jesus and entering into a union with him. The link between the life-giving Spirit and the words of Jesus anticipates 15:3 where the words of Jesus prune the new covenant people of God.

6.7.3 Keeping Jesus' Commands (15:10)

Second, for John the answer is remaining in Jesus' love, shown by obedience to Jesus' words.[92] The words are the teaching of Jesus and those who abide in it have God, are from God, and have seen God (2 John 9; 3 John 11). Obedience to the teaching of Jesus is the only way they are to remain in the covenant relationship. This is not just commitment to a set of teachings but to a person. Yet, commitment to Christ and commitment to his words are synonymous. Christ's teaching awakens the community to the way of the truth that they walk in and abide in God. As we shall see later, mutual indwelling suggests fellowship with God and has strong implications for holiness. Again the model for this is Jesus' obedience to the Father's commands, which for John is central to the Father-Son relationship of God and Jesus, as well as the accomplishment of Jesus' mission in the world. John

---

90. Gen 9:4; Deut 12:23; Lev 7:26-27; 17:11, 14.

91. Malina and Rohrbaugh, *Social-Science*, 136. Cf. 1:12-13.

92. 15:9, 10. Also 8:31 where remaining in Jesus' words is a sign of true discipleship. In 2 John 6a love is defined as walking after the commandments of Christ.

states clearly that Jesus obeyed the Father's commandments out of love. So important are the Father's commandments to Jesus that he does only what the Father has commanded him to do (4:34; 6:38; 8:29, 55). In the same way the new covenant people of God must obey Jesus' commandments out of love rather than fear or obligation (14:15, 21, 23; 15:14).

The significance of the disciples' abiding is made clear by its effects. Without abiding in Jesus the disciples cannot bear fruit (v. 4). We know from v. 2 what happens to unfruitful branches. The two notions of abiding and fruit-bearing are tied together so that "to remain in Christ is to become fruitful."[93] While fruit-bearing is the ultimate reason for the vine's existence and the Father's pruning, it is clear that abiding is the condition for fruit-bearing. If the disciples abide in Jesus and Jesus in them, they bear much fruit (v. 5) and bring glory to the God and thus ensure their place as true disciples of Jesus (v. 8). That is, if they remain in Jesus and let Jesus' teachings remain in them, they will produce the desired fruits of a virtuous life, communal holiness, and witness to the world concerning Jesus. Also, if they abide in Jesus, they will receive answers to their prayers.

6.8 Conclusion

Several conclusions concerning mutual abiding and the shared life of the new people of God can be drawn.

First, mutual abiding is John's way of describing Father-Son, Son-disciple, and disciple-disciple fellowship. Father-Son fellowship exists eternally as a loving relationship and includes obedience and the sharing of all attributes. The descent of the Spirit to make his abode in the incarnate Son suggests that divine coinherence can be seen as Trinitarian. The mutual coinherence of the divine persons is driven by a strong desire to accomplish the Father's will and purpose for the world (1:9-13, 29; 3:16-17). The mutual abiding of the divine persons is the prototype of Son-disciple (divine-human) fellowship. The principles governing Father-Son fellowship

---

93. Beasley-Murray, *John*, 273.

are at work in the relationship of the Son to the disciples. Jesus often uses his relationship with the Father to exemplify how the disciples must relate to him and to one another (15:9, 10; 17:11, 21). The principles governing disciple-disciple mutual abiding are modelled after the Father-Son mutual abiding, but the power to carry them out is received through the Son-disciple mutual abiding. For example, in generosity they are to emulate the divine family by not hoarding resources but sharing with each other.

Second, mutual abiding, at all its levels, must be read in connection with the new temple theme. When God made a covenant with Israel he came and dwelt with them in the tabernacle or temple, just as he had originally dwelt with Adam in the Garden. This dwelling "with" humankind in the old creation was from the beginning a temporary state that pointed forward to the indwelling of Christ and the Spirit (14:16-18). In both the old creation, dwelling "with" humankind, and the new creation, dwelling "in" humankind, there is an analogy to the mutual abiding of the Persons of the Trinity, not in its ontological meaning but in its covenantal significance.

Third, mutual abiding can be interpreted as a call to a life of communal holiness and outward looking love. It is expressed in obedience to the command to love even to the point of laying down life for another. It includes a reliving of true NT fellowship and an honest call to meet the social needs of God's people. The purpose of this covenantal indwelling is the extension of covenant blessing to the entire world (17:21c). Abiding in Christ provides the bridge which links indwelling and mission to the world, for when the world sees obedient disciples, it will believe and the Abrahamic promise will be fulfilled. The next chapter will detail how mutual abiding can be expressed in the community by a life of hospitality.

CHAPTER 7

Mutual Abiding as Johannine Hospitality Language

7.1 Introduction

In this chapter the theme of shared life, introduced in chapter 5 in connection with the mutual abiding motif, is further developed. We suggest that mutual abiding, which carries the giving of room and sharing of one's space with another, is expressed in hospitality language throughout the GOJ. Its climax is 15:1-17 where John draws the reader's attention to the coinherence and sharing of life of the vine and its branches. These are used metaphorically for the coinherence of the holy one of God and the holy people of God. John states clearly that in this coinherence there is reciprocal giving and receiving of another's life (15:4). The hospitality theme, developed throughout John, is linked with the Gospel writer's interest in Trinitarian theology where the divine family models a higher level of hospitality.

This chapter will show how a Trinitarian reading of a range of passages in John helps the reader grasp the rich theme of hospitality at the center of Johannine mutual abiding. Trinitarian hospitality will be discussed at three levels: intra-Trinitarian hospitality, God's hospitality to humankind, and the new people of God as a reflection of Trinitarian hospitality. Before discussing Trinitarian hospitality, the case is made for hospitality in John, and then anthropological insights will be drawn from the Swazi, an African *Bantu* tribe, to show an imperfect human example of hospitality.

Particularly helpful within the *Bantu* is the philosophy of ubuntu with its similarities to ancient Jewish culture.

7.2 The Case for Hospitality in the GOJ

While the word hospitality is not present in the GOJ, the notion is present from the beginning. The Gospel opens with a reference to the archetypal hospitality of the Triune God (1:1-2, 32) and further describes how this divine hospitality extends to the realm of humankind through the incarnation (1:11-14) and the practical acts of Jesus throughout the Gospel. Jesus' transformation of water into wine at Cana and his encounter with the Samaritan woman at Jacob's well are both examples of his ability to move from guest to host.[1] In 15:1-17 the writer portrays a higher level of hospitality where the participants share not just space and possessions but one another's lives. Here the disciples' relationship to Jesus is deepened to "friends" rather than servants, and they are commanded to "love one another as I have loved you" (v. 12-14). Such love is referred to in the 1 John 3:16-18 intratext as "not in word or speech but in deed and in truth" and, as we have seen earlier,[2] expresses itself in empathy and pity. The notion of hospitality introduced in the prologue inaugurates an important theme that will run through the Gospel and forms an important context for John's teaching on communal holiness.[3]

Hospitality language here does not suggest any form of word study; words receive their meanings from the context in which they are used. The words and ideas used here are treated semantically rather than etymologically. As noted, John has carefully chosen his vocabulary to function within the context of his first century audience. So Brower, "the most important axiom in biblical exegesis is that full account must be taken of the context"

---

1. Ellen L. Marmon, "Teaching As Hospitality," *AJ* 63 (2008): 35.

2. See discussion of 1 John 3:16-18 in chapter 6.

3. We refute Meeks' assertion that the GOJ "does not provide moral instruction . . . nor does its narrative directly model character to be emulated." Wayne Meeks, "The Ethics of the Fourth Evangelist," in *Exploring the GOJ: In Honor of D. Moody Smith* (eds. R. Alan Culpepper and C. Clifton Black; Kentucky: JKP, 1996), 322.

and "only as we hear the word as it was to the first readers can we begin to hear it today."[4] It is only in the light of its background and context that the full message of John, including hospitality, can be interpreted.

Hospitality as portrayed in John is not the shallow hospitality portrayed in modern times and perceived as "entertaining relatives, friends, and acquaintances."[5] Nor is it commercialized hospitality marked by "an industry with training courses, certificates, five star ratings, and "meet and greet" attitudes."[6] Unfortunately, such hospitality gains ground in contemporary cultures where patriotism and its xenophobic tendencies increase. Modern cultures view hospitality in terms of kinship and ability of future individual reciprocation. True hospitality, however, is not restricted to friends or family whether immediate or extended. Nor is it restricted to those who are capable of buying it or paying it back. Clearly, this is not acceptable in biblical terms where "hospitality normally refers to hosting a stranger"[7] almost always on the basis of theoxeny.[8]

Abraham offered hospitality to angels in the persons of three strangers who came to his tent (Gen 18:1-4).[9] His hospitality taught later generations the virtue of helping strangers and remains a model for Jewish and Christian hospitality.[10] Later the writer of the Testament of Abraham juxtaposes Abraham's willingness to offer hospitality with his righteousness: "But above all others he is righteous in all goodness, (having been) hospitable and loving until the end of his life" (*T. Ab.* 1:6). Lot received two

---

4. Kent Brower, "Purity of Heart," in *Biblical Resources for Holiness Preaching (2): From Text to Sermon* (ed. by H. Ray Dunning; KC: BHPKC, 1993), 16.

5. Bruce J. Malina, "The Received View and What it Cannot Do: III John and Hospitality," *Semeia* 35 (1986), 188.

6. Cathy Ross, "Creating Space: Hospitality as a Metaphor for Mission," *ANVIL* 25 (2008): 167.

7. Malina, "Hospitality," 188.

8. Ladislaus J. Bolchazy, *Hospitality in Early Rome: Livy's Concept of Its Humanizing Force* (Chicago: Ares, 1977), 7-8, who defines theoxeny as "the belief in the epiphany of the gods, whether in their divine majesty and glory or in the incarnate form of beggars and strangers."

9. See John Koenig, *New Testament Hospitality: Partnership with Strangers as Promise and Mission* (Philadelphia: Fortress, 1985), 3, who suggests in the light of Gen 18:1-4 that "strangers may be God's special envoys to bless or challenge us."

10. See Artebury, *Entertaining Angels*, 59.

angels in the form of strangers (Gen 19:1-2); Matthew echoed this belief in theoxeny when he wrote: "I was a stranger and you took me in" (Matt 25:35); Paul taught Roman believers to "extend hospitality to strangers" (Rom 12:13).Likewise the writer of Hebrews wrote: "Do not neglect to show hospitality to strangers, for by doing that some have entertained angels without knowing it" (Heb 13:2). That this is the nature and direction of Johannine hospitality is clear from the prologue where Jesus comes to his own people and is offered no hospitality, which he then receives from strangers[11] (1:11-12). The hospitable reception of Jesus by strangers and Jesus' reciprocal reception and transformation of these strangers into children and friends unearths the nature and direction of Johannine hospitality throughout the Gospel.

However, to suggest that hospitality applies only to strangers is not adequate when considering John's archetypal hospitality of the Triune God. The Johannine Jesus models a type of hospitality where strangers do not remain strangers but move on and become guests, friends, and family where the creator God is the ultimate Father. Johannine hospitality, like his Trinitarian theology, is based on creation.[12] The Persons of the Trinity are no strangers to each other, yet they model hospitality of the highest level. The disciples are no strangers to one another, yet they are commissioned to practice lifetime hospitality (13:15; 15:12-15). Johannine Trinitarian hospitality is not limited to strangers only. It is first of all creationist, pointing back to the Genesis creation story where God is the source of all life and creator of humankind (Gen 1:1-3, 27). The Genesis creation story is consensually taken to be intertextually present in the Prologue of John.[13] Second, it is intrinsic to the long-term reciprocal life of the holy people of God. Third, it is incarnational, compelling the one who extends it to be

---

11. Note that in 1:10 the strangers are called the world and they do not know Jesus. Yet in 3:16 they are the recipients of God's sacrificial love.

12. Cf. 1:1-3; 17:1-5 and Gen 1:1-3. It is, therefore, not influenced by gender, ethnicity, social class, or any form of classification.

13. See Westcott, *Gospel*, 2; Brown, *John*, I:4; Bruce, *Gospel*, 28-31; Schnackenberg, *John*, 1:232; Beasley-Murray, *John*, 10; Köstenberger, *John*, 25; Brower, *Gospels*, 69-73; Bauckham, "Monotheism"; Ngewa, "John," 1252, who argues that it is limiting to say the Word was present at the time of creation, preferring reference to eternal existence.

personally present in the life situation of the one who receives it. Johannine hospitality emphasizes not only sympathy but also empathy. It emphasizes long-term presence of the one in the other's life situation. It transcends Koenig's[14] and Artebury's[15] definitions of hospitality. An excellent illustration of hospitality is seen in the communal life of the Bantu in Africa, particularly the Swazi.[16]

7.3 Hospitality Among the Swazi: Community, Kinship, and Buntfu

The early history of the Swazi is well documented in the writings of Kuper, Booth, Bonner, Matsebula, Bowen, and Rose.[17] "The Swazi are descendants of the Nguni speaking peoples who came down southward from east central Africa, crossed the Limpopo River, and settled in Tsongaland (Mozambique) in the late fifteenth century."[18] Later in the eighteenth century under the leadership of Dlamini, the father of the Dlamini clan, the Swazi moved into the southern part of what is today Swaziland or the Kingdom of Eswatini.[19] The Kingdom of Eswatini is a small (17,364 sq. km)

---

14. Koenig's definition is limited to the short term reception of strangers and thus lacks the long-term reciprocal nature of hospitality as found in the Mediterranean and the GOJ in particular.

15. Artebury, 6, like Koenig (though he critiques him), narrows hospitality to the assistance of travellers for a limited amount of time.

16. For a significant work on the life and culture of the Swazi, see Hilder Kuper, *The Swazi: A South African Kingdom* (2nd ed.; NY: HRW, 1963), Hilder Kuper, *An African Aristocracy: Rank Among the Swazi* (NY: APC, 1980).

17. Kuper, *The Swazi*; A. Booth, *Swaziland: Tradition and Change in a Southern African Kingdom* (Boulder: Westview Press, 1983); P. Bonner, *Kings, Commoners and Concessionaires: The Evolution and Dissolution of the Nineteenth Century Swazi State* (Johannesburg: Raven, 1983); J. S. M. Matsebula, *A History of Swaziland*, (Cape Town: Longmans, Penguin, Southern Africa Ltd, 1980); Paul N. Bowen, *A Longing For Land: Tradition and Change in Swazi Agricultural Community* (Avebury: Aldershot, 1993); Laurel L. Rose, *The Politics of Harmony: Land dispute strategies in Swaziland* (Cambridge: Cambridge University Press, 1992).

18. Bowen, *A Longing for Land*, 1.

19. The name "Kingdom of Eswatini" functions equally as the name Swaziland and is favorable to the present King Mswati III as evident in his parliament speeches. See http//:www.gov.sz/home under the link "Prime Minister."

land-locked country bordered on three sides by South Africa and on one side, the east, by Mozambique. It has a population of 1,337,186 (July, 2009 est). The Swazi are a homogenous unit, all speaking Siswati,[20] with a mix of Zulu in the South. English is the second official language and the medium of instruction in all Swazi schools. This probably developed from colonial times since the Swazi got their independence from the British just over forty years ago in 1968.

Hospitality among the Swazi is founded on three important aspects of Swazi culture: community, kinship, and *buntfu*. In order to delve into[21] Swazi hospitality, all three will be briefly examined.

First, the Swazi have a corporate perception of human existence, which is characteristic of the *Bantfu*, and makes it naturally easy for them to receive one another. For the Swazi, true life happens only in community. It is only in and through the community that an individual achieves personal self-realization. As with all *Bantfu*, Swazi life is ordered in groups, with reciprocal rights and duties, privileges, and obligations, which determine behavior patterns for each individual member towards other members.[22] For example, Fogelqvist, citing Omer-Cooper,[23] describes Swazi society in the 1860's thus: "Any Swazi was consequently a member of different sub-communities which had a claim on his loyalty. He was a member of his clan, a member of an age-regiment, and a member of the nation as a whole."[24]

Like all African *Bantfu* tribes, the Swazi believe that "umuntfu ngu-muntfu ngebantfu" or "umuntfu ngumuntfu ngalabanye bantfu," meaning,

---

20. An erroneous record is made by Anders Fogelqvist, "The Red-Dressed Zionists: Symbols of Power in a Swazi Independent Church" (PhD Diss., Uppsala University, 1986), 19, that "All Africans are Swazi speakers." Siswati is spoken only in Swaziland and in some parts of South Africa, particularly the Mpumalanga Province where the Swazi tribe dominates.

21. Swazi hospitality is deep and complex, and, this paper will only scratch the surface.

22. A. Winifred Hoernle, "Social Organization," in *The Bantu Speaking Tribes of South Africa: An Ethnological Survey* (ed. I. Schapera; London: Routledge, 1937), 67.

23. John. D. Omer-Cooper, *The Zulu Aftermath: A 19th Century Revolution in Bantu Africa* (London: Longman, 1966), 52.

24. Fogelqvist, *Zionists*, 22. For details on Swazi age regiments see Rose, *Harmony*, 35; Bowen, *A Longing for Land*, 2.

"a person is a person in community" or "a person is a person by or through other people."[25] For the Swazi, a person receives and maintains his or her identity from and through others. As Mbiti puts it, "He is simply a part of the whole."[26] He or she belongs to the community, which must create and make him or her to be what the ultimate creator intended for him to be. In Mbigi's language, this is "collective personhood," and it is important to "encounter the collective we before we encounter the collective I" since "I am only a person through others."[27] Any person who does not identify with the community is treated with suspicion and often branded by the community to discourage individualism. For example, a person can be called *umnyemu* (from the root "nyemu" which means to withdraw) or *umkhwibi* if he or she does not participate in community projects or activities. A person who is an *umkhwibi* is associated with sanity problems and often suspected of harboring criminal or even suicidal thoughts. In short, Swazi culture and thinking has no place for individualistic self-sufficiency. This belief in corporateness of life and being is well expressed by Mbiti with regard to the Bantu:

> Only in terms of other people does the individual become conscious of his own being, his own duties, his privileges and responsibilities towards himself and towards other people. When he suffers, he does not suffer alone but with the corporate group; when he rejoices, he rejoices not alone but with his kinsmen, his neighbors and his relatives whether dead or living. When he gets married, he is not alone, neither does the wife "belong" to him alone. So also the children belong to the corporate body of kinsmen, even if they bear their father's name. Whatever happens to the individual happens

---

25. The proverb is expressed in other Bantu languages: "Umuntu ngumuntu ngabantu" in Zulu; "Motho ke motho ba batho ba bangwe" in Sotho; "umntu ngumntu ngabanye abantu" in Xhosa; "mtu ni watu" in Swahili; "mundu ni andu" in Kikamba; "munhu munhu nevanhu" in Shona, etc.

26. J. S. Mbiti, *African Religions and Philosophy* (London: Heinemann. 1969), 108.

27. Lovemore Mbigi, *Ubuntu: The African Dream in Management* (Randburg: Knowledge Resources, 1997), 2, 5.

to the whole group, and whatever happens to the whole group happens to the individual.[28]

According to Mbiti, the proverb "umuntfu ngumuntfu ngebantfu" means "I am, because we are; and since we are, therefore I am."[29] The individual's whole existence is relative to that of the group. This is manifested in anti-individualistic conduct, ensuring the survival of the group and concomitantly the individual. It is essentially a humanistic orientation towards fellow human beings. The effect of this belief on Swazi communality is the constant awareness of the need for others to complement or even to complete one's life. This need for, and dependence upon, each other permeates every aspect of Swazi life. Collective solidarity is expressed, for example, in the Swazi *lilima*, described as "communal work parties."[30] When a Swazi has much work to do he or she normally invites (ncusa) other members of the community to join him or her do the work at no fee. Pay is normally by reciprocation of the same. Members who cannot attend for any reason contribute by sending *emahewu* (smoothies) or *tjwala* (beer) for the work party. The work party, which normally works through a rhythm of their own music,[31] is common during sowing, weeding, and harvesting seasons. Every member of the community, despite their socio-economic status, has a right to call a *lilima*.

As we shall demonstrate, this belief "umuntfu ngumuntfu ngebantfu" is the hallmark of the philosophy of *buntfu*, the fundamental philosophy that governs all Bantfu relations in Africa. "Umuntfu ngumuntfu ngebantfu" describes group solidarity, which is central to the survival of communities

---

28. Mbiti, *African*, 108.

29. Mbiti, *African*, 108; also Mbigi, *Ubuntu*, 2.

30. Kuper, *The Swazi*, 43.

31. Mbigi, *Ubuntu*, 10, highlights the importance of working "together in the spirit of joyful service and harmony" as a significant characteristic of buntfu. A story is told of Harmon Schmelzembach, a Nazarene missionary who was named *Sibhaha*, meaning, bitter herb, after he saw a joyful work-party weeding at Phophonyane, northern Swaziland. Since they included his converts he reacted bitterly to their joyous mood and singing assuming they were drunk. However, since this was a party of women, it was highly unlikely that they were drunk—they were only a *lilima* working together in the spirit of joyful service.

with a scarcity of resources.[32] According to Mbigi, this belief in collective solidarity is common in other marginalized communities around the world including poverty-stricken cities of developed economies such as Harlem (New York) and Roxbury (Boston) in the USA and Brixton and Handsworth (Birmingham) in Britain.[33] Like all *Bantfu*, these communities perceive generosity as the hallmark of achievement and the primary virtue of *buntfu*. For example, Kuper explains how the Swazi instill generosity at an early age:

> From infancy, children are taught not to be greedy or to take too large a portion of food from the common pot, and they, themselves, soon enforce the rule of sharing. A mother who hides food for her own offspring will be insulted by co-wives and suspected of witchcraft, and the character of a headman is judged by his hospitality. A donor must always belittle his gift, while the recipient must exaggerate its importance and accept even the smallest article with both hands. . . . A person is thanked for a favor by the further request "Do the same tomorrow."[34]

---

32. I do not think, however, that the scarcity of resources contributes importantly to the spirit of buntfu. Buntfu is not the same as collective solidarity as seen in strikes, liberation, mass action, protest marches, consumer boycotts, etc., which are occasioned by circumstances and may be temporary. Bantfu giving is a culture and is not necessarily occasioned by a need on the part of the recipient. Buntfu is at work among all members of the Bantfu tribes in Africa, rich and poor alike. The philosophy stresses the giving of oneself first, then resources. For example, in the case of the Swazi *lilima*, it is the participation of the person in the communal activity that is primary, not the *emahewu* or *tjwala*, which may be sent if personal participation is not possible. The same applies in the case of sickness or death in the community, where it is personal attendance rather than sending gifts that matters most. Habitual failure to attend may result in the identification of the person as *umkhwibi*.

33. Mbigi, *Ubuntu*, 3. I will argue, however, that these communities are not purely Westerners. Roxbury, for example, is inhabited by Afro-American communities. Brixton and Handsworth are Afro-Caribbean communities. The African philosophy of Buntfu, and its belief, "umuntfu ngumuntfu ngebantfu" is practiced wherever the Bantfu are regardless of whether they are rich or poor.

34. Kuper, *The Swazi*, 50.

Second, the Swazi have a deep sense of kinship. Kinship governs the whole life and thinking of the individual and society. It controls social relationships and determines the behavior of one individual towards another. Kinship, as understood by the Swazi, is not the same as Western kinship, which has strong impermeable boundaries. It is permeable and has no rigid boundaries. Swazi kinship embraces "with a single term relatives who, in more specialized and isolating societies, are kept distinct."[35] For example, the term "mother" embraces a person's own mother, his mother's sisters, her co-wives, her co-wives' sisters, and wives of his father's brothers. Kinsmen covered by a single term "share a common identity and, in some situations, can serve adequately as substitutes for each other in case of need."[36] Swazi kinship is a vast network that stretches horizontally in every direction, embracing everybody in any given local group. This means that everybody is related to one another either as brother or sister, mother or father, grandmother or grandfather, uncle or aunt, cousin, brother-in-law, or something else to everybody else.

guanxi

When two strangers meet in the village, one of the first duties is to find out how they may be related to each other. They begin by sharing their surnames, which may potentially lead to a common ancestor through the *sinanatelo* (extended praise name).[37] If one of them is older, they may ask questions like "ungumsawabani?" which means "whose son are you?" or "ungumtukulu wabani?" which means "whose grandson are you?" The hope is that he might know your father or grandfather, or find a connection between his own ancestors and yours. Answering these questions usually calls for reciting one's genealogy, also an important way of establishing links between individuals and groups.[38] When they have found out how the kinship system applies to them, they behave to each other according

---

35. Kuper, *The Swazi*, 27.

36. Kuper, *The Swazi*, 28.

37. Certain *tinanatelo* may have the name of a common ancestor. Where this happens it suggests a link between the clans and thus close relations, to the point of prohibiting intermarriage between the clans. For example, the Kunene, the Shongwe, the Sikhondze, and the Sifundza have a common ancestor, *Ntimandze*.

38. Kuper, *The Swazi*, 18, suggests that Swazi kinship "always involves some theory of descent, some explanation of conception."

to the accepted behavior set down by society. If they find out, for example, that they are brothers,[39] they will treat each other as equals, or as an older and younger brother. If they are uncle and nephew, then the nephew may be expected to give much respect to the uncle as required by society. Once kinship is established, from that moment on the individuals concerned will refer to each other by the kinship term with or without using their proper names. In the light of this, then, among the Swazi a person has hundreds of fathers, hundreds of mothers, hundreds of uncles,[40] hundreds of wives, hundreds of cousins,[41] and hundreds of sons and daughters. This elasticity in Swazi kinship, where everyone is related to almost everyone else, has contributed well to the maintenance of peace among the Swazi. It has made it easy for the Swazi to receive one another not as strangers but as kinspersons.

What happens when kinship ties cannot be established? What if the individuals concerned turn out to be strangers? Three things can be said here: 1) such cases are rare among the Swazi; 2) Swazi hospitality is not dependent upon the existence of kinship ties alone. The Swazi believe in *Mvelinchanti*, the one who was "The First to Emerge." He was already there in the beginning, was uncreated or unborn, has no father or mother, and is the creator. *Mvelinchanti* is perceived by the Swazi (and the Zulu) as the one who "broke off the nations" from a bed of reeds (eluhlangeni).[42] As the creator god he is the source of all human life and thus the common ancestor of all humankind. His depiction in this way is embraced in his other name, *Mkhulumnchanti*,[43] which means the first great grandfather.

---

39. The kinship term "brother" is understood broadly to include all the sons of my mother's sisters, all sons of my father's bothers, and all who share my surname, whether close or distant.

40. The kinship term *malume* used to translate the word "uncle" refers to my mothers' brothers and cannot apply to my fathers' brothers as it is done in the West.

41. The kinship term "cousin" is used for my uncles' children and cannot apply to children of my fathers' brothers as done among Westerners.

42. See W. D. Hammond-Tooke, *The Bantu Speaking Peoples of Southern Africa* (London: RKP, 1937), 210.

43. *Mkhulumnchanti* is a combination of two words: *mkhulu*, meaning grandfather or great grandfather (or ancestor, with no gender, where it can be used with the prefix *bobabe* (father) for a male ancestor or *bogogo* (grandmother) for the female ancestor: *babemkhulu* or *gogomkhulu*), and *nchanti*, meaning first. However, Rev. Samuel Dlamini (in a telephone interview held on 2 January, 2009), former district superintendent of the

And, it is on account of this common ancestor and source of all human life that hospitality will be exchanged. The Swazi, like the Zulu, also refer to the creator God as *Nkulunkulu*. An incarnated form of *Mvelinchanti*, called *Mlentengamunye*, is also known among the Swazi;[44] 3) the Swazi are *Bantfu* and their behavior towards humankind is governed by the philosophy of *buntfu* that governs all *Bantfu* speaking tribes in Africa.[45] For the ✱ Swazi hospitality is an integral part of being human. To be human is to be hospitable and vice versa, and to be inhospitable is likewise to be inhuman. This understanding of humanness or humanity derives from the *Bantfu's* corporate view of human life and existence.

Third, and important for Swazi hospitality, is the philosophy of *buntfu* that underlies Swazi and *Bantfu* behavior towards one another and towards strangers. This philosophy, like many other African philosophies, is not easy to define. Moreover, to define an African notion in a foreign language and from an abstract perspective as opposed to a concrete approach is to defy the very essence of the African world-view. I will, therefore, not promise to define the concept with precision in this work. That would in any case be unattainable. *Buntfu* can best be described as a philosophy of life, which in its most fundamental sense represents personhood, humanity, humaneness, and morality. Among its important values are group solidarity, conformity, compassion, respect, human dignity, and collective unity. *Buntfu* is the world-view of African *Bantfu* societies and a determining factor in the formation of perceptions which influence social conduct. Among those who have *buntfu* respect is mutual and reciprocal irrespective of race, ethnicity,

---

Swaziland South District of the Church of the Nazarene, clarifies that *Mkhulumnchanti* is not an ancestor since the ancestors are said to be closer to him. To suggest that he is an ancestor is to belittle him. The Swazis gave him this name because of lack of sufficient vocabulary to describe his greatness.

44. Rev. Samuel Dlamini says shepherd boys would occasionally be visited by a strange person who would bring them special messages concerning things that will happen to the Swazi. These were messages concerning drought, famine, pestilences, floods, etc. The messenger would tell the people to fast and not breastfeed or take animals to grazing pastures for a period of time in order to avert the disaster.

45. See I. Schapera, ed., *The Bantu Speaking Tribes of South Africa: An Ethnological Survey* (London: Routledge, 1937).

class, age, and gender. *Buntfu* requires one to respect others first if one is to respect oneself. In the words of Desmond Tutu,

> A person with ubuntu is open and available to others, affirming others, does not feel threatened that others are able and good, for he or she has a proper self assurance that comes from knowing that he or she belongs in a greater whole and is diminished when others are humiliated or diminished, when others are tortured or oppressed.[46]

As Tutu suggests, the meaning of the concept becomes much clearer when its social value is highlighted. Group solidarity, conformity, compassion, respect, human dignity, humanitarian orientation, and collective unity have, among others been defined as key social values of *buntfu*. However, the significance of hospitality as an integral part of *buntfu* is clear in Mandela's definition of the concept: "In the old days, when we were young, a traveller through our country would stop at a village, and he didn't have to ask for food or water. Once he stops the people will give him food and entertain him. That is one aspect of *ubuntu*, but it will have various aspects."[47] A telephone interview with Mrs Pauline Dlamini,[48] a retired teacher at Nhlangano, Swaziland, confirms Mandela's definition. According to Pauline, a traveller or stranger was received, given food, asked about his identity and journey, and then offered a place to sleep in order to continue his journey on the next day. Pauline adds that Swazi hospitality is also expressed as people give preference to others on a walkway: "People give preference to one another such that the path would rather have no one as one person drifts in respect for another." Mbigi, who rightly refers

---

46. Desmond Tutu, "Ubuntu," *Wikipedia*, n. p. [cited 23 December, 2008].

47. Nelson Mandela, "Ubuntu," n. p. [cited 23 December, 2008]. Online: http://ubuntu.wordpress.com/2006/06/01/the-meaning-of-ubuntu-explained -by-nelson-mandela/

48. Pauline Dlamini was interviewed on 23 December, 2008. Pauline is an experienced school teacher and wife who has in all her life lived where hospitality was an important part of daily life. She is a pastor's daughter and a district superintendent's wife, who married into a traditional Siswati home where her father-in-law had twelve wives.

to the concept as "the spirit of unconditional collective hospitality" echoes Dlamini and Mandela's definitions: "When you call at an African home, you are immediately made to feel welcome. There is instant hospitality. You are invited into the house and given food, drink or water as a token of the spirit of hospitality."[49]

But what connection might there be between the vine metaphor or Johannine hospitality and Bantfu hospitality? First, *buntfu* is not an idealized way of life. The purpose is not to baptize any one culture over another; for every culture has its own good and bad. Swazi culture, however, has many similarities with 2TP Jewish culture and thus presents itself easily for a near example of biblical or Johannine hospitality. Second, the Swazi ideas of communality, open-ended kinship, and Buntfu present good models for explaining Johannine Trinitarian hospitality. As we shall see below, the Triune God is God-in-community who has deliberately, out of divine hospitality, graciously invited the participation of humankind in the divine family.

Third, the notion of *buntfu* reflects God's image and likeness in humankind. *Buntfu* is humanitarian and corporate in perspective and embraces the communal qualities of respect, trust, unselfishness, caring, sharing, and helpfulness, etc. We can postulate that it is the lack of *buntfu*-like qualities that saw Israel, the choice vine of God, being described as a degenerate and wild vine (Jer 2:21). That is, with *buntfu* Israel was a choice vine, and without *buntfu* she was a wild degenerate vine. As true humanity (Muntfu) Israel was hospitable, trustworthy, caring, helpful, just, and righteous. With the restoration of *buntfu*, the justice and righteousness demanded by the prophets who used the vine metaphor will be realized in abundance among the people of God.

Furthermore, if humankind can embrace the spirit of *buntfu*, the world can soon realize the Prophets' dream for everyone to invite his neighbor under his own vine and fig tree (Mic 4:4; Zech 3:10; 1 Kings 4:25; 1 Macc 14:12). *Buntfu*, like the vine metaphor, is about mutual peace shared among community members regardless of social status, ethnicity, or gender. *Buntfu*

---

49. Mbigi, *Ubuntu*, 5.

demands the beating of swords into plowshares and spears into pruning hooks (Isa 2:4; Mic 4:3). It is about peace and tranquillity whereby equal hospitality is extended to the rich and the poor, the traveller and the neighbor, the widow and the orphan alike with no strings attached. If you like, it is about being the choice vine of God to others, which was Israel's initial, but failed, vocation.

How does the gospel story with its emphasis on hospitality fit in the context of the Swazi and *Bantfu* in the light of their hospitality? First, it is important to note that for John membership in the new covenant community is not automatic. It is for all who receive Jesus by believing in his name (1:12; 3:16). They receive a second birth and become "children of God," where human blood and ancestry do not matter (3:3, 6; 8:39). This is opposed to Swazi hospitality where human blood and ancestry is the beginning point. Second, Swazi hospitality can be open to abuse and, therefore, can only be an imperfect copy of the Trinitarian hospitality portrayed in the GOJ. For example, widows are denied hospitality during their extended mourning period, which prohibits their participation in social gatherings. As we shall show, John portrays the flawless hospitality of the persons of the Godhead before which all human hospitality stands judged. After all, a heightened patriotic response to human culture can lead to deceptive self-righteousness.

7.4 The Case for the Trinity in John: The Nature of Implicit Trinitarian Allusions

The GOJ does not have a fully-fledged Trinitarian doctrine; that would come centuries later in the Church. But the Trinitarian significance of the GOJ has long been noted in Johannine scholarship.[50] The nature of John's implicit Trinitarian allusions needs to be considered briefly for the understanding of the archetypal life of the Godhead. The GOJ provides not only texts for the later theological developments of the doctrine of the

---

50. See, chapter 1 for a list of scholars who resonate with the Trinity in John.

Trinity (e.g. 1:32-34; 3:34; 14:16-17, 25-26; 15:26; 16:13-15), but also texts for accounting for the distinct personhood and divinity of the Father, Son, and Holy Spirit without compromising the unity of God. Out of the text of John also arose matters of intense reflection on the doctrine of the Trinity in the post-apostolic period. While the Father, Son, and Spirit appear as distinct role players in John they are unified, among others, by their common will, work, word, knowledge, love, and mission. But what is the nature of the implicit Trinitarian texts in John?

That an implicit Trinitarian theology functions as an interpretative context in this research is stated clearly in the introduction. This context derives from the opening verses of John's prologue (1:1), which immediately sends the reader to Genesis 1:1. Barrett is right to suggest that "John intends that the whole of his Gospel shall be read in the light of this verse."[51] The texts that lend themselves easily to this reading regard the relationships of the Father and the Son (1:18; 10:38; 14:10-11, 20; 17:21, 23), Father and Spirit (15:26), and Son and Spirit (1:32-34; 14:18). As we show with the example of 1:32-34 below, a Trinitarian interpretation of each of these texts will help us see and learn from the shared life of the Triune God.

John 1:32-34 is set within the context of John the Baptist's ministry and shows the place of the Father and the Spirit in Jesus' life and ministry. The Father is portrayed as the One who sent John in his revelatory mission (cf. 1:6). He instructed John how to identify the One who is to come: the one on whom the Spirit descends. The identity of the Spirit, "like a dove," is similar to that of the Synoptic Gospels (Matt 3:16; Mark 1:10; Luke 3:22). The descent of the Spirit upon Jesus echoes Israel's scriptures concerning the Davidic ruler (Isa 11:1-16; 42:1; 61:1).[52] That the Spirit descends from "heaven" or from "above" implies that God is the giver of the Spirit. Indeed for John the Spirit always proceeds from God (14:16, 26; 15:26).

When read together with other texts where the Spirit shares the Father and the Son's knowledge and speaks only what he hears from the Father, it also alludes to the Spirit's deity (16:13-15) and intimacy with the Father and the Son. According to Gruenler, "the hearing passages resonate with

---

51. Barrett, *Gospel*, 156.
52. See Bruce, *Gospel*, 53-54.

the complete unity of the Triune Family in which there is mutual defer-
ence and availability."[53] Not only is Jesus the bearer of the Spirit, but he is
also "the One who baptizes with the Spirit" (1:33). This becomes clear as
Jesus bestows the Spirit upon his disciples and all believers (7:37-39; 20:22;
14:15-17, 26; 15:26; 16:5-15). The portrayal of the Messiah as the bearer
of the Spirit is familiar in Jewish thought (*1 En.* 49:3; *Pss. Sol.* 17:37; *T.
Levi* 18:2-14; *T. Jud.* 24:2-3).[54] This must also be read in the light of God's
promises through Israel's Prophets to cleanse his people and put a new
spirit in them (Ezek 36:35-37). The testimony that Jesus is the Son of God
is linked to Jesus' claim for deity and equality with the Father and is used
throughout the Gospel. Thus we have in 1:32-34 the three Persons of the
Godhead collaborating to inaugurate Jesus' earthly ministry.

7.5 Intra-Trinitarian Hospitality: The Model of Hospitality in John

As seen in chapter 6, the Father, Son, and Holy Spirit are mutually available
to and for each other as a hospitable home. They each mutually indwell one
another. This hospitality of the divine Persons, including the mutual love
which is at its center, the humble coinherence, and the mutual availability
to and for each other, become the prototype of the communal life of the
new people of God in the GOJ. However, failure to perceive the Triune
God in this way, that is, as a "social being of relationality" and "a perpetual
movement of love,"[55] sends the church askew. It is unfortunate that questions of hospitality are seldom addressed on the grounds of Trinitarian
theology. While our theology is Trinitarian in theory, "in actual practice,
the doctrine of the Trinity has no bearing on the lives and practices of
Christians."[56] As a result the archetypal life of the divine Persons of the

---

53. Gruenler, *Trinity*, 53.
54. Köstenberger, *John*, 70; Colin G. Kruse, *John* (TNTC 4; Nottingham: IVP, 2003), 83.
55. Brower, *Gospels*, 80.
56. Millard J. Erickson, *God in Three Persons: A Contemporary Interpretation of the Trinity*
(GR: Baker Books, 1995), 112.

Trinity is seldom reflected in the ethical life and practice of the people of God. Instead, an individualistic form of Christianity that is built upon an inadequate Christology develops, where Christ is the example for each individual member in the new community.[57]

An ecclesiology founded on inadequate Christology may fit well with modern individualism, but in the GOJ ecclesiology is wrapped in the fabric of Trinitarian language.[58] So central is the Trinity in John that even his "Christology is Trinitarian Christology."[59] For John it is the three Persons of the Trinity who establish the ethical patterns and hospitality forms an important part of their character. And, if hospitality is a crucial dimension of the life of the Triune God, and a portrayal of the very character of the Triune God, it is expedient that the hospitable character of God be reflected in the lives of God's holy people. Just as the Triune God is a social being, a being-in-communion, so also his holy people are social beings and beings-in-community.[60] This is at the heart of the GOJ as evidenced by the writer's appeal to the Trinity in his Prologue. Far from being an arcane doctrine best left alone, "the doctrine of the Trinity is ultimately a practical doctrine with radical consequences for the Christian life."[61]

Necessary for a proper understanding of the message of John is "concrete trinitarian thinking."[62] From its inception, the GOJ invites inclusive and corporate thinking, pointing the reader to the divine community deliberating together in mutual hospitality. The opening words, "In the beginning was the Word, and the Word was with God, and the Word was

---

57. C. F. D. Moule, "The Individualism of the Fourth Gospel," *NovT* 5 (1962): 171-186, for example, is representative of scholars who approach the GOJ from a Christological perspective and can see nothing more than a strongly individualistic writing.

58. Tatiana Cantarella, "Hospitality Language in the Gospel of John and its Implications for Christian Community," (M. A. Diss., Nazarene Theological Seminary, 2006), 31.

59. Andreas J. Köstenberger and Scott R. Swain, *Father, Son and Spirit: The Trinity in John's Gospel* (NSBT; DG: IVP, 2008), 111.

60. John Zizioulas, *Being as Communion* (NY: VSP, 1985); also Brower, *Gospels*, 71.

61. Cathrine LaCugna, *God for Us: The Trinity and Christian Life* (San Francisco: Harper, 1991), 1.

62. Colin E. Gunton, *Father, Son and Holy Spirit: Toward a Fully Trinitarian Theology* (London: T&T Clark, 2003), 7.

God" (1:1), are "a statement of inclusion."[63] They introduce the reader to
the divine community and establish the equality and the social relationship
of the Persons of the Trinity. It is not only co-existence or closeness that is
in view here but an active personal relationship, sharing, and having-in-
common. It emphasizes interaction and communion with, and yet, also,
the separateness from God.[64] In the opening verse the Gospel writer tells us
that the Word and the Father are on the one hand "two distinct persons of
the Godhead," and yet on the other hand they share "in the most intimate
relations."[65] Thus from the start, John presents us with a picture of God
who is a community of Persons, a socially related being within himself,
characterized by mutual hospitality expressed in love, communication,
respect, assistance, teamwork, mutual service, and enjoyment.[66]

    A clarifying statement regarding John's Trinitarian theology is neces-
sary at this point. The participation of the Holy Spirit in a Trinitarian
mutual relationship with the Father and the Son in John is denied by
some scholars who view the Holy Spirit as only an agent and emissary who
enters the world and perpetuates Jesus' mission without looking back to
heaven.[67] Crump sees a triad of Father, Son, and disciple rather than that of
Father, Son, and Spirit and argues that the Spirit is inextricably bound to
Johannine ecclesiology and his role entirely soteriological.[68] As argued, this
re-examination of the Johannine Trinity is unconvincing. It demonstrates
a lack of awareness of John's intratexts and allusions, treating the text as if
it stands alone without connectedness to other scripture. The relegation of
the Spirit to a lesser being who does not participate in the mutual indwelling of the Father and the Son is not accepted in this research.

---

63. Erickson, *God in Three Persons*, 199.

64. Erickson, *God in Three Persons*, 201.

65. G. A. McLaughlin, *Commentary on the Gospel According to Saint John* (Salem, OH:
Convention Bookstore, 1973), 8.

66. Bruce A. Ware, *Father, Son and Holy Spirit: Relationship, Roles and Relevance*
(Wheaton: Crossway Books, 2005), 21.

67. Crump, "Johannine Trinity," 405.

68. Crump, "Johannine Trinity," 407.

It is quite clear, however, why the Holy Spirit has become a casualty to exegetes who do not see references to the Trinity in John.[69] Because the GOJ does not present a perfectly symmetrical picture it creates a problem. It is true that the Holy Spirit does not feature as prominently in the Gospel as Father and the Son do. Thus "the personhood of the Spirit is much more inferential than is the case with the Father and the Son."[70] Nevertheless, that does not make the Spirit a lesser being or an insignificant member of the divine family.

Three passages in John, including their intertexts, should resolve this problem. First, in 1:32-34 the Spirit descends (from the Father in heaven) upon and abides in Jesus at his baptism and inauguration. This descent and abode of the Spirit upon Jesus inaugurates a partnership with Jesus in all that he says and does throughout the Gospel. This "continuous habitation" is in contrast to the merely temporary inspiration experienced by Jewish prophets in the OT.[71] Jesus' whole ministry must not be perceived as individualistic. In this particular passage, the writer clearly relies on available tradition.[72] The Synoptic writers make it clear that the Spirit who baptizes Jesus also drives him as he does the works of the Father.[73] John incorporates this by framing his pneumatology in a large *inclusio* (1:33; 14:26; 20:22).[74]

Second, in 14:14-16, 26 the Holy Spirit is sent from the Father in Jesus' name. His work is to continue the presence of Jesus in the disciples' company, to take what is of Jesus (which is also of the Father) and teach it to the disciples, and to remind the disciples of all that Jesus taught them. If the Spirit teaches and reminds of all that Jesus taught, and according to Jesus all came from the Father (for Jesus said and did nothing of himself), then the Spirit must be perceived as functioning at the same level with

---

69. See Crump, "Johannine Trinity."

70. I. Howard Marshall, *New Testament Theology: Many Witnesses, One Gospel* (DG: IVP, 2004), 522.

71. Keener, I:460. Cf. Num 11:25-26; 24:2; Judg 3:10; 6:4; 11:29; 14:6, 19; 15:4; 1 Sam 10:6, 10; 11:6; 16:13; 19:20, 23.

72. A reference to the Synoptic intertexts (Mark 1:8-10; Matt 3:11, 16; Luke 3:16, 22) may illuminate this.

73. Luke 4:1, 14, 18, gives a helpful chronicle of the Spirit's significant role in the life and ministry of Jesus.

74. See Keener, I:458.

the Father and the Son. The Holy Spirit shares equally in the mutuality of the Father and the Son and in carrying out the work of the Triune God (14:16-17, 26; 16:13-15).

Third, in 16:13-15 the Spirit continues the work of the Son among the people of God. However, like the Son (5:19, 30; 14:10), he speaks not of his own account but whatever he hears. The picture given is of active involvement of the Triune God in the work and ministry of the Holy Spirit. That is, behind the Spirit's voice are the voices of the Father and the Son. In addition to sharing the Father and the Son's knowledge of all the teaching of Jesus, the Spirit also has knowledge of future things (16:13). Scholars are divided in the interpretation of the future things known to the Spirit with some suggesting an eschatological interpretation of the passion events while others suggest predictive prophecy.[75] The Spirit, like the Father and the Son, shares the attributes of foreknowledge and omniscience. The Spirit is, therefore, not a lesser being who serves only as an emissary or agent of the Father and the Son.

But how are the texts where the Son and the Spirit are portrayed in subordination to the Father to be understood? Where John portrays the Son and the Spirit in subordination to the Father, it must not be read as referring to subordination of importance or nature. The subordinate state is "voluntarily assumed and flows out of the dynamic and mutual hospitality of the divine family as a unity" and does not make the Son and the Holy Spirit "second and third class members of the Family."[76] It points to "a convention, an agreement among the persons of the Trinity."[77]

Unlike the Spirit, the participation of the Son in the mutuality is commonly accepted. However, the question of subordination still remains. It is commonplace in John to find the Son speaking of his submission and total dependence upon the Father in subordination language: 1) the Father is greater than the Son (14:28); 2) the Son has not come on his own but he

---

75. Keener, II:1040, relates the division of scholarship in interpreting the future things in the Spirit's knowledge. Deciphering the future things known to the Spirit is beyond the scope of this thesis.

76. Gruenler, *Trinity*, xvii.

77. Erickson, *God in Three Persons*, 303.

has been sent by the Father (8:42); 3) the Son speaks not on his own but says what the Father tells him to say (12:50); 4) the Son can do only what he sees the Father doing (5:19; 8:28); 5) the Son derives his life from the Father (5:26). All these texts suggest a continuing secondary status for the Son in relation to the Father. However, to be properly understood, these texts must be interpreted in their context. They must be balanced by other Johannine passages that support the Son's equality with the Father and his full participation in the Triune mutuality.

For instance, Jesus' claim to "have life" is a claim to deity and would be confusing to Jewish hearers.[78] Jewish literature attributes life to God alone as the "self-begotten,"[79] "unbegotten"[80] or "uncreated."[81] Speaking of God in these terms set him apart from creation and properly describes his self-sufficiency.[82] This is what the Son is claiming for himself: the Father's prerogative to have life. Jesus, however, makes it clear that this prerogative is imparted to him by the Father. The OT states repeatedly that God grants life to others.[83] But the Son's life, though derived from the one who grants life to others, is unique in that the Son does not only possess it but can communicate it.[84] This prerogative to life does not begin with Jesus' "ministry on earth or his incarnation; it is an eternal act, part and parcel of the unique Father-Son relationship which existed already 'in the beginning.'"[85] Thus for the Son to "have life in himself" (5:26) and to be able to impart that life to others as he does throughout the Gospel (3:16; 4:14; 5:21, 24; 6:33-54; 10:28), is essentially to participate in the unity and mutuality of the divine family. Such participation in the unity of God, existing from the beginning, is the hallmark of Bauckham's "Christology of divine identity,"[86] by which he explains Jewish monotheism in light of the coronation of Jesus as God.

---

78. See Keener, I:653-654.
79. *Sib. Or.* 1:20; 3:12, 33; *Apoc. Ab.* 17:19.
80. Josephus, *Ag. Ap.* 2.167.
81. *Sib. Or.* Frg. 7.
82. Keener, I:654.
83. Gen 2:7; Job 10:12; 33:34; Ps 36:9.
84. Beasley-Murray, *John*, 77.
85. Bruce, *Gospel*, 132.
86. Bauckham, "Monotheism," 148, 149.

Another claim clearly asserting the Son's divinity and equality with the Father is his claim to be the Son of God (5:18). According to Erickson, it is natural to assume that the use of the term "Son" indicates subordination and derivation of being.[87] However, this is not true of John. In the GOJ the development of the title, "Son of God" (1:34, 49; 3:18; 5:25; 11:4, 27; 19:7; 20:31) suggests that its meaning is more than messianic, as it is in the OT and the Synoptic tradition. In John when the term "Son" is applied to the second Person of the Trinity, it is his equality with the Father rather than his inherent subordination that is being affirmed. "Jesus is presented everywhere in the fourth Gospel as equal yet obedient to God the Father."[88] This is confirmed by the Jews' response to Jesus' claim for Sonship (5:18). Also, on several occasions Jesus emphasizes his oneness with the Father (10:30; 17:11). Even when the Son reveals submission to his Father's will through coming into the world in his name and receiving from the Father all that he says and does, the Son can still claim the Father's name and equality with him. The description of the unity and mutuality of the divine Persons in John as a "divine family characterized by the generous hospitality and love of Father and Son in concert"[89] must be supported.

A final statement is necessary regarding the participation of the Father in the mutual hospitality of the divine Persons of the Triune God. The question is whether the Father reciprocates the hospitality and submission accorded him by the Son and the Holy Spirit. Is the Father an equal and committed partner or a self-sufficient unmoved mover who is only concerned with the doing of his will and work by the Son and Spirit? The Father's participation in the reciprocal hospitality and mutuality of the divine family is clear in John.[90] The Father loves (3:35; 5:20; 10:17), honors, hears (11:42), and bears witness (5:32) to the Son. The metaphor of the vine, in particular, is one place where the Father as vine dresser makes himself vulnerable by

---

87. Erickson, *God in Three Persons*, 301-302.
88. Köstenberger and Swain, *Father, Son and Spirit*, 105.
89. Gruenler, *Trinity*, 76.
90. Gruenler, *Trinity*, 38.

depending on the vine for the production of fruits. Gruenler interprets the Father's care to the vine (15:1-2) in terms of the Father "serving" the Son.[91]

It is evident that the proper picture of the Trinity in John is not of a hierarchy of Persons with the Father at the head, and the Son and Spirit as second and third class members. It is plausible to view the three persons of the divine family as making themselves dependent on each other's hospitality and service and acting hospitably on behalf of and always pointing to one another. John speaks of all three Persons of the divine community ministering to one in hospitable love and acting on behalf of one another. John clearly uses hospitality language to describe the divine community in which three distinct Persons are unified by such phenomena as reciprocal love, communication (hearing, seeing and speaking), mutual knowledge, giving and indwelling, as well as glorifying one another, and sharing their common will and work.

As the divine Persons are not a hierarchy, but fundamentally equal partners in their mutual unity and interpenetration,[92] we must ask what it is that keeps the enduring mutual unity: What "social glue"[93] binds the Persons of the Trinity together? Trinitarian scholars concur with one another that it is "love" that binds the Trinity together in the GOJ.[94] This is probably why the Triune relationship is described as "an unceasing movement of mutual love."[95]

The significance of the mutuality and interdependence of the Persons of the divine family is necessarily matched by the dominance of the love theme that runs through the Gospel. Integral to this unifying love is the propensity to undertake an action to the advantage of the loved one. John 3:35 shows how love prompted the Father to give all divine prerogatives

---

91. Gruenler, *Trinity*, 38.

92. Miroslav Volf, *After our Likeness: The Church as the Image of the Trinity* (GR: Eerdmans, 1998), 217.

93. Malina's term.

94. See, for example, Stanley J. Grenz, *Theology for the Community of God* (GR: Eerdmans, 1994), 68-69; Kallistos Ware, *Orthodox Way* (London: Mowbray, 1979), 33; Brower, *Gospels*, 68.

95. Ware, *Orthodox*, 33.

to the Son.[96] In reciprocation the Son loves the Father and demonstrates his love by laying down his life (10:17). The Son's love for the Father is demonstrated in his obedience to the Father, for he does exactly as the Father commanded him (14:31). In 15:10 the Son is described as abiding in the Father's love, an act that includes the hospitable reception of the Father's love as well as willingness to obey the Father's commands at all costs.[97] Chapter 17:27 shows that the Son demonstrates the Father's love by announcing the name of the Father who has loved the Son to the believers. In 17:24 the writer states the eternal character of the Father's love for the Son: the Father loved the Son before the foundations of the world and has given him glory.

The efficacy of love in effecting the bond between the Persons of the Trinity is great. The three "mutually constitute one another to such a degree that we cannot speak of them as 'individuals.'"[98] To speak of one is to imply the three. Thus within the community of perfect love, between the Persons who share all the divine attributes, a notion of hierarchy and subordination is unthinkable. The Persons of the Trinity relate to one another on an equal footing. As Volf suggests, in the relations between the divine Persons, the Father is not the one against the other, not the first, but rather the one among the others[99] who are bound in love expressed in a mutual relationship of hospitality. For Gunton, "the Triune God is a God in whom the one is not played against the many, nor the many against the one."[100] Gruenler explains the outworking of this Triune relationship: "The Father and the Spirit are both deferring to the Son who is to act as spokesman for the divine community, and the Son is deferring to the Father and the Spirit in accepting their mission to represent the one gracious will of the divine family."[101]

---

96. Gruenler, *Trinity*, 33; Also 5:20 where the Father demonstrates his love for the Son by showing him all he is doing.

97. Watt, 306.

98. Cunningham, *These Three Are One*, 181; Brower, *Gospels*, 68.

99. Volf, *After our Likeness*, 217.

100. Gunton, *Father, Son and Holy Spirit*, 15.

101. Gruenler, *Trinity*, vii.

7.6 Trinitarian Hospitality to Humankind

In the GOJ the outward-looking hospitality of God is evident from the prologue and occurs on at least four levels: first, in God's reaching out to humanity with gracious and loving inclusiveness (e.g. 1:12-14, 29; 3:16); second, in God's special care for those who by receiving his hospitality become his friends and participants of the mutual indwelling of the Trinity (e.g. 15:1-17); third, in God's hospitable restoration and reinstatement of children who return after denying him (21:15-23);[102] fourth, in the promise of God's eschatological hospitality through the future ministry of the Spirit in the church.

7.6.1 Trinitarian Hospitality to the World

The extension of Trinitarian hospitality to humankind can be traced back to the Genesis creation story alluded to in the first part of John's prologue (1:1-4). The creation of humankind (Gen 1:27) is a definitive expression of the outward-looking nature of God's love. The Triune God is a social being who exists in relationality. However, this relationality is not only witnessed by the Persons of the Godhead. It is generously extended to humankind. The creation of humankind in the image and likeness of God points to God's desire for fellowship with humankind, a result of God's relationality and hospitality. In creation God's relational nature is extended to include humankind and, through humans, to all God's creation. Humankind, therefore, is the reflection of God's relationality and hospitality, not created for solitude but for fellowship with God and with fellow human beings. When we see humankind and all God's created order in his or her trust, we are reminded of the relationality and hospitality of God. Creation itself is an act of generosity and hospitality and a refusal to hoard life but a willingness to give it away to others. The creation of humankind in God's image and likeness has great implications for the relationality of humankind.

The story of the fall of humankind in Genesis, however, represents the disruption and distortion of the relationships God intended. Trinitarian

---

102. See Blomberg, *Contagious Holiness*, 124-126, who treats John 21:1-14 as a meal of reinstatement, with Peter's reinstatement story following in vv. 15-23.

hospitality is revealed in the GOJ as the Father, seeking to show his love for fallen humanity, communicates to us through the Word and the Holy Spirit. John's allusion to the Genesis creation story in his prologue suggests a new beginning and a restoration of the relationships disrupted by the fall.[103] The One through whom "all things came into being" (1:6) comes into the world he created, gathers around him a new covenant community, and hospitably receives humankind back to God. In reiteration of the creation of humankind in Gen 2:7 and the Ezekiel 37 prophecy of a new covenant, the Lord of life infuses the Spirit of life into his new covenant people (20:21-23). Thus John uses not only new creation language but also covenant language to express the Triune God's hospitality to lost humankind.

The Triune God extends hospitality to humankind through covenant relationship with his chosen people.[104] In the GOJ OT covenantal figures such as Abraham, Moses, and David testify to the person and work of Jesus. For instance, Abraham rejoiced to see Jesus' day (8:56-58), Moses bore witness to Jesus (5:45-47), and Jesus is the king of Israel (1:49; 12:13) fully within the royal line of the Davidic covenant. God's hospitable election of Israel as his chosen covenant people is in view where Jesus stresses his choosing and appointing of the disciples (15:16). As was the case with the Triune God's election of Israel, love, not merit, is the basis of this election (13:1). The covenantal motif of divine presence in 1:14, also an important theme in 15:1-17, points back to Exod 25:8; 29:45-46 where God dwells among his people.[105] Also expressing divine-human hospitality is the shepherd-sheep covenantal motif in John 10 which shows Jesus as the true shepherd gathering his sheep, not by racial exclusiveness, but out of all nations (10:16). As the true shepherd Jesus protects the sheep by giving his life for them (10:11, 15) and thereby gives them eternal life (10:28).

In the GOJ Trinitarian hospitality to humankind is also expressed through the generous gifts to humanity. One of the Triune God's major

---

103. Brower, *Gospels*, 71.

104. We treat this as hospitality to humankind because of the inclusiveness of the covenants. As with Israel, God chose the disciples (apostles) not for themselves but for others.

105. Also Num 14:14; Deut 12:11; 1 Kings 18:36.

characteristics in the GOJ is that he is a generous giver. The greatest gift of God to humankind is the gift of his Son and is given for the salvation of the world (3:16-17). The motivation behind this gift is God's love for the world rather than the world's merit or ability of reciprocation. Thus through the Son, the love of the Triune God reaches and embraces undeserving humankind and the entire created order. The relationship of this love to God's love for the Son and the Spirit is noted by Pinnock: "God loves sinners in history because, prior to that, God loves the Son and the Spirit, and loves us in relation to them."[106] A strong love relationship exists among the persons of the Trinity, which in John is unselfishly and generously extended to humankind. It is important to note that this gift of God has no apartheid[107] or discrimination of any kind but comes equally and inclusively to all humankind: "Jews were familiar with the truth that God loved the children of Israel; here God's love is not restricted by race."[108] The positioning of the love message (3:16) suggests an understanding in the context of the cross (3:14) and the incarnation (3:17), both inclusive acts for all humankind. This all-inclusive out-going love of the Triune God, which is hospitably open to all humanity, is "the background of the canvas on which the rest of the Gospel is painted."[109] For the GOJ is an inclusive Gospel generously reaching wide to all humankind with the love of the God.

God's gift of his Son to humankind comes with countless blessings given by the Son to humankind on behalf of the Triune God. Lacking words to describe the plethora of gifts to humankind, John says, "From his fullness we have all received, grace upon grace" (1:16). According to Bruce, "'We all' probably denotes not only the Evangelist and his associates . . . but the readers of the Gospel also, and indeed all who share the blessing pronounced in 20:29 on 'those who have not seen and yet they believe.'"[110] The

---

106. Pinnock, *Flame*, 30.

107. Here we particularly recall a sad time in South Africa when a political system was in force whereby members of different races had different political and social rights, when they lived, travelled, shopped, schooled, worshipped, etc. apart from each other.

108. Carson, *Gospel*, 205.

109. Beasley-Murray, *John*, 51.

110. Bruce, *Gospel*, 43. For a contrast see Keener, I:420, who suggests that the "all" refers only to those who believe the light (1:7, 9). However, this is unlikely since the light of 1:9

last phrase, "grace upon grace" must be understood as grace in abundance rather than a reference to the replacement of the law.[111] That is, the measure of grace received through Christ is greater and remains more inexhaustible than that of the Law: "an ocean from which all his people may draw without ever diminishing its content."[112]

The most significant gift God gives to humankind in John is the gift of eternal life (3:16). The Son, who is himself life, was the source of life in the Genesis creation, and now in his incarnation he makes life abundantly available to humankind. All that he is has something to do with life: he gives the waters of life (4:14; 7:37-38); he is the bread of life (6:35); he came that humankind may have life (10:10); he is the life (14:6); he is the resurrection and the life (11:25). There is a connection between the Word's giving of life to all things in creation and the incarnated Word's coming into the world as the giver of life. After crowning the Word with all the work of creation, John attributes life to him saying, "What has come into being in him was life, and that life was the light of all people"[113] (1:3-4). The theme of "life" runs through the Gospel and normally represents God's hospitable offer to humankind.[114] The writer of John speaks of the three persons of the Trinity as giving life to humankind (5:20-21; 6:63). With mutual outward looking love, they collaborate to generously open to humankind an opportunity to participate in this divine prerogative of life and to share in the life of God.

Trinitarian hospitality to humankind in the GOJ is also expressed through inclusive fellowship meals and drinks where, as the host, Jesus provides food and/or drink for the people. In the GOJ Jesus often meets people as a stranger or ordinary guest, but when the need arises he becomes the stranger-turned-host or guest-turned-host. We shall give three examples for this.

---

is also inclusive and enlightens everyone, not a particular group.

111. See Carson, *Gospel*, 132, on the unlikely suggestion for replacement of the law.

112. Bruce, *Gospel*, 43.

113. Edward L. Miller, *Salvation-History in the Prologue of John: The Significance of John 1:3/4* (NovTSup 60; Leiden: Brill, 1989); Keener, I:381-82.

114. E.g. 3:15-16, 36; 4:14; 5:24; 6:47, 53; 17:3.

First, Jesus and his disciples are invited to a wedding in Cana where Jesus changes water into wine (2:1-11). Jesus arrives at the wedding as a guest, but when the host runs out of wine, he transforms a desperate situation and becomes a guest-turned-host providing wine to the host and his wedding guests. He extends unmatched hospitality to both the host and his guests by providing sweet wine at a traditionally wrong time. By his provision of better quality wine at a time when lower quality wine is usually offered, Jesus does more than what is generally expected of a host. He "gave the most valuable present of all: valuable for its quality, its quantity, its timeliness, and its non-reciprocating character."[115] Jesus' use of the water jars kept for ritual purification represents his priority of mercy over ritual: "Jesus favors a semi-religious host's social standing above ritual purification."[116] Thus in this wedding Jesus, on behalf of the Triune God, shows great mercy and takes action for humanitarian purposes. As argued earlier, humanitarian action is integral to Johannine holiness. For John to refer to this as the beginning of signs (2:11), which for him are synonymous with the works, indicates that John does not isolate social needs from spiritual needs. Faith and holiness include, as an important part, practical humanitarian service. Acts of hospitality, therefore, are integral to the character of the Triune God, and, it is the will of the Triune God that humankind should mirror such hospitality.

Second, in his encounter with the Samaritan woman[117] Jesus approaches her as a desperate stranger asking for water to quench his thirst. As the conversation progresses, however, Jesus turns and offers her water that would become in her "a spring gushing up to eternal life" (4:14), thus becoming the host. This hospitable offer culminates in yet another incident of hospitality where Jesus is invited to "abide" with the Samaritans (4:30, 40).

---

115. Köstenberger, *John*, 95.

116. Keener, I:512. The consequences for failing to supply wine to the end of a ceremony are stated by Leon Morris, *Reflections on the Gospel of John* (4 vols. GR: Baker, 1986-1988), 1:69-77. Culturally, running out of wine was not only embarrassing. The host for the wedding feast was responsible for securing a sufficient supply of wine for the guests and could be subject to legal charges if it failed to do so.

117. Arterbury, *Entertaining Angels*, 113-118, offers a fuller interpretation of Jesus' encounter with the Samaritan woman in the light of Mediterranean hospitality.

The Samaritan recognition that Jesus is the "Savior of the world" (4:42) again marks the universality of Jesus' hospitality, an important theme in John. Indeed throughout the conversation with the Samaritan woman, John "employs words that are typically associated with hospitality"[118] in accordance with the hospitality customary in antiquity.

As noted, this story is particularly important because it represents the breaking of barriers and the removal of all boundaries affixed by humankind to hospitality. True biblical hospitality knows no boundaries. Jesus comes not only as a stranger but as a "hated stranger." Intending to destroy boundaries, he asks for hospitality from an unlikely person, a Samaritan, and a woman with strained relationships. Notably, while Jews usually sought hospitality from a kinsperson or fellow Israelite, Jesus goes far beyond that. As a divine stranger who represents God, Jesus offers hospitality not only to those who could expect it (the Jews) but to the excluded Samaritans and to all the marginalized, inviting them also to come and partake in the life of God.

A third example of Jesus' extension of hospitality to humankind is the sign of the feeding of the multitudes (6:5-14). Here Jesus takes five loaves and two fish and, as host, generously feeds five thousand. The Markan version of this sign begins with an allusion to Ezekiel 34 where God's people lack godly leaders and are thus like "sheep without a shepherd" (Mark 6:34). Although John does not make the connection here, the idea is present and clearly illustrated, especially when the sign is read in relation to the Good Shepherd discourse (10:1-19).[119] In John the sign is followed by a discourse, which interprets and applies it, bringing out a deeper meaning both of the sign and of Jesus' true identity. This deeper meaning is seen in the abundance of food. The food offered in the context of wilderness, Passover (6:4), and Jesus-the-prophet (Deut 18:15) reflects the eschatological celebration of the feast of the Kingdom of God[120] prepared for and

---

118. Arterbury, *Entertaining Angels*, 117.

119. See Beasley-Murray, *John*, 88, who sees it proper to assume that the passage is an act of compassion.

120. Beasley-Murray, *John*, 88.

hospitably offered to the people. The setting has the people reclining[121] and Jesus as the "good host"[122] (6:11) distributing the bread and the fish himself.[123] This miraculous act of hospitality is an obvious sign of the greater hospitality of the Triune God to the world. Taking place up on the mountain, "a well-attested place for communing with God,"[124] this meal is not only a generous provision for the physical needs of the people. It is a working of the hospitality of God who gives the enduring bread of life to mankind.

It is clear from the above discussion that in John the Triune God is a community of persons bound together by outward-looking love that is expressed in generous hospitality to humankind. John's choice of a Trinitarian frame for his Gospel, evident in the Prologue, opens his Gospel to a Trinitarian[125] interpretation and thus enables humankind to learn and live the life of the Trinity. The three are selflessly open to humankind's needs and offer the possibility of joining the mutual relationship of Trinitarian life. They openly minister "to a world that is thirsty for hospitality and communion."[126] Nevertheless, the GOJ is also clear about the Triune God's extension of hospitality to the children of God. This is a level of hospitality that John portrays in parallel with his agenda for hospitality to the lost humankind.

7.6.2 Trinitarian Hospitality to Children of God

A significant characteristic of the hospitality of the Triune God in John is that it is available and can be received by all. Throughout the GOJ two opposing factions can be observed: 1) those who receive Jesus and believe

---

121. According to Keener, I:668, this is a sign of a special meal rather than a usual daily meal during which people were simply seated.

122. Keener, I:668.

123. We note that the Synoptic Gospels have Jesus delegate the disciples to distribute the food to the crowds.

124. Malina, "The Received View," 126.

125. In John 1:12 humans who receive the Son by believing in his name receive power to become "children of God." These are described in various terms throughout John, such as, "born of God" (1:13), "sheep" (10:1-8), "children of light" (12:36), "branches of the true vine" (15:5), and "friends" (15:14).

126. Gruenler, *Trinity*, 54.

in him as the Son of God; and 2) those who do not believe in Jesus and reject him. To the former he is the "Son of God" (1:49), the Messiah (1:41), king of Israel (1:49), the prophet (6:14; 7:40; 9:17), the one whom the prophets and Moses wrote about (1:45), and the holy one of God (6:69). To the latter he is mere man (10:33), a deceiver (7:12), illegitimate (8:41, 48), a Samaritan (8:48), and demon possessed (8:48). These factions first appear in the prologue (1:11-12), and throughout the Gospel they appear either honoring Jesus (1:49; 12:13) or opposing him, seeking to kill him and those who speak well of him (5:18; 7:19-25). Those who receive him into their lives and become children of God, however, are in turn treated to hospitality of the highest level: they participate in the mutuality and shared life of the Triune God.

In 15:1-17 the writer illustrates how divine hospitality is extended to the new people of God and through them to the world. The mutuality and the sharing of life is so deep that they are described in the most intimate language: branches of Christ the true vine. That is, they are received into the life of Christ and through him the Triune God, so that, as 1 John suggests, they can properly testify: "we are in him who is true, in his Son Jesus Christ" (1 John 5:20). As demonstrated, Paul expresses the same notion when he says, "in him we live and move and have our being" (Acts 17:28). So deep is the love and hospitality that what is shared is not just space or gifts but life itself so that the one can claim the other as his or her own.[127] Paul's words to the Thessalonians offer the best intertextual reading of this hospitality: "So deeply do we care for you that we are determined to share with you not only the gospel of God but also our own selves, because you have become very dear to us" (1 Thess 2:8).

The GOJ records at least two occasions where Jesus extends Trinitarian hospitality to the children of God by means of a meal. Both these occasions

---

127. In 13:1 Jesus refers to the disciples as "his own." Early in 1:11 the same term is used with reference to Israel. However, here it signifies the new relation that Jesus has with the new people of God. The farewell discourse describes this relationship in deeply intimate terms, such as, mutual indwelling (15:1-11), friends (15:16), branches of the vine (15:1-6), etc. In 17:10 the disciples are Christ's and God's. In reciprocation, the disciples also claim Jesus as theirs. E.g. Thomas (20:28).

are connected to his death and resurrection.[128] First, is the occasion of foot-washing (13:1-17), and, second, the "meal of reinstatement"[129] (21:1-14).

The occasion of the footwashing (13:1-17) is a practical example of the Trinitarian hospitality accorded the new covenant people of God.[130] The writer sets the scene by drawing on three significant Johannine themes: "the Passover," "the hour," and "love to the uttermost" (13:1). These impor-tant themes converge at the cross as Jesus gives himself as a paschal lamb, completes the task for which he is sent, and reveals love in its highest form. Love stretched to the end is probably comparable to the greater love of John 15:13 where sacrificial love is in view—laying down one's life for one's friends. It also recalls Jesus' proclamation of himself as the good shepherd who lays down his life for the sheep (10:11, 15). Thus when Jesus enjoins the new people of God to lay down their lives for one another he asks them to do no more than he has done and will do for them (15:12-15).[131] This sacrificial love is the basis of Johannine Trinitarian hospitality and is clearly the focus of John 13:1-17.[132]

Here Jesus, representing the divine family, hosts the disciples to a meal where he gives himself to them in selfless service. He takes a towel, girds himself with it, and stoops down to wash the disciples' feet. Jesus' removal of clothes and girding of himself with a towel "are symbolic of a change of status from master to slave."[133] Contrary to conventional hospitality, the one who should have his feet washed disregards his status and gives himself in selfless hospitality to his friends. The symbolism of suffering and death in this act is clear in two NT parallels. First, Jesus, referring to the death by

128. Keener, II:907.

129. See Blomberg, *Contagious Holiness*, 124, for the reading.

130. See Malina, *Social Science Commentary*, 223, who indicates that footwashing was a conventional hospitality to guests in the ancient world. Also Cantarella, *Hospitality*, 73.

131. Dwight Moody Smith, *The Theology of the Gospel of John* (Cambridge: Cambridge University Press, 1995), 146.

132. Westcott, *John*, 189, sees self-sacrifice as the central idea of 13:1-20; D. Moody Smith, *John* (ANTC; Nashville: Abingdon, 1999), 252; Keener, II:901-2, who sees Jesus as taking the role of the Suffering servant in accordance with Isa 52:13-53:12.

133. Ford, *Redeemer*, 139; J. C. Thomas, *Footwashing in John 13 and the Johannine Community* (Sheffield: JSOT, 1991), 26-56; Ruth B. Edwards, "The Christological Basis of Johannine Footwashing," in *JOHNLC*, 368, notes that "In the ancient world the washing of guest's feet was normally the work of slaves."

which Peter was to glorify God, warns Peter that another will "gird" him and take him where he does not wish to go (21:18-19). A second parallel is Acts 21:11 where Agabus takes Paul's girdle and binds his own feet and hands to symbolize Paul's impending arrest. Thus by becoming a slave, hospitably serving his friends, Jesus suggests that knowing and loving God includes readiness to die for him and the fellow believer.

The acts of "taking up" and "laying down" are symbolic of Jesus' death and resurrection.[134] They are also reminiscent of an earlier passage where Jesus says, "For this reason the Father loves me, because I lay down my life in order to take it up again. No one takes it from me, but I lay it down of my own accord. I have power to lay it down, and I have power to take it up again. I have received this command from my Father" (10:17-18). The acts of "taking up" and "laying down" also anticipate the impending death and resurrection of Jesus.[135] The description of Jesus' death as the "laying down" of life suggests that Jesus knew of it and that it was his choice rather than that of his enemies (10:17; 13:3).[136] His control over the events is also displayed in his final words on the cross, "It is finished" (19:30), following which he deliberately gives up his spirit. Jesus voluntarily gives his life in loving service to his friends. This is clearly the view of 13:1 where the writer sets the context by referring to "the hour"[137] and Jesus' selfless love for "his own." That Jesus will give his life in death as a sacrifice for the salvation of lost humankind is clear in the Gospel (1:29; 3:17; 11:50-53). However, a second objective is also clear here: Jesus gives his life in selfless love for "his own" in order to set an example that they will follow as a holy community.

The significance of Jesus' posture in this narrative is clear. "Whereas masters and banqueters would sit or recline, servants might stand to serve them; Jesus 'rises' (13:4) to wash their feet. That the disciples reclined

---

134. Keener, II:908.

135. R. Alan Culpepper, "The Johannine Hypodeigma: A Reading of John 13" *Semeia* 53 (1991), 137; James D. G. Dunn, "The Washing of the Disciples' Feet in 13:1-20," *ZNW* 61 (1970): 248.

136. Cantarella, *Hospitality*, 74. Also Culpepper, *"Hypodeigma,"*134-137, on the recurrence and use of Jesus' knowledge in the GOJ, especially chapter 13.

137. Keener, I:507-508, offers background information and commentary on the use of "the hour" throughout the GOJ.

(13:12, 23, 28) sheds light on the posture of the washing (13:5)."[138] As noted, Jesus assumes the role of a slave whose duty it is to wash the master's and the guests' feet.[139] More light on the classification of slaves with regard to the humble duty of feet-washing is shared by Edwards.[140] She asserts that feet-washing was particularly suitable for women and female slaves and was also expected of Jewish wives as a wifely act of personal service, like preparing a husband's meals and making his bed. Also joining the practice are Jewish children who might do it for their parents[141] and devoted rabbinic students who performed the service for their teachers. In light of this it is plausible to suggest that Jesus' act is highly counter-cultural as it comes from one who has often been rightly regarded as master.[142] "For a person of status, particularly a patron host, to wash his guests' feet as if a servant would be unthinkable."[143]

Thus Peter, seeking to be true to culture and expectation, objects.[144] However, upon Jesus' insistence and explanation of the significance of the washing, Peter accepts and asks for the cleansing of his hands and feet as well. In this counter-cultural act Jesus does at least two things. First, he redefines what it means to be in power and authority and, second, he repudiates the culture of slavery including all forms of discrimination. According to Ford, "Jesus surrenders his life . . . so that he might be conscious of the mode of existence of the most humiliated and jested of humankind, the slaves and 'personless.'"[145] Indeed, "when Jesus washes his disciples' feet he is reversing

---

138. Keener, II:908.

139. That the culture of footwashing existed as a form of hospitality in early Jewish culture and practice is clear in the OT (Gen 18:4; 19:2; 24:32).

140. Edwards, "Johannine Footwashing," 368.

141. Some African cultures, for example, the Swazi, carried this practice to about late twentieth century. I can recall my mother taking a basin and towel and kneeling down to wash my father's feet as my father returned from work. Occasionally my mother would also ask my sisters to wash her feet as she returned home from a busy day.

142. The disciples, who themselves are Jews and are familiar with the culture, have always regarded Jesus as Lord and master, and would, therefore, not expect him to wash their feet. Jesus also refers to himself as master in the passage in order to make his lesson clear.

143. Keener, II:907.

144. See Culpepper, *Hypodeigma*, 138, who properly states that Peter's response would be readily appreciated by first century readers.

145. Ford, *Redeemer*, 140.

the world's values and doing the work of the lowest of the low—Gentile slaves, women, children, and students!"[146] Failure to grasp the meaning of power and authority leads to abuse and manipulation of others. In Jesus, the Triune God shares all circumstances of humankind. God is "a fellowship of Persons who are open to the joy and pain of the world."[147]

The use of water is significant, linking the scene to the theme of water and cleansing introduced earlier in the Gospel. It is interesting to note that water is used almost always in the context of hospitality in the GOJ. The cleansing function of water is first introduced in 2:1-11, where Jesus swung from guest to host hospitably changing water into wine and saved the host from embarrassment. John 4:7-42, in parallel with 7:37-39, describes the water that Jesus gives as that which leads the one who drinks it to springs of water gushing to eternal life. Both these texts portray God's hospitality to lost humankind and thus may easily be interpreted in relation to salvation. Cleansing water here (13:10) almost certainly anticipates 15:3 where the writer focuses on the disciples and states that they are cleansed by the water of the words of Jesus. However, the roles played by Peter and Judas Iscariot in 13:1-17 lead to another possibility: hospitality to children who drop out. This is represented more clearly by the "meal of reinstatement" (21:1-14).

7.6.3 Trinitarian Hospitality to Children Who Drop Out

In the GOJ, where reference is made to large numbers of disciples turning their backs on Jesus, our task would be unfinished if we don't address the plight of disciples who lapse or drop out. Moreover, the vine metaphor does include branches that are cut off from the vine. In John, Trinitarian hospitality is not only extended to lost humankind and children of God, it is also extended to children and friends who lapse or drop out and turn from following Jesus. Does Johannine discipleship include the possibility of lapsing or drawing back? The work of Matsunaga[148] is indispensable here.

---

146. Edwards, "Johannine Footwashing," 369.

147. Pinnock, *Flame*, 41.

148. Kikuo Matsunaga, "Is John's Gospel Anti-Sacramental? – A New Solution in the Light of the Evangelist's Milieu," *NTS* 27 (1981): 516-524, uses the title, "drop outs"

Matsunaga, seeking to answer the question of John's engagement in *Spiritualisierung*, offers an extended discussion of the special attention that the GOJ gives to "drop outs." In his language, "the Fourth Gospel alone records explicitly the presence of 'drop outs' from Jesus' disciples."[149] Moloney concurs, suggesting that "disciples always have and always will display ignorance, fail Jesus, and deny him, and that some may even betray him in an outrageous and public way."[150] Matsunaga focuses on the text where the Gospel writer reports disciples opting to withdraw from following Jesus: "Because of this many of his disciples turned back and no longer went about with him" (6:66). The reason for the withdrawal is stated early in the passage: it is the words of Jesus, which the disciples describe as hard (6:60). Jesus' words are hard, harsh, or rough, not in the sense of "difficult to understand" but "unacceptable, harsh, offensive."[151] Matsunaga understands the words of Jesus in view as either 6:51-58 or 6:26-51b and to represent the *kerygma* of John's church. He compares the explicit records of disciples dropping out in the GOJ to the Gospel of Mark where no record of the disciples' retreat is made until the moment of Jesus' arrest (Mark 10:32; 14:50).

According to Matsunaga, Judas Iscariot, whose name is mentioned eight times in the GOJ in association with the betrayal of Jesus, is "the representative figure of the drop outs from John's church."[152] By contrast there is Simon Peter who "may be portrayed as the representative figure of those who accepted 'the word of Jesus' and remained in John's church."[153]

---

and suggests that the GOJ alone records explicitly the presence of "drop outs" from Jesus' disciples. See also Terry Griffith, "'The Jews Who Had Believed in Him' (8:31) and the Motif of Apostasy in the Gospel of John," in *The Gospel of John and Christian Theology* (eds. Richard Bauckham and Carl Mosser; GR: Erdmans, 2008), 183-192.

149. Matsunaga, "Anti-Sacramental?," 517.

150. Moloney, *Glory not Dishonor*, 23.

151. Barrett, *Gospel*, 302.

152. Matsunaga, "Anti-Sacramental?," 519; Rensberger, *Johannine Faith*, 74-5.

153. Matsunaga, "Anti-Sacramental?," 517; Westcott, *Gospel*, 111. However, to say that he remained in John's church does not exclude the possibility of failure or denial. Rather it includes the courage to rise up and receive the hospitality and love that the Triune God extends to all "drop outs." This is the essence of the sharp contrast between Peter and Judas: Peter had the courage to return and be reinstated whilst Judas adamantly went into the dark, despite being offered hospitality to return.

Two passages are crucial for our discussion here: 6:60-71 where a record is made of disciples who were scandalized by Jesus' teaching and stopped following him, including Judas Iscariot who is called a devil; and 21:1-25 where a meal is recorded in connection with Jesus' rehabilitation and reinstatement of Peter and the disciples.

Chapter 6:60-71 states that many of Jesus' disciples found his teachings hard, murmured at them, and eventually drew back and stopped following him. It is also clear that the scandalized "many" are not just the misunderstanding multitude of 6:22-40 or the ill-disposed Jews of 6:41-59 but the disciples who had followed him. The scandalizing message includes chewing Jesus' flesh and drinking his blood,[154] which for John is a means of abiding[155] in union with Jesus. Therefore, these disciples fail to abide in Jesus and thus walk away. They fail to remain in Jesus' love or obey his commands and prove their true discipleship (8:31; 15:7, 10). Indeed, "they rejected the teaching of Jesus and deserted him."[156] Malina suggests, on account of the ambiguity of the Greek of 6:60, that this "could also mean that because of the hard teaching, Jesus was difficult to accept."[157] The use of "at that time" or "because of this" in 6:66 suggests a later stage of their walk with Christ when these disciples renounced their discipleship and fell away. The warning against falling away is an important subject in 15:1-17, especially in Jesus' emphasis upon abiding (15:4-11).[158]

If Matsunaga is right in his assessment regarding John's portrayal of scandalized disciples murmuring and falling away from following Jesus, we must inquire about the extension of hospitality to these disciples. This includes Peter who, though often regarded as the leader[159] of the twelve, denied the Lord three times. Earlier it was argued that hospitality is an

---

154. Bruce, *Gospel*, 162; Ngewa, "John," 1265; See chapter 5 on the interpretation of John 6:56 and its connection to notion of abiding.

155. See chapter 6 on the meaning and importance of abiding in Christ. Also our discussion of the image of removing barren branches in chapter 5.

156. Beasley-Murray, *John*, 97.

157. Malina and Rohrbaugh, *Social-Science Commentary*, 137.

158. See I. Howard Marshall, *Kept By The Power Of God: A Study of Perseverance and Falling Away* (Revised ed.; London: Epworth, 1995), 183-184, who treats the verb "to abide" as an equivalent of the verb "to persevere."

159. Carson, *Gospel*, 668, calls Peter "the unofficial leader" of the twelve.

important part of the character of the Persons of the Triune God. Such hospitality is generously extended to humankind and the children of God. Here it is clear that the GOJ shows that the hospitality of the divine family does not exclude those who return after dropping out. Blomberg's classification of the post-resurrection fish meal (21:1-14) as "a meal of reinstatement" should give a clue to the treatment of drop-outs in John. This passage "focuses on the reinstatement of Peter, who has proved to be a notorious sinner of a very different kind: in the threefold denial of Christ (cf. 18:15-18, 25-27)."[160] Blomberg's suggestion that the passage concerns Peter's reinstatement is a consensus among scholars.[161]

While it is clear that Peter lapsed in his threefold denial of Jesus, there is no scholarly consensus regarding whether it was apostasy for the disciples to return to fishing. On one hand Hoskyns, Barrett, and Brown concur that the disciples acted in apostasy.[162] On the other hand Westcott, Beasley-Murray, Bruce, Carson, Milne, Keener, and Ngewa do not see any apostasy in the apostles' behavior.[163] Ngewa, for example, states that the disciples went fishing "not because they wanted to return to their original occupation. It was because they needed to be fed. Hunger comes to everyone, even a disciple of Jesus!"[164] Nevertheless, in view of Peter's representative status in the GOJ, the argument is that his restoration and reinstatement represents that of all disciples including later children of God. John's discipleship includes the disciples' potential for being lost.[165] Also, in view of Peter's leadership position among the disciples, divine hospitality is equally extended to leaders who drop out. Smith, then, rightly states that "Peter is reinstated as a leader of Jesus' disciples, literally as a pastor (i.e.

---

160. Blomberg, *Contagious Holiness*, 124.

161. See, for example, Gruenler, *Trinity*, 139; Carson, *Gospel*, 675, 678; Smith, *Theology*, 124; Beasley-Murray, *John*, 405; Milne, *Message*, 316; Köstenberger, *John*, 596; N. T. Wright, *Surprised by Hope* (London: SPCK, 2007), 84.

162. Hoskyns, *Gospel*, 552; Barrett, *John*, 579; Brown, *John*, 2:1096.

163. Westcott, *Gospel*, 300; Beasley-Murray, *John*, 399; Bruce, *Gospel*, 399; Carson, *Gospel*, 669; Milne, *John*, 309-310; Keener, II:1227; Ngewa, "John," 1296.

164. Ngewa, "John," 1296.

165. See Marshall, *Kept*, 184. Cf. 16:1; 17:11, 12, 15, 24.

shepherd) alongside the enigmatic Beloved Disciple."[166] Thus, the generous hospitality of the Persons of the divine family offered to humankind and the children of God does not discriminate against drop-outs, including those in leadership.

An unfortunate situation is that of Judas Iscariot who, though offered the loving hospitality of the Triune God in the morsel (13:30), chose to reject God's unfailing hospitality and went into darkness. His immediate retreat into the darkness after taking the morsel is a sharp contrast to Nicodemus' coming out of the darkness earlier in the GOJ (3:1). Judas, given the gift of love,[167] departs immediately: "a radical rejection of the love of God."[168] John's interest in portraying divine hospitality is postulated in the striking differences between this passage and the Synoptic Gospels. Mark 14:20, for example, records that Judas dipped with Jesus in the dish while in John Jesus actually gives the sop to Judas (13:26). According to Bruce, "For the host or master of a feast (as Jesus was on this occasion) to offer one of the guests a particularly appetizing morsel was a mark of special favor."[169] Jesus treats Judas with great hospitality despite having full knowledge of the condition of Judas' heart and what he was about to do (6:64, 71; 12:4-6; 18:4). As indicated, Johannine hospitality can be resisted or rejected, and Judas' story is a typical example of someone who rejects God's love and hospitality to the end. Despite being singled out for a special mark of favor, Judas persists with his treachery and resists Jesus to give room to the adversary. Again it helps to compare him with Peter who, even though he had shamefully denied the Lord at the trial, remembered the Lord's unfailing hospitality and proceeded to Galilee to meet him. By contrast, Judas last appears in the garden (18:5) and makes no effort to return to the Lord thereafter.[170] Should he have returned to join the band

---

166. Smith, *Theology*, 124.

167. Moloney, *Glory not Dishonor*, 23.

168. Moloney, *Glory not Dishonor*, 24.

169. Bruce, *Gospel*, 290.

170. The Synoptic Gospels portray a remorseful Judas who appeared when Jesus was sent to Pilate for trial and confessed that he had betrayed innocent blood bringing the money to the chief priests (Matt 27:3-10). Even there Judas never returns to Jesus or the disciples to repent and receive the hospitality that he had known for three years. Instead, he hanged

of disciples who met the resurrected Lord, we do not doubt that he would have received unconditional hospitality.

Nevertheless, some scholars[171] do not see Judas as an apostate, basing their arguments on Judas' lack of sympathy with the mission of Jesus. In Guthrie's words, "Judas is clearly a special case and can hardly be regarded as evidence for a general possibility of falling away."[172] This suggestion is hard to accept. Judas was not only appointed as a disciple but also treasurer for Jesus and the disciples. Did Judas himself share in Jesus' foreknowledge that he was going to be the traitor? It is not likely that Judas harbored thoughts of betraying Jesus throughout the three year period he spent as a disciple. Judas did, however, share the common misunderstanding that Jesus was a political messiah which opens the possibility that he may have been speeding up a revolution that could possibly restore the kingdom to Israel (Acts 1:6).[173] Judas is a clear example of a branch in the vine that fails to abide and bear fruits. Simply put he was a disciple (12:4) consumed with love of money, and that finally destroyed him (12:6).[174] However, despite his full knowledge of Judas' character, including the betrayal, Jesus continued to show the love and hospitality of the divine family to Judas, just as to the other disciples.

Jesus' offer of a morsel to Judas, together with his post-resurrection fish meal with his disciples, show clearly, however, that lapsers and apostates are graciously welcome in John's Trinitarian hospitality. The risen Lord, on behalf of the divine family, serves the disciples again and "meets their tiredness after a time of toil with a hot breakfast."[175] Here again Jesus, now risen, is still committed to giving humble service to his disciples, giving them an example.

himself. See Frederick Dale Bruner, *Matthew: A Commentary Volume 2: The Churchbook* (Revised and expanded ed.; Michigan: Eerdmans, 1990), 703-712. Also Leon Morris, *The Gospel According to Matthew* (GR: Erdmans, 1992), 694-95, who suggests that Judas may have come to the chief priest to find spiritual guidance after realizing his sin.

171. Guthrie, *Theology*, 615; Marshall, *Kept*, 181.

172. Guthrie, *Theology*, 615.

173. Morris, *Matthew*, 694.

174. Matt 26:14-26; 27:3-10. Cf. 1 Tim 6:10; John 2:13-16.

175. Carson, *Gospel*, 671.

The conversation that ensues between Peter and the risen Lord (21:15-25) raises a question regarding the need for rehabilitation of lapsed disciples.[176] Three times Peter is required to confess his love for the Lord mirroring and offsetting his threefold denial of the Lord during the trial (18:15-18, 25-27). It is important for those who return to reaffirm their love for Christ. This is "a pastoral conversation."[177] It does not issue in a time of probation or penance.[178] The focus is in correction and encouragement. "What is important is that Peter reaffirms his love for the Lord and is rehabilitated and recommissioned."[179] The call to love echoes 15:13 and actually questions Peter's readiness to die for his friend(s), a subversion of his previous unwillingness to die evident in his denials.

7.7 The Children of God as a Reflection of Trinitarian Hospitality

As demonstrated in the GOJ, Jesus as the creator of a new community graciously invites all to participate in a new community that will reflect the hospitality of the Father, Son, and Spirit (1:7, 12; 3:16; 12:32). Those who receive this invitation become the new covenant people of God through whom God extends divine hospitality to humankind. These new covenant people of God believe and abide in Jesus, the Word-become-flesh, and are called children of God, the flock, the branches, friends, and his own. They participate in a mutual hospitality with Jesus where each finds a hospitable home in the other. This new relationship is initiated through the self-giving

---

176. Whether the conversation between Jesus and Peter was private or public is a matter of scholarly debate. On one hand Bruce, *Gospel*, 404, suggests from v. 20 that "Jesus took Peter for a short walk, and held this conversation with him in private." On the other hand Carson, *Gospel*, 675, says Jesus' initial question, "Simon son of John, do you truly love me more than these?" (21:15), suggests a public nature for Peter's reinstatement. Bruce's suggestion is more persuasive since the word "these" in v. 15, referring to either the disciples or the fishing equipment, makes sense even if Jesus and Peter were walking away from the group of disciples.

177. Smith, *Theology*, 124.

178. Blomberg, *Contagious Holiness*, 126.

179. Bruce, *Gospel*, 405.

love of Jesus who, on behalf of the Triune God, demonstrates the hospitality of the divine community to humankind. It is inaugurated when humankind hospitably receive the Word-made-flesh by believing in him and entering into a mutual union with him.[180]

What does Trinitarian hospitality have to do with the new covenant people of God? How are the new covenant people of God to live in view of their reception of the archetypal hospitality of the divine family? These questions relate to our concern for how the new people of God live out the hospitality of the divine family with regard to humankind as a whole, members of the covenant community, and those who turn their backs on the community.

First, efforts have been made in recent scholarship to relate Trinitarian theology to Scripture and practical Christian living.[181] Barton rightly suggests that there is "a profound connection between who God is and what it means to be a member of the people of God."[182] The life of the people of God "has to be measured against the greater reality of the life of the Trinity."[183] Our discussion of the intra-Trinitarian hospitality previously shows that the life of the divine family is characterized by unity, corporateness, mutuality, love, humility, obedience, and unselfishness, to mention but a few. These characteristics are necessary for the new covenant people of God especially since the mutual hospitality of the divine family is here considered archetypal.

---

180. See 1:12 where "receiving" and "believing" are placed as parallels and are synonymous. That those who believe enter into a union with Jesus is the subject of 15:1-11 where the mutual sharing of life is in view.

181. Cunningham, *These Three*; Gunton, *Christ and Creation*; Gunton, *The Promise of Trinitarian Theology* (2nd ed.; Edinburgh: T&T Clark), 1997; Gunton, *The Creator*, (Edinburgh: Edinburgh University Press, 1998); Pinnock, *Flame*; Volf, *After Our Likeness*; Stephen C. Barton, "Christian Community in the Light of the Gospel of John," in *Christology, Controversy & Community: New Testament Essays in Honour of David R. Catchpole* (eds. David G. Horrell and Christopher M. Tuckett; Leiden: Koninklijke Brill, 1999), 279-301; Gruenler, *Trinity*; Leonardo Boff, *Holy Trinity, Perfect Community* (NY: Orbis Books, 2000); Brower, *Gospels*; Köstenberger and Swain, *Trinity*.

182. Barton, "Christian Community," 293.

183. Barton, "Christian Community," 279.

Second, Nyerere's article, "The Church's Role in Society,"[184] is particularly helpful in thinking corporately about humanity and the world as the context in which children of God practice their faith (17:14-15). Nyerere argues persuasively for the involvement of the Church in the creation of a more just and equal society where humankind will live with dignity and well-being. He urges the church to work for the eradication of exploitation and the sharing of wealth. Nyerere rightly argues that "Poverty is not the real problem of the modern world. For we have the knowledge and resources which could enable us to overcome poverty. The real problem—the thing which creates misery, wars and hatred among men—is the division of mankind into rich and poor."[185] Indeed the division of humankind into rich and poor, strong and weak, powerful and powerless creates an unnecessary dichotomy. The rich see their wealth as a source of controlling power and use it to manipulate and exploit the poor.

Nyerere sees this division at two levels: individual and national. On the individual level, he describes a few wealthy individuals within a nation who with wealth acquire great power whilst within the same nation a vast majority of people suffer from varying degrees of poverty. On the national level Nyerere describes a repetition of the same pattern with a few wealthy nations dominating the whole world economically and politically whilst a mass of smaller and poor nations struggle to survive. Elaborating on the division of people in the world, Nyerere states:

> They are divided between those who are satiated and those who are hungry . . . between those with power and those without power . . . those who dominate and those who are dominated . . . those who exploit and those who are exploited. It is the minority which is well fed, and the minority which has secured control over the world's wealth and over their fellow

---

184. Julius Nyerere, "The Church's Role in Society," in *A Reader in African Christian Theology* (ed. John Parratt; London: SPCK, 1987), 117-130. The reader will note that Nyerere's language is not gender sensitive. The present writer will not correct direct quotations but would like to dissociate from this insensitivity and send an apology for the difficulty it might cause for some readers.

185. Nyerere, "The Church," 117.

men. Further, in general, that minority is distinguished by the color of their skins and by their race.[186]

The situation described by Nyerere is tragic, despicable, and is a gross violation of God's purposes and plans for creation. It is reminiscent of the situation described by Isaiah with reference to the corrupt vineyard of Israel and Judah: "he expected justice, but saw bloodshed; righteousness, but heard a cry!" (Isa 5:7). God never intended for humankind to be divided into a rich minority and a poor majority whether as individuals or as nations. Wealth is a gift of God and must not be hoarded but used to the glory of God to care for his creation. And among God's creation, humankind must be priority.

The division of humankind into rich and poor is an evil that the people of God, living within societies that perpetuate it, must confront. The holy people of God must refuse to accept this situation and must break silence[187] and speak and act against this evil.[188] It cannot be acceptable to the Triune God who exists as a hospitable family and has sent his only Son as the "Savior of the world" (4:42). Nor is it acceptable to those who have received his divine hospitality and are sent to show it to God's creation (13:14-17). The people of God must never accept as immutable any social, economic, political, or religious framework that imposes division and inequality on humanity. As Nyerere says, what is important "is the creation of conditions, both material and spiritual, which enable man the individual, and man the species, to become his best."[189] Those who are branches of the true vine

---

186. Nyerere, "The Church," 120.

187. The Swazi say "kubindvwa kubonwa." The saying derives from two words, *kubindza*, meaning "to keep quiet," and *kubona*, meaning "to see." It bluntly translates, "you keep quiet even if you notice." It means that when you see someone do some wrong you must ignore it and pretend as if you did not notice. The impact of "kubindvwa kubonwa" is seen in the amount of resources that are stolen from government turning selfish ordinary civil servants into millionaires.

188. I would like to acknowledge efforts made by leaders of the Council of Swaziland Churches (CSC), particularly the bishops of the Anglican Church and the Roman Catholic Church who have often made their voice heard on social issues in Swaziland. Although they are accused of "forgetting their job" and interfering in political and social issues, they have not stopped fighting against injustice.

189. Nyerere, "The Church," 118.

must work with the God of peace to usher in, if possible, the dream of the oppressed people of God when "they shall all sit under their own vines and under their own fig trees" with no one to make them afraid.

Third, like their God, the people of God must have a corporate view of life. They must perceive humankind as a larger family and members of one another. Unity and corporateness are central to the life of the holy people of God in the GOJ. This is evident in the writer's allusions to the creation and the Trinity in the prologue (1:1-3) and is underpinned by his careful choice of language throughout the gospel (10:30, 34-35; 11:52; 14:10-11; 15:5; 17:11, 21). All people are God's people. They are created by God in his image and likeness (Gen 1:1-3), and, as Brower states, "The image of God is a plurality because God exists in plural form."[190] Since they are taken from the same dust, God's people belong together despite their differences in ethnicity, age, nationality, gender, wealth, or poverty, etc. Before God they all stand as equals and must, therefore, respect each other and seek to exist in relationality.

The people of God must lead the way in shedding all forms of injustice, discrimination, apathy, selfishness, indifference, and unconcern and embrace the hospitality of the divine family treating all humankind equally as God's treasured creation. As Nyerere suggests, "everything which prevents a man from living in dignity and decency must be under attack from the church and its workers."[191] The new covenant people of God must offer hospitality including feeding the hungry, clothing the naked, housing the homeless, and receiving and caring for the discriminated and marginalized. Where possible they must help people find sustainable means of living so that they gain confidence and take control of their lives and become helpers rather than just receivers of help. Jesus exemplified this in the resurrection fish meal: although he had already made a meal he did not stop his disciples from fishing. He still helped them fish for more.

Fourth, an aspect of the church in society that is missing in Nyerere's article regards the hospitality of the new covenant people of God to one another. The new covenant people of God must love sacrificially and not

---

190. Brower, *Gospels*, 70.
191. Nyerere, "The Church," 124.

give up that love at any cost, including life itself (13:34, 35; 15:12, 17). For John this is how the world knows true followers of Jesus (13:35). The standard for this love is clear: "Just as I have loved you" (13:34). That is, the new people of God must first consider the love they have received from Jesus (3:16; 1 John 3:1). The disciples have a living experience of that love since they have basked in it for at least three years. They know the privilege of being chosen for intimacy with the Son of God and the King of Israel; They know the patience of Jesus in their many failures; they witnessed Jesus' impartiality in dealing with people of differing social standing; they have known Jesus' compassion for poor and marginalized; they have seen and heard Jesus' passion for unity and *buntfu*. All these characteristics and more are to shape their life and ministry on earth.

Particularly important here is 15:12-17 where sacrificial love is the proper application of the vine metaphor.[192] The command to love flows from and builds upon unity or mutual abiding which is the main theme of 15:1-10. Thus in the Johannine vine metaphor, the trajectories of unity and love are placed together, each a requisite of the other. This makes love and unity the primary characteristics of the new covenant people of God in the GOJ. They are to live out the mutual love of the Trinity to which they have been invited. They must show, in miniature, the love of the divine family.

There is clearly recognizable here an intertextual link to Paul's words (Rom 12:9-10; 13:8-10). Although both John and Paul stress the mutuality of this love, "one another," Paul includes the details of ethical application: no dissimulation (v. 9); in honor outdo one another (v. 10); contribute to the needs of the saints (v. 13); practice hospitality (v. 13); rejoice with those who rejoice and mourn with those who mourn (v. 15); live peaceably with all (v. 18); and do not revenge (v. 19). In the GOJ these ethical details are embedded in the life and ministry of Jesus. For example, John's emphasis upon sacrificial love and loving "as I have loved you" (15:12-13), which is modelled by Jesus' death "for the people" (12:50), clearly allows no room for dissimulation. Similarly, his attendance of and compassionate works in

---

192. Segovia, "Theology and Provenance," 119, sees love as the proper explanation of the vine imagery.

weddings (2:1-11) and funerals (11:17-44) offers a perfect example of the call to rejoice with those who rejoice and mourn with those who mourn.

7.8 Conclusion

In closing, hospitality is an important aspect of Johannine communal holiness and three factors must be noted.

First, as demonstrated in the introduction, the absence of "hospitality" as a term must not suggest the absence of the notion in the GOJ. John's allusion to the creation in the prologue points to the hospitable character of God. God includes. He includes the other Persons of the divine family. He also includes humankind sharing his image and likeness with him or her and generously placing them in the Garden. He includes humankind in sending his Son so that through him humankind can participate in a union with God. It is in the mission of the Son that acts of hospitality are shown from beginning to end, as we have painstakingly shown. The farewell discourse is a summation in word-and-deed of the hospitality that Jesus portrayed to the world and the disciples in the years of his ministry. The washing of the feet and the last supper, including the teaching that links to it, is hospitality in action. The metaphor of the vine, including the explanation linking it to sacrificial love, is hospitality in word. Here hospitality is enveloped in mutual abiding, a term describing the mutual giving and receiving and sharing of one another's life. There is no greater hospitality than this.

Second, drawing on *buntfu* does not suggest that *Bantfu* hospitality needs no reworking. Human ideas have limitations when used to explain divine truths. However, two aspects concerning the *Bantfu* support the work of this chapter: 1) their corporate perception of life as taking place only in community—"umuntfu ngumuntfu ngebantfu" which follows closely the biblical Israelite culture that is in view in John.[193] God is God in

---

193. The link between the OT and the GOJ is clear in the images that John uses from the OT. Examples of these include water jars for ceremonial cleansing (2:6), Jacob's well (4:6), Moses (2:45), Festivals (7:10-24), Abraham (8:52-58), the vine (15:1-8), etc.

community and, therefore, has designed for humankind that a person be completed by the presence of others in and around him or her. It is here that the *Bantfu* become useful as an example of Johannine hospitality. 2) *Buntfu* is all-encompassing in communal life especially in matters of generosity, hospitality, availability, mutuality, preferring one another, and solidarity in times of difficulty. In this way what is shared is not just possessions, which are often minimal, but life itself. 3) The *Bantfu* perception of porous boundaries of kinship matches ideas of the new covenant community. This makes it easy for believers to think corporately of themselves as belonging together. It facilitates comprehending the notions of "children of God" and "family" in a church setting where biological relations are secondary. In our opinion, the Bantfu, despite their weak areas, offer a useful example of hospitality as portrayed in the GOJ.

Third, the pattern of hospitality presented here must lead to a rethinking and reworking of the ethics of the people of God. Response to the following questions may help facilitate this process: 1) Do the people of God think and live corporately as responsible custodians of God's creation including treating all humankind as significantly important before God? 2) Does the way the people of God live and treat each other as members of the new covenant community reflect the character of God? 3) Do the people of God respond to those who reject them and their message with unconditional love and hospitality as the GOJ shows such response from the divine family? These questions are crucial for Johannine holy living. Children of God must show hospitality towards one another, those who drop out from the community, and humankind as a whole.

CHAPTER 8

Towards a Johannine Theology of Corporate Holiness

8.1 Introduction

The previous chapters have shown that ideas of covenant, corporateness, mutuality, holiness, sharing, and hospitality are present in the vine metaphor. In John these ideas are embedded in the mutual abiding motif that is central to the vine metaphor. In this chapter John's corporate metaphors for the new people of God are juxtaposed with his portrayal of the new people of God as a holy community. Beginning with the scholarly debates on individualism and corporateness in John, we discuss corporate metaphors and argue that Johannine holiness is embedded in them. These metaphors serve to underscore the covenant relationship between God and his holy people. Any study of John that neglects the context of communality and corporateness is likely to misinterpret John's holiness theology. We propose, therefore, that it is within the backdrop of communality and corporateness that Johannine holiness must be explained: For John, holiness is primarily corporate.

The notion of corporateness has been given the priority it demands in this research. The motif of mutual abiding and John's concern for Trinitarian hospitality, at the center of the Johannine vine metaphor, has emphasized this. But corporateness in John goes beyond the mutual relations of the Father, Son, and Spirit. John's language is both personal and corporate and it is on his corporate message that his call to holiness is embedded. The reference both to creation and to the divine family in John's Prologue show that community is always a starting point.

The significance of the covenant motif for understanding corporate holiness in John raises one important question in relation to the motif in the OT: which covenant?[1] A study of the OT narratives suggest that YHWH made covenants with Noah (Gen 6:18; 9:9-10), Abraham (Gen 15:18; 17:7), Moses (Exod 24; Deut 5:3; 29:1), and David (2 Sam 23:5; cf. 7:12-16; 2 Chron 13:5; Ps 89:3-34; 132:12). The word "covenant" is used in this thesis with reference to the Mosaic covenant. Although this covenant is based on the divine promises to the Fathers, emphasis is placed on human obligations in maintaining the covenant relationship with God.[2] The OT also shows many references to the renewal of the covenant between YHWH and Israel (Exod 34; Josh 24; Jer 31; Ezek 16).

The argument for holiness in this chapter is based upon three important interpretative contexts: first, postulation of the mutual life of the Divine family as a model in Johannine spirituality; second, use of the vine as a covenant metaphor suggestive of a special relationship with God and obedience to his commands. Seen in the light of God's covenant relationship with Israel, for John there is no discontinuity between the new covenant people of God and the story of Israel. The third is careful interpretation of the language John uses for the people of God. Reading the GOJ in this way shows that the holiness of believers is a significant theme closely related to the holiness of the Divine family.

---

1. See D. J. McCarthy, "Covenant in the Old Testament," *CBQ* 27 (1965): 217-240; McCarthy, *Treaty and Covenant* (Rome: BIP, 1981); D. G. Hillers, *Covenant: The History of a Biblical Idea* (Baltimore: John Hopkins University Press, 1969); Paul R. Williamson, *Abraham, Israel and the Nations: The Patriarchal Promise and its Covenantal Development in Genesis* (Eds. David J. A. Clines and Philip R. Davies; Sheffield: SAP, 2000); Chennattu, *Discipleship*, 50-52, for the origin and historical development of the covenant motif in the ANE and OT.

2. See D. N. Freedman, "Divine Commitment and Human Obligation: The Covenant Theme," *Interpretation* 18 (1964): 419-431; David Noel Freedman and David Miano, "People of the New Covenant," in *The Concept of the Covenant in the Second Temple Period* (Ed. Stanley E. Porter and Jacqueline C. R. de Roo; Leiden: Brill, 2003; Chennattu, *Discipleship*, 53-54. Cf. Pryor, *John*, 161-163.

Two questions are important for our portrait of the holy community: First, how far can we press the notion of the corporate people of God in John in the light of Moule's[3] argument for individualism? Second, to what extent can this new community be said to be holy in the GOJ?

8.2 Individualism and Corporateness in Recent Studies

In 1962 Moule, responding to the diversity of the doctrine of the *ecclesia* in John, drew scholarly attention to the tension between the corporate and the individual. His thesis stated that John is "one of the most strongly individualistic of all the New Testament writings."[4] In another study where he compared eschatology in the Gospel and the epistles of John, Moule suggested that in the Gospel, John "is concentrating mainly on the individual's relation to Christ."[5] On the corporate metaphors of John, such as temple, shepherd, and vine, which so distinctively describe John's view of Christ's relationship to the *ecclesia*, Moule stated that they include an individual reference. He emphasized that this individual reference in the corporate metaphors is more important and is balanced by the same individualistic emphases elsewhere in the Gospel.

In 1971 Smalley agreed with Moule on the presence of a clearly sounded individualistic note in John: "the Fourth Gospel as a whole possesses a strongly individualistic character."[6] However, he disagreed with Moule's thesis especially on the Son of Man Christology in John.[7] Smalley suggested that in John "the complementary theme of corporate belonging, to

---

3. C. F. D. Moule, "The Individualism of the Fourth Gospel," NovT 5 (1962): 171-186.

4. Moule, "Individualism," 172.

5. C. F. D. Moule, "A Neglected Factor in the Interpretation of Johannine Eschatology," in *Studies in John Presented to Prophessor Dr. J. N. Sevenster on the Occasion of his Seventieth Birthday* (NovTSup. 24; Leiden: Brill, 1970), 159.

6. Smalley, *John*, 263.

7. Stephen S. Smalley, "Diversity and Development in John," NTS 17 (1971): 276-292.

Christ and to other Christians, is not absent."[8] For Smalley, John shares an equal awareness for both the individual's faith in Jesus and the community in which believers share the life of the Spirit (10:16; 20:22-23), and his ecclesiology is "nicely balanced between the one and the many."[9] Smalley suggested that "we need not press for one emphasis or the other in the Johannine presentation of the church."[10]

In 1979 Cook echoed Smalley affirming both the individual and the corporate, suggesting that "God makes individuals only in the context of community."[11] He described two extremes within the church. First, the Protestant evangelical individualistic approach to salvation: "Jesus died for me. I receive Christ into my heart. Christ lives in me. I am on my way to heaven."[12] Second, the social gospel, where emphasis is upon changing society, transforming communities, changing living conditions, and creating new opportunities in life. He observed that "the extreme stress on community alone destroys individuality, and substitutes totalitarian control for personal responsibility."[13]

In 1982 Whitacre echoed Moule's thesis on the prevalence of individualism in John.[14] However, his later suggestion that "the Gospel is not simply concerned with individuals but with two communities in conflict"[15] shows that he followed Smalley's suggestion of a nice balance between individualism and corporateness. In view of what he described as unbalanced individualism in the opponents of the Johannine community in 1 John, Whitacre cautioned that autonomy of individuals must not be stressed to

---

8. Smalley, "Diversity," 282.

9. Smalley, "Diversity," 282.

10. Smalley, "Diversity," 282.

11. E. David Cook, "Man in Society," in *Essays in Evangelical Social Ethics* (ed. David F. Wright; Exeter: Paternoster, 1979), 144 (hereafter called *EESE*).

12. Cook, "Man in Society," 143.

13. Cook, "Man in Society," 144.

14. Rodney A. Whitacre, *Johannine Polemic: The Role of Tradition and Theology* (SBL 67; Chico: Scholars, 1982), 135.

15. Whitacre, *Polemic*, 166.

the neglect of identity as members of the community.[16] He also cautioned that corporateness must not be overstressed.

In 1988 Rensberger lamented the relegation of John's corporateness to "a rather remote subsection of a late chapter of our thinking about John."[17] He studied passages in John previously used to support the argument for individualism and concluded that these passages are crucial for developing the corporate aspect of Johannine salvation. Rensberger argued, for example, for a view of John 3 as communal appeal.[18] He suggested that Nicodemus, individualistically perceived by Bultmann[19] as representing "man as he is" in need of salvation, plays the role of a communal symbolic figure. In Rensberger's words, "Throughout the gospel . . . Nicodemus appears as a man of inadequate faith and inadequate courage, and as such he represents a group that the author wishes to characterize in this way."[20] Rensberger suggests that being "born again" has a strong communal dimension as it means "belonging to the community of such believers."[21] This approach to texts previously viewed as individualistic strengthens the argument that John is primarily corporate.

In 1991, Fee, examining the language the NT uses for the people of God, demonstrated 1) the strong sense of continuity with Israel, and 2) "their basically corporate nature."[22] He studied OT and NT motifs for the corporate people of God and showed how they suggest a corporate nature.[23] In his own words, "the New Testament knows nothing about individual

---

16. Whitacre, *Polemic*, 167.

17. Rensberger, *Johannine Faith*, 15.

18. Rensberger, *Johannine Faith*, 38. Also Koester, *Symbolism*, 12, who sees Nicodemus as representing "a benighted world, squinting with incomprehension at the light of God that has appeared in Jesus."

19. Bultmann, *John*, 133-143.

20. Rensberger, *Johannine Faith*, 40.

21. Rensberger, *Johannine Faith*, 55. Köstenberger, *John*, 124, advances the same argument on the basis of the plural "you" and concurs that "this requirement does not extend solely to Nicodemus but to the entire group he represents."

22. Gordon D. Fee, *Gospel and Spirit: Issues in New Testament Hermeneutics* (Peabody: Hendrickson, 1991), 124. Fee is not particularly Johannine but helps give the bigger picture of the NT.

23. Fee's list lacks Johannine corporate motifs. The only one he has, "chosen" (15:16), has no reference to the GOJ.

'saints,' only about Christian communities as a whole who take up the Old Testament calling of Israel to be 'God's holy people' in the world."[24] On the covenant concept of election, also present in John, Fee observes that "in the OT the term refers not to individual election, but to a people who have been chosen by God for his purposes."[25] It is by incorporation into and belonging to the chosen people of God that an individual is elect.

What then do we make of individualism and corporateness in John in light of these varied arguments? First, the suggestion that John is individualistic rather than corporate reflects a Western individualistic perspective. According to Sundermeier, "for the Westerner, life means individuality. We know each other as individuals; the development of life is seen as enhancing individuality. Community, being with others is secondary."[26] Unfortunately, this individualism is found within the church and is manifest in individualistic interpretation of scripture and deficiency in communal holiness.

Second, Smalley's suggestion for a nice balance between the one and the many must be supported. As we have shown, this suggestion is followed by Cook and Whitacre and has clear textual support. In John 3, for example, the writer addresses Nicodemus on two levels, both as singular (3:3, 5) and as plural (representative of society, 3:2, 11).[27] Another example is the Samaritan woman (4:4-42) who, though encountering Jesus personally, is not named but called the Samaritan woman, identifying her with the people called Samaritans.[28] Jesus' conversations with Nicodemus and the Samaritan are in the plural since, in John, the life of one person is bound with another's suggesting that the corporate reference is equally important.

Third, Smalley and scholars following his suggestion for a balance between individualism and corporateness contribute significantly to

---

24. Fee, *Gospel*, 127.

25. Fee, *Gospel*, 127.

26. Theo Sundermeier, *The Individual and Community in African Traditional Religions* (Hamburg: LIT, 1998), 17. See also, Paul Lehman, *Ethics in a Christian Context* (NY: Harper&Row, 1963); David F. Wright, "Introduction," in *EESE*, 9; Adewuya, *Community*, 194; Brower, *Gospels*, 68.

27. See Carson, *Gospel*, 187; Rensberger, *Johannine Faith*; Brodie, *Gospel*, 194; Louis J. Martyn, *History and Theology in the Fourth Gospel* (3rd ed.; Louisville: WJK, 2003), 88; Waetjen, *Gospel*, 144.

28. See Brodie, *Gospel*, 216-217.

Johannine scholarship. However, do they go far enough in challenging Moule's individualism? Moule's suggestion that John's corporate metaphors include an individual reference which is "more important" needs reviewing. How can an individual reference within a corporate metaphor be more important? Does John use corporate metaphors for an individualistic purpose? This is highly unlikely. John's corporate metaphors are carefully selected to underpin the writer's interest in unity and solidarity. Corporateness is the starting point for John. Not only the ruling metaphors (sheep, vine), but also the covenantal motifs John uses, such as tabernacle, temple, birth, family, fatherhood, election, witness, abiding, and fruit-bearing, underscore John's corporateness. We suggest, therefore, that while John's ecclesiology is nicely balanced between the personal and the corporate, it is the corporate that is the foundation and core.

8.3 John's Corporate Metaphors for the People of God

8.3.1. The Vine Branches

Jesus' designation of the people of God as branches of the vine suggests corporate existence, belongingness, and solidarity with Jesus and with one another. John's characterization of the disciples as branches of the vine can be easily misinterpreted as a reference to individual existence. The image mitigates against such thinking. Branches are one in the vine from which they grow before they are many. This oneness continues as long as they are in the vine and share the same nourishing sap. The primary interpretative context here is the notion of mutual indwelling. Therefore, the figure is of one complete vine with all branches vital and intact. "We cannot conceive of a vine without branches."[29] Jesus' categorization of the disciples as branches underpins the mutual union. There is no suggestion that any one branch can be detached and still continue to live. The consequences of detachment are unbearable—no abiding, no life, and no fruit bearing. To be removed

---

29. B. F. Westcott, *The Gospel According to John: The Authorized Version with Introduction and Notes* (London: John Murray, 1908), 217.

from the vine and the community is to cease to live since true life flows from the vine to and through the community. In fact the polemic in the metaphor is upon any one disciple who may break the solidarity and divide the new covenant community in any way. Unfortunately this "vine-branch" motif has been used to promote a person's individualistic relationship with Christ,[30] disregard corporateness, and offer the false impression that faith is a private affair.

8.3.2. The Sheep/Flock

Another motif identifying the new people of God with corporateness in John is the metaphor of the Good shepherd (10:1-21). Reference to the people of God as God's sheep/flock suggests corporate belongingness to God and to each other. The stress is upon "one shepherd" and "one flock" (v. 16). The reference to "other sheep," which is an allusion to gentiles or Diaspora Jews, suggests the absence of all discrimination and the inclusiveness of this flock. According to Koester, v. 16 suggests the "oneness of believers," which transcends the boundaries of language and ethnicity.[31] Exclusion, discrimination, or any harm to the unity is the work of a violent thief and robber who does not care for the sheep. Like the vine-branches, the shepherd-flock relationship between God and his people has its background in the OT and 2TP.[32] The repeated references to sheep and a shepherd evoke the well-known OT background in which the corporate people of God are referred to as a flock, and "shepherd" is used of such central characters as Moses (Exod 2:16-3:1), Joshua (Num 27:6-7), David (1 Sam 16:11; 2 Sam 5:2; 7:8), and above all God's own self (Ezek 34). The rulers, however, are portrayed as wicked shepherds (Ezek 34:1-10). The shepherd/flock metaphor is thus covenantal, describing the relationship between God and his corporate people. On one hand God is depicted as the nourisher

---

30. See Malina and Rohrbaugh, *Social-Science*, 234, who wrongly suggest that "the metaphor of vine and branches describes a one-to-one relationship between a disciple and Jesus."

31. Koester, *Symbolism*, 264.

32. Ps 23:1-6; Jer 23:1-8; Ezek 34; Zeph 3:3; Zech 10:2-3; 11:4-17; *1 En.* 89:12-27, 42-44, 59-70, 74-76; 90:22-25; *T. Gad* 1:2-4.

and protector of his people[33] and, on the other, the people as followers and faithful adherents of God's law. That the shepherd calls his sheep by name and the sheep recognize the shepherd's voice conveys a sense of belonging and intimacy.[34] The shepherd shows a high level of care for his flock when he lays down his life (10:15, 17), an act attributed to a true friend in 15:13.

8.3.3. The Children (1:12; 11:52; 12:36)

In John those who hospitably welcome the Word of God become the new community of "children" of God. The reference to the new people of God as "children" has family overtones. It suggests unity and corporate belonging to God as Father/Mother and to each other as brothers or sisters. The use of the "children" motif here is covenantal and is an allusion to the perception of those who are in a covenant relationship with God in the OT and 2TP.[35] For example, the Deuteronomist could address the Israelites: "You are children of the Lord your God" (Deut 14:1). That this refers to corporate Israel in a covenant relationship with God is underscored in the following verse where Israel is addressed corporately as "a people holy to the Lord your God" and people whom "the LORD has chosen out of all the peoples on earth to be his people, his treasured possession" (Deut 14:2). In John the motif carries the similar sense of the corporate people of God in a covenant relationship with God.

Here we must think of the fatherhood of God where there is no discrimination between humans. As children of God, people of all social status stand equal before God. The criterion is stated clearly: reception of the Word of God by believing in his name (1:12). As Bruce says, it "has nothing to do with racial or national or family ties."[36] The importance of faith is even clearer in a Pauline intertext: "For you are the children of God by faith in Christ Jesus" (Gal 4:26). In 1 John 3:10 "children of God" is contrasted

---

33. Köstenberger, *John*, 301, who suggests that "the leading out of sheep was a delicate task."

34. Keener, I:806.

35. R. Alan Culpepper, "The Pivot of John's Prologue," *NTS* 27 (1980): 1-31, surveys the common OT synonym "sons of God." The title "Son of God" is reserved for Jesus in the GOJ. Believers are called "children of God," a title never applied to Jesus in John.

36. Bruce, *Gospel*, 38.

with "children of the devil," and the children of God are associated with righteousness and love of a brother or sister.

The title "children of God" is directly tied to ethical behavior. According to Culpepper, it carries "the obligations and promises of the covenants of Abraham, Moses, and David. Israel, like a child to its natural father, was to be subject to God, receive his teaching, and enjoy his loving kindness."[37] In John the "children" motif is also juxtaposed with the "light" motif so that the corporate people of God are not only "children" but are "children of light" (12:36). For John "children of light" is a variation for "children of God" since "God is light" (1 John 1:5). Because of the union and solidarity Jesus has with God, Jesus can claim the divine prerogative of being light (8:12; cf. 1:4-9). This new designation of the people of God as children of God may have brought great comfort to the Johannine believers in the light of the excommunication from their religious home in the synagogue. Jesus' words meant that once again they have a place they can call home and a family to confide in. They are all together fathered by God whom they love and whose commands they obey.

8.4 The Case for Holiness in John's Corporate Thought

Having shown that John's theology of the people of God is corporate, questions regarding the place of holiness in this corporateness must now be addressed. To what extent can the people of God be conceived as holy? Does the Gospel writer have any interest in the holiness of this new community? Until the recent groundbreaking work of Bauckham,[38] Johannine scholars have ignored the topic. Bauckham argues persuasively that "the Gospel does in fact treat the holiness of Jesus' disciples as a significant theme which

---

37. R. Alan Culpepper, "Anti-Judaism in the Fourth Gospel as a Theological Problem for Christian Interpreters," in *Anti-Judaism and the Fourth Gospel: Papers for the eLeuven Colloquium, 2000* (ed. R. Bieringer, D. Pollefeyt, and F. Vandecasteele-Vannneuville; Assen, The Netherlands: Royal Van Gorcum, 2001), 87.

38. Bauckham, "Holiness." Bauckham's work is indispensable for this chapter and to some extent we will expand upon his ideas.

is closely related to the holiness of Jesus, the Father, and the Spirit."[39] He rightly observes that at first sight John does not seem to have much to offer in the theme of "holy church." For Bauckham the holiness language the writer uses with reference to the Father, Son, and Spirit, though not dominant, is an important pointer to the holiness of the disciples. Bauckham notes that "The word [holy] appears four times, with reference to God (17:11: "Holy Father"), Jesus (6:69 "the Holy One of God"), and the Holy Spirit (14:26; 20:22)"[40] and that the verb sanctify (to make holy, to consecrate) occurs four times (10:36; 17:17, 19), two with reference to the sanctification of the disciples (17:17, 19). Again connected to the disciples is the word pure/ clean (13:10; 15:2-3), associated with holiness in the LXX and suggesting purification from sin.[41]

Bauckham offers a useful analysis of the relationship between holy and pure in the OT and 2TP in connection with the sanctuary and the cultic practice of the temple. Holiness belongs properly to God, an expression of his uniqueness and distinction from all creation. God's holiness is the premise on which scripture stands in inviting the people of God to be holy: "You shall be holy, for I the LORD your God am holy" (Lev 19:2; cf. 11:44-45; 20:26). The people of God are holy insofar as they are related to the holy God and set apart for his holy purposes. In the OT, objects and places set apart for God's use are called holy.[42] As it is with objects and things, the people of God derive their holiness from their relationship with God. This is the kind of holiness at work at Qumran[43] and in the NT where the people of God are addressed as "saints" or "holy ones" (Rom 1:7; 1 Cor 1:2; Eph 4:12). This holiness has been termed by scholars as relational holiness or derived holiness.[44]

---

39. Bauckham, "Holiness," 95.

40. Bauckham, "Holiness," 95.

41. The double reference in 13:10 may also suggest a reference to purification rites. See Beasley-Murray, *John*, 234.

42. E.g. Mt. Sinai (Exod 19:23), Sabbaths (Exod 16:23; 20:8, 11), the ark of the covenant (2 Chron 35:3), vessels (1 Kings 8:4; 2 Chron 5:5), priests' garments (Exod 28:2; 35:19), anointing oil (Exod 37:29), the Temple (Hab 2:20), etc.

43. See Swanson, "Holiness," 19-39, for a helpful exegesis of selected scriptures dealing with commitment to holiness in the sect.

44. W. T. Purkiser, *Exploring Christian Holiness Vol. 1, Biblical Foundations* (KC: BHPKC,

But how do these intertexts illuminate our reading of John? In John there is no question that the disciples are pure (13:10; 15:3). As a covenant term, "pure" enhances continuity with the OT where purity is a requirement relating to the holiness of the people of God. As covenant partners of the holy God through "the Holy One of God," the disciples can be said to be holy. This includes the "temple" metaphor and the mutual abiding motif where we think of God's people as his holy habitation. The mode of cleansing, Jesus' teaching (15:3), suggests understanding in light of the Torah, which was the covenant charter. The disciples are cleansed by receiving and following Jesus' words. This become clearer when read against 6:63 where the words of Jesus are infused with spirit and life. In this regard Johannine holiness embraces both inner purity and outward performance of the commands.[45] God's people are obligated to replicate the character of God by doing Jesus' commands (14:15; 15:10-17). This can be read in light of what God did with Israel: "God consecrates Israel by giving them the commandments, and Israel maintains holiness by keeping them (Exod 31:13; Lev 11:44-45)."[46]

Another aspect of the disciples' holiness is introduced in 17:17. Here Jesus prays for their sanctification. What Jesus asks the Father to do, sanctify, is what Jesus himself has done while he was with them (17:12). However, now that he is leaving this will be the work of the Father which he will do by sending the Spirit (14:16-17). The word which featured in 15:3 as the agent of cleansing now features as the agent of sanctification (17:17). God is committed to keeping those who abide in him and his words. A second way of reading the sanctification of the disciples links to the sanctification of Jesus (10:36) where the theme is consecration.[47] Consecration for the Father's use can be seen in light of the covenantal notion of fruit-bearing,

---

1983), 19; Adewuya, *Holiness and Community*, 9; Brower, *Gospels*, 15, 24; Bauckham, "Holiness," 110; Kent E. Brower and Andy Johnson, "Introduction: Holiness and the Ekklēsia of God," in *HENT*, xix-xx. John A. Knight, *The Holiness Pilgrimage: Developing a Life-Style that Reflects Christ* (KC: BHPKC, 1986), 19, refers to this holiness as "positional" holiness.

45. Bauckham, "Holiness," 96.

46. Bauckham, "Holiness," 111.

47. See our discussion of John 17:17 following.

which in 15:16 is linked to the *missio Dei*. Fruit-bearing is integral to being the vine as seen in the imagery of Israel who was created and cultivated for the *missio Dei* (Isa 5:1-7).

The Gospel writer carefully links the moral purity of the disciples to the vine metaphor. He does this by using the word clean/pure to refer both to the pruning of the vine branches and the holiness of the disciples. It is significant to note that it is the themes of the vine metaphor (15:1-17) that form the prayer of 17:1-26 where the sanctification of the disciples is an important feature. This must not be surprising since the vine metaphor is the primary imagery of the last discourse (13:31-17:26). The focus of the prayer is the union that also forms the main theme of 15:1-17 illustrated by the vine and its branches. The sanctification of the believers will be expressed corporately in their union with God and one another and in their participation in the *missio Dei*.

8.5 Aspects of Holiness in John

8.5.1 Holiness as Covenant Fidelity

The vast expanse of covenant language spreading throughout the GOJ including, most importantly, the vine metaphor has already been identified. Two things must be emphasized: First, that to be involved in a covenant relationship with the creator God, whose quintessential nature is holiness, is to be holy. In John the new people of God are holy by virtue of their covenant relationship with the holy God. It follows that everything given to or belonging to God, whether places, objects, or humans, is holy on the basis of relationship to the source of holiness.[48] The holiness of the new people of God is relational, assumed on the basis of their right relationship with the holy God. For Johannine believers this right relationship consists in mutual indwelling, the deepest relationship ever possible between any two covenant partners.

---

48. Bauckham, "Holiness," 95; Adewuya, *Community*, 9; Brower, *Gospels*, 24.

Second, as shown previously, covenant relationship with God includes fidelity. The OT reveals that God's holy covenant with his people was not without a commitment to ethical holiness on their part. Such holiness was clearly defined in terms of social justice and righteousness, which consisted much in their relationship with one another and hospitality to the orphan, the widow, and the stranger (Jer 22:3; Zech 7:10). If their social life was skewed then the vine of God was contaminated and deserved punishment. Holiness was defined in terms of relationship with one another which often reflected their relationship with God. The call to abide and keep commandments, central to 15:1-17, clearly defines the character of this covenant relationship. The strong emphasis on sacrificial love as a sum of the commandments expresses the outward-looking nature of love. This is what John calls "love not in word or speech but in truth or action" (1 John 3:18). According to Chennattu, "A certain commitment and way of life— manifesting God's life-of-love and revealing God's creative presence—are expected from the disciples of Jesus."[49] In Bauckham's language, "people make themselves holy."[50] This is much like Paul's exhortation to the people of God at Philippi to "work out your own salvation with fear and trembling; for it is God who is at work in you, enabling you both to will and to work for his good pleasure" (Phil 2:12-13). Thus we can infer that covenant representation of holiness is two-faceted: It is derived by virtue of relationship with the holy God and is expressed in fidelity to the covenant Lord.

8.5.2 Holiness as Cleansing from Sin (13:10; 15:3; 1 John 3:3)[51]

The cleansing of the new people of God is an important feature of the vine metaphor in the GOJ. This should be anticipated since cleansing, either of the sanctuary or some part of it or of the people of God, does form an important feature at points where the vine metaphor appears in the OT and 2TP.[52] In Zechariah 3:10 the metaphor is used in the context

---

49. Chennattu, *Discipleship*, 115.
50. Bauckham, "Holiness," 96.
51. See Chapter 5.
52. See for example, Zech 3:10 where the vine metaphor is used in the context of the

of the cleansing of Joshua the high Priest,[53] which in the Prophet's words anticipates the cleansing (removal of guilt) of the people of God under the new covenant to be ushered in by God's servant the Branch (vv. 8-10). The cleansing will make the people of God fit to be made the sanctuary of the Holy One and the priests of YHWH in accordance with their calling: "You shall be unto me a kingdom of priests and a holy nation" (Exod 19:6; Isa 61:6).[54] In the prophet's writing there is a connection between the cleansing of the people of God and God's abiding in their midst. Their cleansing is also important for their participation in God's mission in the world. Similarly, in 1 Macc 14:12 the vine metaphor is used in the context of the cleansing of the sanctuary following its earlier profanation by Antiochus Epiphanes.[55] These texts are important for establishing the holiness of the people of God in the GOJ, particularly as they combine the notions of purity, dwelling place, and sanctification.

For the writer of the Gospel of John cleansing is symbolized by the pruning of branches. This pruning becomes the occasion for fruit bearing. For the disciples, who are already fruitful branches, cleansing has already occurred. The Gospel writer makes it clear in 15:3 that the disciples, the new covenant people of God, are pure. Here, as is his custom, the writer uses pure with double meaning to refer in a literal sense to the pruning of the vine branches and in a symbolic sense to the spiritual cleansing of the disciples from sin. The statement, "And you are clean" (15:3) harks back to 13:10, "And you are clean, though not all of you," where on the occasion of feetwashing Jesus alluded to the disciples' purity. Here again he uses pure

---

cleansing of the High Priest and the people of God.

53. See Lena Sofia Tiemeyer, "The Guilty Priesthood (Zech 3)," in *The Book of Zechariah and its Influence* (ed. Christopher Tuckett; Aldershot: Ashgate, 2003), 1-19, for a significant discussion of the purity and impurity of the high priest.

54. See David Baron, *The Visions and Prophecies of Zechariah* (GR: NKP, 1972), 86.

55. Antiochus Epiphanes' desolating sacrilege is recorded in 1 Macc 1:59; 4:53-54. The importance of 1 Macc 14:12 and its intertexts for the interpretation of the vine metaphor in John 15 is highlighted in chapter 3. The aspects of cleansing or worship of YHWH present in these texts is important for our understanding of cleansing and worship in John, especially 15:1-17. See Bauckham, "Holiness," 98-108, where 1&2 Macc are properly used for the interpretation of the idea of cleansing in the GOJ.

with double meaning, referring both to the disciples' physical purity after washing and to their spiritual purity after Jesus cleansed them from sin.[56]

The Gospel writer uses this double meaning to give new meaning to common Jewish images and metaphors. His purpose, however, is always to derive a new meaning rather than the conventional one. This is clearly what he does with the notion of purification. In 2:6 where purification first appears in the Gospel, it is used with reference to water as a common Jewish means of purification. The depiction of the Jewish water jars as empty has long been interpreted as symbolic reference to the emptiness of Jewish rites of purification.[57] Indeed in John these Jewish rites are displaced by placing them against the reality to which they pointed. In the language of the writer to the Hebrews, they were shadows of the reality that was to come (Heb 10:1). Thus the disciples, who are targeted for faith by this first miracle, behold the glory of Christ and put their faith in him (2:11). It is this faith in the lamb who takes away the sin of the world that cleanses them and marks them out as children of God (1:12-13, 29).

In 13:10 pure appears with reference to water for the ritual of feetwashing. Here the writer uses ceremonial washing as a symbol for the purification of the disciples from the defilement of sin. In v. 8 it is this purification from sin's defilement that guarantees fellowship with Christ. The imperative of this purification from sin is underscored by the imperative of ritual purification for participation in the table fellowship: "Unless I wash you, you have no share with me" (v. 8). On a symbolic note, it is those whom Christ washes who have a share in the eschatological feast (14:1-14).

However, it is necessary to distinguish a second type of washing mentioned in vv. 9, 10. Here reference is made to the washing of the entire body which makes the whole person pure. According to Mediterranean customs, "A person invited to a dinner party takes a bath (at home or in the public baths) before coming to supper. Upon arrival the individual needs only to

---

56. See Bauckham, "Holiness," 98.

57. See Barrett, *John*, 160, who adds on the basis of the six jars that the number six is also symbolic of the imperfection of the Jewish dispensation since seven is the number for completeness and perfection; Talbert, *Reading John*, 85; D. Moody Smith Jr., *John* (ANTC; Nashville: Abingdon, 1999), 84.

have his feet washed before the meal."[58] Since the disciples have had this bath, their whole body is clean and they do not need another bath only the ritual washing of the feet. It is this cleanness of the whole body that Jesus uses to symbolize the purification of the disciples.[59] There is a possible echo here of the hospitable reception that makes believers children of God (1:12) and the truth concerning the disciples' cleansing faith in Jesus (2:11).

It is, therefore, plausible to suggest that the disciples are pure on the basis of their acceptance of Jesus and putting their faith in him as the Son of God and the lamb of God who takes away the sin of the world (1:12; 6:69). The ritual cleansing of the feet, which is meant to remove dust accrued on the path to the supper, must be interpreted as symbolic of the continued need for cleansing of the believer on the journey with Christ. This sugges- tion, which clearly falls into John's employment of the "already but not yet" motif, becomes clearer when read in the light of the use of pure in 15:2-3 where it is at play again.

In 15:2-3 the writer uses pure again with double meaning to refer to the vinedresser's pruning work as well as to the disciples' spiritual cleansing by their faith in Christ. The latter is already accomplished (v. 3) while the former is presented as on-going (v. 2). The spiritual cleansing (v. 3) is attributed to the word they have heard from Christ. This does not militate against our suggestion that they are cleansed by their faith in Christ. Faith in Christ is the same as faith in Christ's words since Christ is one with his words. Moreover, it is the one who is of God who hears the words of God (8:47), the very words that Christ speaks (3:34), and are spirit and life (6:63). John 15:2-3 harks back to the disciples' purification in John 13. There the disciples have had a bath for the whole body and they are wholly clean, yet the footwashing must proceed. The proclamation that the disciples are already clean parallels the whole bath alluded to in 13:9-10 whereas the cleansing suggested by the pruning (itself continuing in nature) parallels the necessary feetwashing, interpreted as the need for continuing cleansing for the believer. The disciples, who are already wholly clean and fruit bearing, will only need the vinedresser's pruning so that they bear

58. Talbert, *Reading John*, 192.
59. See Bauckham, *Holiness*, 98.

more fruits.[60] They will only need the removal of dust accrued on the Christ journey.

8.5.3 Holiness as Hospitality in John[61]

A helpful connection between the motifs of purity and hospitality is made by Chilton[62] in his discussion of "Jesus' theory of purity." He views Jesus' meal practice as an enactment of the kingdom's purity. Jesus redefines purity by engaging in meals with suspect people who may have been pronounced ceremonially profane and marginalized. In John, as elsewhere in the Gospels, Jesus' hospitality culture prevailed over taboos he would have been expected to observe as a law-abiding Jew. Presented with a choice between the popular culture of ceremonial purity and a culture of hospitality, Jesus chooses hospitality. In chapter 7 we dealt with the meals in the GOJ where Jesus moved from stranger or guest to host, creating opportunities for hospitality to the despised and marginalized of society. For Jesus hospitality knows no bounds. It is offered equally to the rich or poor, saints or sinners, and to all people without discrimination. However, the question remains, what has hospitality to do with holiness?

First, hospitality is the way of life of the Persons of the Trinity. As we have seen, the life of the divine family is characterized by selfless outward-looking love. This love is expressed mutually among family members and towards humankind and all creatures. That the life of the divine family is the archetype of the life of the people of God is underscored by our previous chapter. When the people of God practice hospitality they reflect the holy life of the divine family. Hospitality is humanity in God's design. It is the true reflection of the *imago Dei* in humankind. If the creator God is hospitable then it is unthinkable for the people of God to be apathetic,

---

60. See Talbert, *Reading John*, 212, who concurs with us that v. 3 relates to branches that are alive but need pruning to be fruitful. However, it needs clarified that the branches are already bearing fruit. The vinedresser's pruning enables them to bear much fruit. See chapter 4 for the meaning of pruning and fruit bearing, including the efficacy of the word to cleanse.

61. See chapter 7, where hospitality as the hallmark of the mutual abiding motif.

62. Bruce Chilton, A *Feast of Meanings: Eucharistic Theologies form Jesus through Johannine Circles* (Leiden: Brill, 1994), 46.

unwelcoming, and condemning (3:17). If God is sensitive to the needs of humankind and all his creation, then the reverse is apathy. It is unholy to be indifferent or insensitive to the needs of humankind and other creatures. God's holiness could not allow him to wait and watch in apathy while the world perishes (1:14; 3:16). This is outside the scope of his holy character and would have seriously compromised his holiness. Apathy is ungodly and unholy. For John, holiness involves being moved with compassion and pity towards humankind and all God's creation.

Holiness that ends with pity and compassion, however, is not a true reflection of God's holiness and is not what John portrays. For John hospitality is holiness in action. God's hospitality moved him into salvific action (1:12-14; 3:16). Similarly, hospitality must move his people to act. Holiness is not a feeling but an action. It is not enough to be reeling with pity when no salvific action is taken (1 John 3:17-18). Jesus, the Holy One of God, lived out his holiness in hospitality. He was often criticized for his table fellowship with wrong people;[63] his critics assumed that Jesus' fellowship with sinners implied an approval and endorsement of their shabby behavior. They also thought fellowship with sinners would compromise his holiness. What they misunderstood was that "Jesus, 'the Holy One of God,' is not contaminated by impurity but rather, as the bearer of the Holy Spirit of God, is characterized by a holiness that is contagious and transforming as it confronts the impure and the sinful."[64] Jesus knew that his holiness is contagious and that by contact with him sinners may be transformed.[65] As a result he endeavored to host sinners and outcasts, drawing them into the sphere of his transformative holiness. There is a great lesson for the people of God here: rejection hardens people, but hospitality makes transformation possible. By accepting people into his presence just as they were, with all their problems and imperfections, Jesus exposed them to his example and to his message of love.

---

63. Jesus' meeting with the Samaritan woman culminates in his hospitable invitation by the Samaritans where he spent two days. Keener, I:585, identifies three barriers that Jesus overcomes in this story: the socioethnic barrier of centuries of Jewish-Samaritan prejudice; the gender barrier; and a moral barrier imposed by this woman's behavior.

64. Brower and Johnson, "Introduction," in *HENT*, xix.

65. Craig L. Blomberg, *Contagious Holiness: Jesus' Meals with Sinners* (DG: IVP, 2005).

When God's people ignore Jesus' message of holiness embodied in his acts of hospitality, the church becomes individualistic, divisive, judgemental, and exclusionary. A dividing wall builds up between believers and non-believers, true believers and false believers, in-groups and out-groups, so that an us-them attitude prevails.[66] Unfortunately, this is the opposite of the holy community portrayed in the GOJ and elsewhere in the Christian scriptures. John portrays a holy community where love, showing itself in hospitality, is the norm. Such love opens no room for division, hatred, and factionalism. The love ethics of 1 John 3:11-24, where Cain is postulated as an example of inhospitality, suggests that hatred of one's brother can lead to murder. The writer states clearly that no murderer has eternal life. It is unthinkable to have faith in God or to be holy and still harbor hatred. The Gospel writer states clearly that eternal life is for those who have a faith relationship with God, and, for holiness' sake, these will not murder.

8.5.4 Holiness as Sanctification in John (17:17)

The holiness of believers in John is also described in terms of sanctification. Bauckham gives a helpful analysis of the occurrence of the "holy" group of words in the GOJ.[67] His analysis, however, shows that the words are mostly used in relation to the holiness of the Father, Son, and Spirit, with only two uses regarding the dedication of the disciples. Although the "holy" group of words is not frequent in John, the sanctification of believers is one of the major themes of Jesus' prayer on behalf of the disciples (17:17). We concur with Smith who treats the prayer for the sanctification of the disciples as the climax of John 17.[68] Jesus prays that the disciples may be sanctified in truth. Again the OT and 2TP where "holy" and its cognates are used to denote consecration for a sacred duty sheds light here. For example, Aaron and his sons were consecrated or set apart for the priesthood (Exod 28:41). In a similar way John uses the verb sanctify to denote a relationship

---

66. The division of the Christian Church in Swaziland into the Conference, League, and Council has created a notion that Christians are not one. Strong boundaries exist and the us-them mentality prevails as one camp remains out of bounds to the other. One wonders if differences in theological persuasions need to go that far.

67. Bauckham, *Holiness*, 95.

68. Smith, *John*, 315.

of belonging to God and being set apart for his use. In denoting a sacred relationship and use by the holy God, sanctify intrinsically carries implications for ethical purity and social holiness. This must be understood in light of the calls to the people of God to sanctify themselves (e.g. Lev 21:8; 2 Chron 35:6).[69] There is careful moral conduct that goes hand in hand with the believer's dedication to God, the pure way of life, and the upright behavior. As Oswalt says, "it is precisely in the context of human behavior that God calls for his people to demonstrate their holiness."[70] The sanctified people of God also make their sanctification sure by living the life of God. As we shall show, the life of God in view here consists of love.

Second, they are sanctified in relation to Jesus' own sanctification (v. 19). In 17:19 the writer juxtaposes the sanctification of the disciples with that of Christ. Christ sanctifies himself so that the disciples may be truly sanctified. This text links to 10:36 where the writer refers to Jesus as "the one whom the Father has sanctified and sent into the world." The immediate context of 10:36 is a discussion of the question of the identity of Jesus beginning in 10:24. As the Jews object to his Sonship and deity, Jesus raises the question of how one whom God has sanctified and sent to the world cannot legitimately claim equality with God. The trajectory here is that of union with God and solidarity with him in fulfilling his mission to the world. These ideas are echoed in the prayer of 17:20-26. Jesus is one with the Father who sanctified and sent him, and in solidarity with him he will fulfil his mission on the cross. The oneness of the disciples with God is the theme of the vine metaphor (15:1-17), and here it remains for the disciples to fulfil, in solidarity with God, fruitfulness and mission in the world. However, Jesus must first fulfil his mission on the cross as "the Lamb of God who takes away the sin of the world" (1:29, 36), since "when I am lifted up from the earth, I will draw all people to myself" (12:32).

---

69. Bauckham, *Holiness*, 96.

70. John N. Oswalt, *Called to be Holy: A Biblical Perspective* (Nappanee: Evangel, 1999), 32.

8.5.5 Holiness as Mutual Abiding in John (15:4-7)[71]

The motif of mutual abiding lends itself to being interpreted as John's chosen way of referring to the holiness of the new people of God. This is due to its allusions to the covenant[72] and its description of a theosis or deification of the new people of God.[73] First, it suggests union with the Holy Triune God through union with the Holy one of God, a union intrinsically bearing much fruit (v. 5). That this union is holiness is iterated by Taylor: "Holiness is not first life 'for' Christ, 'before' Him or through Him, but 'in' Him."[74] The new covenant people of God, who are bound to God and are nourished by union with him, share the holiness of God. The futility of life outside God, the ultimate source, is clear: "apart from me you can do nothing" (v. 5c). The motif suggests continued faith in Christ and his word in all circumstances. For John holiness consists in that and more.

Second, it concerns drawing life from and living the life of the Holy one of God. Particularly helpful here is Dodd's association of the motif with expressions "indicating the life of virtue or wisdom, divinely given or directed, lived in dependence on God, in conformity with His will."[75] Receiving the life of Christ by believing in his name is the purpose of the GOJ (20:31). The motif of life is introduced in the prologue with Christ illumining his creation: "In him was life and that life was the light of all people" (1:4; cf. 14:6).[76] In the Lukan tradition he is the (source/prince) of

---

71. Chapters 6 and 7. The Johannine notion of abiding, including its intertexts, is explicated.

72. See the work of E. Malatesta, *Interiority and Covenant: A Study of* εἶναι ἐν *and* μένειν ἐν *in the First Letter of Saint John* (AnBib 69; Rome: BIP, 1978), 25-6, 31.

73. The notion of theosis or deification is properly understood by the Eastern Orthodox Church. Although the terminology is later, probably in the fourth century, the notion can be traced back to the apostles Paul (Rom 8:1; 2 Cor 5:17), Peter (2 Pet 1:3-4), and John (10:34; 15: 4; 1 John 4:16). It is a difficult notion for the Western church, especially in Reformed Protestantism, where justification is viewed forensically. See Brower, Swanson, and Thomas, *CHBP*, 3-4.

74. A. Wingrove Taylor, "Holiness Values from the Heavenly Vine," *WTJ* 37 (2002): 219-223.

75. Dodd, *Interpretation*, 192.

76. See Martin Hengel, "The Prologue of the Gospel of John as the Gateway to Christological Truth," in *The Gospel of John and Christian Theology* (eds. Richard Bauckham and Carl Mosser; GR: Eerdmans, 2008), 276, who suggests that for human beings "life" alludes to the *imago Dei*. Also Malatesta, *Interiority*, 314.

life (Acts 3:15). To abide in Christ is to abide in the source of life. Drawing life and light from God is not different from drawing holiness from him. Since God is holy, and his law is holy, abiding in him and his word is abiding in holiness. Again, it must be stressed that the notion of branches abiding in the vine suggests corporateness and belonging to one another. Mutual abiding also links to other Johannine motifs of corporateness such as "one another," which has implications for brotherly love. The believer does not only abide in Christ and his words but also abides in Christ's love (vv. 9-10). Such abiding in Christ's love has as a precondition, keeping the commandments. 1 John 3:17 defines the meeting of people's social needs as the precondition for the abode of God's love in a person or the community. Thus holiness drawn from Christ has compassion at its center.

Third, mutual abiding suggests that the new people of God are God's temple, and God's temple is holy (1 Cor. 3:17). That Christ is the temple of the Father, the Spirit, and the disciples is plainly stated in John (2:21; 14:11; 1:32; 15:4). The invitation to the disciples to "abide in me and I will abide in you" suggests mutuality and that the people of God also function as temple (15:4).[77] The reference to people of God as temple is commonplace in the 2TP. According to Swanson the piling up of terms of holiness, purity, and perfection in the Community Rule represents "a view of life with temple imagery at its center in which the function of the community is to do atonement/expiation."[78] Brooke concurs, and adds that the community at Qumran understood itself as "a temple with a priesthood."[79] God's temple is holy, not only because all things and people belonging to God are holy, but also because it is the place of God's abode in the midst of his people. Not only that, it is the place where sacrifice and atonement takes place, a place where sins are forgiven. It alludes to God's sanctifying presence on earth through his holy covenant people. The ethical implications of belonging to God and to each other are great, Our suggestion that mutual abiding is also ethical and includes a mutual concern among the people of

---

77. Cf. 1 Cor 3:16; 6:19; 2 Cor 6:16.

78. Swanson, "Holiness," 25.

79. George J. Brooke, "The Dead Sea Scrolls and New Testament Eschatology," in *HENT*, 13.

God for the well-being of each other finds support.[80] According to Dodd the motif is "closely related to the idea of the solidarity of all believers in the body of Christ."[81]

8.5.6 Holiness as Fruit Bearing in John[82]

Evidence from 2TL suggests that fruit-bearing could be interpreted with regard to holiness. In chapter 5 we made reference to the self-understanding of the Qumran sect as those "who drink the waters of holiness" (1QH XVI.13) and bear "the fruit of holiness" (1QS 10:22). The possibility of a connection between the GOJ and the Qumran covenanters has almost reached a consensus in recent scholarship.[83] Here we suggest these texts as a plausible background for understanding the notion of fruit-bearing in John 15. Strong support for this is found in the recurrence of a similar interpretation of the notion in the Odes of Solomon (*Odes Sol.* 8:2) about a century later.

The Essenes' notion of "drinking waters of holiness" is echoed in two references to water in the GOJ, both of which focus on salvation. First, in John, Jesus promises the Samaritan woman that those who drink his water will never be thirsty, and that the water he gives will be "a spring of water gushing up to eternal life" (4:14). Second, on the last day of the festival of Tabernacles, where water featured as an important symbol, Jesus announces again that those who believe in him will drink and in their hearts shall flow "rivers of living water" (7:37-38). It would not be far-fetched to think of the waters that Jesus, the Holy One of God, gives as "waters of holiness." And, since in the background scriptures the drinking of "waters of holiness" was associated with bearing "fruits of holiness," it is plausible to think of the fruits in John 15 as holiness in the new community.

That being so, the new people of God drink the waters of holiness, and, as abiding branches of the vine, they bear the fruits of holiness. In 7:39,

---

80. Bogart, *Perfectionism*, 80.

81. Dodd, *Interpretation*, 193.

82. See our interpretation of the image of fruit-bearing in chapter 5.

83. James Charlesworth's *The Dead Sea Scrolls and the Historical Jesus* (London: Doubleday, 1992) highlights several points of contact between the Essenes at Qumran and Jesus' teaching.

where a connection is made between the living waters and the Holy Spirit, the reader is prompted to think of the fruits of the Holy Spirit as described elsewhere in the NT. Particularly helpful here are Paul's words to the people of God in Galatia where the fruits of the Spirit are associated with "love, joy, peace, patience, kindness, generosity, faithfulness, gentleness, and self-control" (Gal 5:22-23). It is possible that John's audience shared with the Pauline corpus the notion that the Holy Spirit could express himself practically in the holy life of the people of God. There is no doubt that the fruits in the Johannine corpus were perceived as a reference to the holiness of the new people of God.

Another important theme connected to the notion of fruit-bearing is the theme of mission. In 15:16 the Gospel writer juxtaposes the motifs of "election," "appointing" and "going" to underscore the importance of the *missio Dei* to the disciples. These motifs are covenantal, suggesting understanding with regard to the election and mission of Israel in OT. The writer imposes on the people of God a missionary task that is "universal in scope."[84]

8.5.7 Holiness as Incarnation in John (1:14)

Another Johannine motif that must be viewed as a reference to holiness is the incarnation of the Word of God. Like other themes, the incarnation is introduced in the prologue (1:14) and is developed further as John's story unfolds. It becomes more explicit in 15:1-17 and 17:6-26 where Jesus and the believers mutually indwell one another suggesting intimate sharing of one another's life including all its joys and perils.[85] The Word of God becomes all that humankind truly is and is subject to all the conditions of human existence.[86] The ascription of eternal divinity and agency of creation to the Word in the opening verses (vv. 1-3) suggests that the incarnation be read as God's goodwill to humankind. This is underscored by the descrip-

---

84. Smalley, *John*, 263.

85. Jesus tells the metaphor of the vine and branches "so that my joy may be in you and that your joy may be complete" (15:11); the believers are to have the full measure of Jesus' joy (17:13). It is clear in John that the believers are to participate in Jesus' suffering (15:18-16:4).

86. Westcott, *John*, 10.

tion of the Word as "full of grace and truth" (v. 14), where grace must mean "a kindness, a manifestation of good will, a gift, an expected favor."[87] In an intertext, Paul describes the incarnation as "self-emptying" where the Word of God must be perceived as voluntarily humbling himself and hoarding the privileges of divinity (Phil 2:6-11). In Hebrews 2:14-18 a similar portrait of the incarnation is given where the Son is "made like his brothers in every way" with a view to destroying the author of death (Satan) and saving humankind.

But what has the incarnation of the Word of God to do with the holiness of the people of God? We suggest that the incarnation of Christ, like the Trinity, be viewed as an archetype of the holy life of the people of God. In John the incarnation is the outworking of the consecration and sending of the Son. If incarnation is important for the Son's consecration and sending into the world (10:36), it must be important also for the disciples whose consecration and sending are analogous to the Son's. Practical theologians view the incarnation of Christ as a model for ministry.[88] In line with this perspective, incarnational holiness can be spoken of. Incarnational holiness demands a corporate and non-hierarchical view of life. It is the kind modelled by Jesus' participation in the lives of people of all social status in John, both social élites and those in the margin of society. The incarnation of the Word of God is a model to be followed. Earlier, the importance of interpreting mutual abiding as hospitality and sharing of life, with important implications for the social life of the people of God, was stressed. Incarnational holiness carries the same implications but puts a strong emphasis in participating in one another's plight in community. Its hallmark is entering practically into another's life with a view to transforming his or her circumstances not as an outsider or a non-resident charitable savior but as an insider. It is expressed in Paul's testimony: "I have become all things to all people, that I might by all means save some" (1 Cor 9:22).

---

87. Molony, *John*, 45.

88. See Dean Borgmann, *When Kumbaya Is Not Enough: A Practical Theology of Youth Ministry* (Peabody: Hendrickson, 1997), 30-33, who talks about an incarnational style of theology and ministry.

Although it does not exclude charity, incarnational holiness does not allow for charity that will keep other community members as "Other", but participation in another's problem as "our" problem. In other words when one has a problem "we" have a problem, not "he/she" has a problem. When one has a blessing "we" are blessed rather than "she/he" is blessed. The idea is to enter into the life situation of fellow humans and become what the other person is including in their situations and circumstances. It is about the people of God living together as a family both locally and internationally: not in a patron-client relationship where one is celebrated, but together as one family where everyone is lifted and Christ celebrated. Incarnational holiness demands a corporate view of life and opposes the hoarding of God-given wealth and resources. Taken in this way, holiness becomes "a power reaching out to heal, as opposed to creating exclusive boundaries."[89] As noted earlier, it is exemplified by the community of the new people of God in Jerusalem in the days following Pentecost (Acts 2:44-47).

8.5.8 Holiness as Love in John (15:9-17)[90]

There is scholarly consensus relating to at least one ethical appeal in John: the command to love.[91] Three concepts are particularly important with regard to John's portrait of love: First, love is an essential characteristic of God—God is love (1 John 4:8, 16). John states categorically that the relationship between the Father and the Son is a love relationship (3:35; 5:20; 14:31).[92] In John love is the social glue that holds together the Father, Son, and Spirit. Second, this love relationship of the divine persons is inclusive rather than exclusive, extending indiscriminately to the realm of humankind in the world (3:16). Trinitarian love is outward-looking and is the context for the incarnation of the Son and the inclusion of humankind in the love circle of the divine family (3:16). Humankind, the object of

---

89. Borg, *Conflict, Holiness and Politics*, xv.

90. Contents of this section reflect work done as part of a presentation for an MA seminar at Nazarene Theological College in 2004. I am indebted to lecturers Dr. Dwight Swanson and the late Rev. Gordon Thomas and my fellow students in that seminar.

91. See, for example, Meeks, *Ethics*, 318; Brower, *Gospels*, 81; Cf. 13:34; 15:12, 17; 1 John 3:11, 23; 2 John 5.

92. Brower, Swanson, and Thomas, *CHBP*, 3.

God's love, will also respond to the divine serenade with love, so that the relationship between God and humankind thrives on mutual love. Just as love glues the divine family, love also becomes the glue that holds together the Triune God and the disciples. According to Dodd, "the Father, the Son, and the disciples dwell in one another by virtue of a love which is the very life and activity of God."[93] Third, the love culture of the divine family is a model for the disciples' love for one another. Since God's very nature is love, it is not possible to relate to him without being affected by his perfect love. The call to the disciples to "love one another just as I have loved you" (13:34), together with the reference to a true friend laying down his life for his/her friends (15:13), underscores the intrinsic ethical dimension of the love command. As Smith suggests, love is a fundamental aspect of Johannine theology and ethics.[94]

However, at this point something must be said on the limits of love in John. There is an ongoing scholarly debate on the use of the words "one another" which for some scholars suggest a limiting of the love to the disciples' family.[95] Nevertheless, the present writer, following Dodd and others,[96] takes an inclusive view and thinks the delimiting view results from a non-Trinitarian reading of the Gospel. Johannine love is Trinitarian, and such love is outward-looking and open-ended. We propose that love in John be read in the light of other important Johannine themes such as the Trinity and the incarnation, where the world is the receptor of God's generosity. "Love one another" is, therefore, not delimiting and carries an intrinsic sense of the possibility of the world being drawn into the disciples' circle of mutual love. In John the mutual love of the disciples is outward-looking and its practice is a revelation of true discipleship to the world (13:35).

The important question here, however, regards how John integrates love into his holiness theme. To respond to this we suggest a reading of 15:9-17 and its intratexts, where love functions within the context of the vine

---

93. Dodd, *Interpretation*, 196.

94. Smith, *John*, 259.

95. See for example, Brown, *John*, II:613; J. C. Fenton, *The Gospel According to John* (Clarendon: Oxford University Press, 1970), 17; Sanders, *Ethics*, 91. This suggestion is often used as support for the view that the Johannine community is narrow and sectarian.

96. Dodd, *Interpretation*, 404, 428; Barrett, *Gospel*, 377.

metaphor in connection with the themes of unity and fruit bearing. Note that important themes arising from this text have already been discussed previously. First, it opens with reference to God, the ultimate source and prototype of love (v. 9). God has loved Jesus and, following the same pattern, Jesus has loved the disciples. Thus to love is to reproduce the life of the divine family. According to Barrett, "it is of the essence of the Christian life that all who are Christians should love one another, and in so far as they fail to do so they fail to reproduce the divine life which should inspire them and should be shown to the world through them."[97]

Second, having the assurance of Jesus' love for them, the disciples respond by abiding in Jesus' love (v. 10), which they show by keeping Jesus' commands. It is important to note here that for John the love of Christ is the sphere in which the disciples live continuously.[98] Also, abiding in Christ and his love is inseparable from obeying the commands. To love God is to keep his commands (14:15, 21, 23, 24), and, to keep the commands is to live in holiness (*T. Benj.* 10:11). Again Jesus' love and obedience to the Father's commands is postulated as a model for his disciples.[99] Jesus loved God and obeyed his commands, the disciples are to love Jesus and obey his commands. There is an echo here of the Testaments of the Twelve Patriarchs where the themes of love and the commands are juxtaposed and illustrated with the virtues and vices of the patriarchs (e.g. *T. Iss.* 5:1-2).

Third, the measure of the disciples' love for one another is Christ's sacrificial death on the cross (vv. 12, 13). Since love is the way of Christ, the disciples must let Christ determine its extent. According to Bruce, "no Christian should speak readily of his love for others unless he is prepared, if need be, to show that love as Christ showed his, by giving up his life for them."[100] That Christ gives his life on the cross as a gesture of love is clear from the beginning of the Gospel (1:29; 3:14, 15; 10:17). For example, in chapter 13, where the command to love is first introduced, Christ is said to love his own "to the end" (13:1), meaning both "to the end" and

97. Barrett, *Gospel*, 377.
98. Westcott, *John*, 219.
99. Köstenberger, *John*, 456.
100. Bruce, *Epistles*, 96.

"absolutely."[101] There is no doubt that this love "to the end" is a reference to his death. These words are echoed in 1 John 3:16 where the new community knows love through the sacrifice of Christ. Here the invitation to the disciples to follow Christ's example and lay down life for one another is stated categorically. True love excludes inhospitality, selfishness, exploitation and oppression of the weak, and disregard of the poor and those on the margins of society. It is practical and includes active participation in one another by meeting communal and personal needs.

8.6 Conclusion

Three things must be said in concluding this chapter. First, a Trinitarian approach to reading the GOJ helps not only to unearth corporateness but also the centrality of holiness to the Gospel. It follows that when we begin with the Trinity as John does, everything falls into place. Second, the identification of covenant motifs in the GOJ in recent scholarship[102] sets the base for understanding the ecclesiology of the Gospel. The link between the corporate metaphors and the covenant motifs legitimizes thoughts concerning the centrality of holiness in John. Third, contrary to popular suggestions regarding the absence of a strong ethic in the GOJ, this chapter has endeavored to show that holiness is integral to John's aim for his Gospel. If the aim of the Gospel is saving faith (20:30), a right relationship with the holy God through the Holy One of God, it is plausible to suggest that the Gospel is aimed at sharing the holiness of God with humankind.

---

101. Bruce, *Gospel*, 278.

102. See Chennattu, *Discipleship*, who brings fresh thoughts on Johannine discipleship and the covenant language of the Gospel.

CHAPTER 9

Conclusion

9.1 Summary

This thesis shows the extent to which communal holiness is central to John's use of the vine metaphor. This is developed in line with usage of the metaphor elsewhere in the OT and 2TP and further elucidated in light of John's Trinitarian theology and African hospitality. In the Johannine corpus, holiness is modelled by the mutual abiding of the divine family and enabled as the community is invited into participation in the divine family, with all its implications for the ethics of the new covenant people of God. For the people of God mutual abiding implies a deep relationship with God, a relationship that issues in the love life of the community (13:34; 15:9-17). The thesis argues that communal holiness expressed in corporateness, solidarity, hospitality, empathy, and care for the poor and marginalized is central to the Johannine vine metaphor.

A survey of secondary literature on the vine metaphor shows that scholars do not demonstrate the extent to which OT and 2TP usage of the metaphor illumines understanding of John. Scholarly consensus that refers to Israel as God's vine serving as the plausible backdrop to the metaphor is helpful. However, since the scholars do not engage the polemical tone of the metaphor, they give insufficient attention to the notion of communal holiness, particularly with regard to hospitality and care for the poor. This thesis attempts to breach this scholarly gap. Chapter 3 shows that viticulture, the vine, and the vine metaphor form an important part of the culture of the people of the OT and its milieu in the ANE. As a treasured product of the vine, wine is particularly important for social and religious reasons. In Egypt, Mesopotamia, and Palestine the vine is perceived symbolically as imparting divine life and particularly denoting the participation of the worshipper in the deity. The OT writers adopt the metaphor to depict Israel's union with YHWH in a covenant relationship in which Israel is bound by a covenant charter. As covenant partners of YHWH, Israel is holy and has an obligation to seek purity, ethical holiness, and to engage in YHWH's mission. Thus the OT writers modify the metaphor to include a strong ethical aspect. The modification includes coining a new way of living in righteousness and communal holiness: inviting one another "under the vine and fig tree." It is this ethical aspect that is highlighted in 2TP as writers use the metaphor negatively as a polemic against deficiency in communal holiness. Where Israel is unfaithful to YHWH the writers describe her as a fruitless vine or the vine of Sodom and Gomorrah that bears fruits of the serpent's venom. Where Israel is faithful to YHWH she is described as "pleasant trees" bearing fruits of justice and communal holiness. We build upon this backdrop as we interpret John's vine metaphor as a call to communal holiness. Although the formula is incomplete in John, appearing only as "under the fig tree" (1:47-49), its usage suggests understanding in continuity with 2TP and OT.

Drawing on this background the Johannine vine metaphor is seen as a covenant relationship in both its vertical and horizontal aspects. As a covenant metaphor the vine suggests comparison with Israel's covenant relationship with YHWH where issues of corporateness, holiness, purity, monotheism, and the *missio Dei* are pertinent. Careful intertextual examination of the aspects of the vine helps us show how John uses them in 15:1-17 to enhance the themes that are pertinent to a covenant relationship. Particularly conspicuous is John's description of a covenant relationship as a mutual indwelling, the highest thinkable intimacy in a relationship. For John this intimacy is modelled by the Father and the Son, who as a divine family mutually indwell one another, are open to one another, and live a life of sharing and having in common.

Since 15:1-17 steps up a covenant relationship to a mutual indwelling of the parties involved, the research follows John and gives priority to the mutual abiding theme. When read within the context of John's Trinitarian theology, the mutuality of the divine family presents a perfect model for the call to mutual abiding that dominates John 15:1-17. In this research we highlight this mutuality and juxtapose it with John's hospitality language to illuminate the hospitality, solidarity, and shared life of the new people of God. In line with the purpose of the thesis, corporateness and shared life are emphasized showing how they are underscored by the vine metaphor in John's stress upon mutual abiding.

We further redefine mutual abiding in culturally relevant language: hospitality, a language which, though not foreign to ancient Israel, is relevant to our context in Africa. The African ideas of communality, solidarity and open-ended kinship present good models for interpreting the vine metaphor. The philosophy of *buntfu* illuminates biblical hospitality by highlighting the participation of one in another's life in a community setting where hospitality and solidarity in times of difficulty are integral to being human. While there is no suggestion that the *Bantfu* are perfect, the suggestion is made that these cultures have something to offer to contemporary western cultures where the individual has priority sometimes to the virtual exclusion of concern for the community. We suggest that the notions of community, kinship, and *buntfu*, which form three pillars of *Bantfu* hospitality, provide living examples of mutuality and shared life within the community. *Buntfu* corporateness is compatible with Trinitarian life and is true of life among the new covenant people of God.

Finally, we suggest that a combination of the themes of corporateness and holiness illuminate the GOJ. Both themes are clearly articulated from the inception of the Gospel and have antecedents in OT and 2TP. Holiness and corporateness are linked to covenant theology. Holiness within the covenant is contingent upon a right relationship with YHWH and obedience to Torah, suggesting strong ethical implications. For John the vine metaphor is a perfect vehicle for combining these two themes. The various aspects of 15:1-17 such as fruit-bearing, cleansing, mutual abiding, and love are John's language of holiness. They are matched elsewhere by the

writer's motifs of incarnation (1:14), new birth (1:12; 3:1-21), and sanctification (17:17), all of which include communal holiness as an important
aspect. We, therefore, end by discussing the aspects of the vine metaphor
that function as holiness language and strengthen our argument by discussing relevant motifs in John where holiness is pertinent.

9.2 Contribution to Scholarship

Several aspects of this thesis show the contribution it makes to
Johannine scholarship.

First, it undertakes a reading of the vine metaphor in the light of its
background in ANE viticulture and religion and draw on that background
to interpret the vine metaphor in 15:1-17. Research on the Johannine
vine metaphor has often lacked important historical details relating to
viticulture and vine metaphorical speech in the ANE, OT, and 2TP. A
wealth of background knowledge is available in the works of Goodenough
(1953-1965), Seltan (1957), and the recent works of McGovern (2003)
and Unwin (2003). Keener (2003) makes some use of this resource but
could have gone further. He leaves out some necessary cultural details and
implications for the contemporary church, which this thesis provides.

Second, interpreting 15:1-17 as a communal holiness text is another key
contribution. The recent works of Brower and Bauckham[1] identify holiness
as an important theme in John. Neither pays particular attention to the vine
metaphor. Nevertheless they present arguments supporting the concept of
holiness as a significant theme in John. The uniqueness of this research
is in the reading of the vine metaphor as a holiness text and weaving of
this metaphor into the whole tapestry of Johannine holiness theology. To
substantiate the claim that the vine metaphor fits well into John's holiness
theology, we have demonstrated how the various images within the metaphor might be read, embedding John's language of holiness in the vine. In
chapter 7 other motifs that inform the writer's language were addressed

---

1. Brower, *Gospels*; Bauckham, "Holiness," in *HENT*, 95-113.

to show that holiness is not only a theme within the vine metaphor but runs through the Gospel. Each of these "aspects of holiness" include inter/intratexts and so represent contributions to scholarship of the GOJ.

Third, our interpretation of the mutual abiding motif is another significant contribution. It takes into consideration how the motif is used elsewhere to allude to the covenant and to invite the people of God to show their covenant status by practising communal holiness. Although Kanagaraj[2] identifies mutual abiding as the central theme of 15:1-17, emphasizing unity and communal life, he misses the link to the temple motif and the presence of hospitality as an expression of communal holiness. Thus the thesis argues on the basis of the intra/intertextual links that mutual abiding refers to the hospitable reception of one another, including meeting social needs. The postulation of hospitality as the proper application for mutual abiding, though building upon other scholars,[3] includes aspects only addressed here. For example, the post-resurrection offer of Trinitarian hospitality to Peter and how that incident becomes a model for dealing with apostates and lapsers in the church.

Fourth, the writer's use of anthropological insights from the African philosophy of *buntfu* and its emphasis upon hospitality is unique in vine metaphorical scholarship. The relevance of this is found in the similarities the Swazi have with the Jews in culture and an example of a culture whose hallmark is in corporate existence. The perception that "a person is a person in community," although expressed differently, is shared by scholars of Trinitarian theology who emphasize the practical implications for the life of the church.[4] For the *Bantfu* hospitality, mutuality, generosity, and solidarity in difficulty sum up what it means to be human. The use of a familiar philosophy to illustrate the complex notion of Trinitarian hospitality in the GOJ will no doubt help the writer's audience in his context in Africa. Hopefully it will also challenge readers to evaluate and rework the

---

2. Kanagaraj, *Mysticism*; Ford, *Redeemer*.
3. For example, Cantarella, *Hospitality*.
4. See Cunningham, *These Three*; Gunton, *Promise*; Barton, "Christian Community"; Gruenler, *Trinity*; Boff, *Holy Trinity*; Brower, *Gospels*.

imperfections in Bantfu hospitality in the light of the perfect hospitality of the divine family.

Fifth, this research raises consciousness of the need to call readers to response.[5] This writer sees the vine metaphor as offering a polemic against social injustice and a public declaration of identification with the marginalized of society. It is an outright rejection of war and a vote for justice, peace, and solidarity. This is deliberately set out because of the way in which the vine metaphor is used in OT prophetic speech. Since the vine metaphor is almost always wrapped in the fabric of polemic and call to response, the thesis suggests that interpretation of the Johannine vine metaphor must invite response. This is also in line with John's purpose for his Gospel to invite a faith response from readers (20:31).

9.3 Implications for Further Research

Due to limitations in space, this research leaves gaps which may be filled by further study. Some of the themes introduced in this research are never developed fully and this can be done in a study germane to them.

First, the idea of the Father as Gardener in 15:1 needs to be developed further drawing on various methodological approaches. For example, an intertextual approach can lead to texts referring to the fatherhood of God or texts representing the people of God in plant metaphors. This research has only managed to scratch the surface in both directions. There is no doubt that a study dedicated entirely to this idea can yield significant results.

Second, the idea of fruit-bearing in the GOJ also remains fertile ground for research. The centrality of the idea as the sole purpose for engaging in viticulture is the reason it must attract scholarly attention. Fruit-bearing has received little attention from scholars yet it is an important aspect of Johannine discipleship. The failure to reach a consensus regarding what sort of fruits are in view where the idea is used is another reason it must be researched. The idea may be explored from its backdrop in the OT

---

5. See chapter 5.

and 2TP literature, where there is no speculation regarding the possible interpretation of fruit.

Third, the possible connection between John's vine metaphor and the use of the metaphor in Zechariah to refer to a messianic dream time of peace ushered by YHWH's servant the Branch needs further careful examination. This can be done in connection with John's portrayal of Jesus as Jewish Messiah and later Jewish texts linking the vine to the Messiah (e.g. 4 Ezra 7:28-29).

Bibliography

Abelson, J. *Jewish Mysticism*. London: G. Bell and Sons Ltd., 1913.

Adewuya, James Ayodeji. *Holiness and Community in 2 Corinthians 6:14-7:1: Paul's View of Communal Holiness in the Corinthian Correspondence*. New York: Peter Lang, 2003.

Adeyemo, Tokunboh, General ed. *Africa Bible Commentary: A One Volume Commentary Written by 70 African Scholars*. Nairobi: WordAlive Publishers, 2006.

Akpunonu, Peter Damian. *The Vine, Israel and the Church*. New York: Peter Lang, 2004.

Albright, W. F. "Recent Discoveries in Palestine and the Gospel of St. John." Pages 153-171 in *The Background of the New Testament and its Eschatology*. Edited by W. D. Davis and D. Daube. Cambridge: Cambridge University Press, 1956.

Alexander, T. Desmond. *New Dictionary of Biblical Theology*. Edited by T. Desmond Alexander and Brian S. Rosner. Leicester: Inter Varsity Press, 2000.

Anderson, Paul N. *The Fourth Gospel and the Quest for Jesus: Modern Foundations Reconsidered*. New York; London: T&T Clark, 2007.

Artebury, Andrew E. *Entertaining Angels: Early Christian Hospitality in its Mediterranean Setting*. Sheffield: Sheffield Phoenix Press, 2005.

Ashton, John. *Understanding the Fourth Gospel*. Oxford: Clarendon, 1991.

Aune, David E. *Revelation 1-5*. Word Biblical Commentary 52. Dallas: Word Books, Publisher, 1997.

Bach, Robert. „Bauen und Pflanzen." Pages 7-32 in *Studien zur Theologie der alttestamentlichen Überlieferungen*. Neukirchen: Neukirchener Verlag, 1961.

Bammel, Ernst, "The Farewell Discourse of the Evangelist John and its Jewish Heritage." *Tyndale Bulletin* 44 (1993): 103-119.

Barclay, William. *The Gospel of John* Vol. 2. Revised edition. Philadelphia: Westminster Press, 1975.

Baron, David. *The Visions and Prophecies of Zechariah*. Grand Rapids: New Kregel Publications, 1972.

Baron, Salo Wittmayer. *The Jewish Community: Its History and Structure to the American Revolution* Vol.1. Westport, Connecticut: Greenwood Press Publishers, 1942.

Barrett, C. K. *The Gospel According to John: An Introduction with Commentary and Notes on The Greek Text*. 2nd ed. London: SPCK, 1978.

Bartlett, John R. *1 Maccabees*. Sheffield: Sheffield Academic Press, 1998.

Barton, Stephen C. "Christian Community in the Light of the Gospel of John." Pages 279-301 in *Christology, Controversy & Community: New Testament Essays in Honor of David R. Catchpole*. Edited by David G. Horrell and Christopher M. Tuckett. Leiden: Koninklijke Brill, 1999.

Bauckham, Richard. "Monotheism and Christology in the Gospel of John." Pages 148-166 in *Contours of Christology in the New Testament*. Edited by Richard N. Longenecker. Grand Rapids; Cambridge: Eerdmans, 2005.

———. "The Holiness of Jesus and His Disciples in the Gospel of John." Pages 95-113 in *Holiness and Ecclesiology in the New Testament*. Edited by K. E. Brower and Andy Johnson. Grand Rapids; Cambridge: Eerdmans, 2007.

———. "Synoptic Parousia Parables and the Apocalypse." *New Testament Studies* 23 (1977): 162-176.

———. *The Testimony of the Beloved Disciple: Narrative, History, and Theology in the Gospel of John*. Grand Rapids: Baker Academic, 2007.

Baumgarten, Joseph M. "4Q500 and the Ancient Conception of the Lord's Vineyard." *Journal of Jewish Studies* 40 (1989): 1-6.

Beale, G. K. *The Book of Revelation*. New International Greek Testament Commentary. Grand Rapids; Cambridge: Eerdmans, 1999.

Beasley-Murray, George R. *John*. Word Biblical Commentary 36. Nashville: Thomas Nelson Publishers, Second edition, 1999.

———. *John*. Word Biblical Commentary 36. Waco: Word Books Publisher, 1987.

Beirne, Margaret M. *Women and Men in the Fourth Gospel: A Genuine Discipleship of Equals*. *Journal for the Study of the New Testament* 242. Sheffield: Sheffield Academic Press, 2003.

Beyerlin, Walter., ed. *Near Eastern Religious Texts Relating to the Old Testament*. Old Testament Library. London: SCM Press, 1978.

Bimson, John J. Consulting ed. *Illustrated Encyclopedia of Bible Places*. Leicester: InterVarsity Press, 1995.

Blomberg, Craig L. *Contagious Holiness: Jesus' Meals with Sinners*. Downers Grove: InterVarsity Press, 2005.

Boff, Leonardo. *Holy Trinity, Perfect Community*. New York: Orbis Books, 2000.

Bogart, John. *Orthodox and Heretical Perfectionism in the Johannine Community as Evident in the First Epistle of John*. Missoula: Scholars Press, 1977.

Bolchazy, Ladislaus J. *Hospitality in Early Rome: Livy's Concept of Its Humanizing Force*. Chicago: Ares Publishers, 1977.

Bonner, P. *Kings, Commoners and Concessionaires: The Evolution and Dissolution of the Nineteenth Century Swazi State*. Johannesburg: Raven, 1983.

Booth, A. *Swaziland: Tradition and Change in a Southern African Kingdom*. Boulder: Westview Press, 1983.

Borg, Marcus J. *Conflict, Holiness and Politics in the Teachings of Jesus*. Pennsylvania: Trinity Press International, 1998.

Borgmann, Dean. *When Kumbaya Is Not Enough: A Practical Theology of Youth Ministry*. Peabody: Hendricksen Publishers, 1997.

Borowski, Oded. *Agriculture in Iron Age Israel*. University Macrofilms International, 1979.

Bowen, Paul N. *A Longing For Land: Tradition and Change in Swazi Agricultural Community*. Avebury: Aldershot, 1993.

Brodie, Thomas L. *The Gospel According to John*. Oxford: Oxford University Press, 1993.

Brooke, George J. "The Dead Sea Scrolls and New Testament Ecclesiology." Pages 1-18 in *Holiness and Ecclesiology in the New Testament*. Edited by Kent E. Brower and Andy Johnson. Grand Rapids/Cambridge: Eerdmans, 2007.

———. "Christ and the Law in John 7-10." Pages 102-112 in *Law and Religion: Essays in the Place of the Law in Israel and Early Christianity*. Edited by Barnabas Lindars. Cambridge: James Clarke and Company, 1988.

———. *The Dead Sea Scrolls and the New Testament: Essays in Mutual Illumination*. London: SPCK, 2005.

Brower, Kent E. and Andy Johnson. "Introduction: Holiness and the Ekklēsia of God." Pages xvi-xxiv in *Holiness and Ecclesiology in the New Testament*. Edited by Kent E. Brower and Andy Johnson. Grand Rapids; Cambridge: Eerdmans, 2007.

———. *Holiness in the Gospels*. Kansas City: Beacon Hill Press of Kansas City, 2005.

———. "Purity of Heart." Pages 15-26 in *Biblical Resources for Holiness Preaching (2): From Text to Sermon*. Edited by H. Ray Dunning. Kansas City: Beacon Hill Press of Kansas City, 1993.

———. Dwight Swanson, and Gordon Thomas. *Christian Holiness in Biblical Perspective: Introductory Essays for BS600*. Nazarene Theological College. Revised edition, 2002.

Brown, Raymond E. *The Gospel According to John*. 2 vols. The Anchor Bible Vols. 29, 29A. New York: Doubleday, 1966-1970.

———. "The Qumran Scrolls and the Johannine Gospel and Epistles." Pages 183-207 in *The Scrolls and the New Testament*. Edited by K. Stendahl. London: SCM Press, 1958.

Brown, Tricia Gates. *Spirit in the Writings of John: Johannine Pneumatology in Social-scientific Perspective*. Edited by Stanley Porter. Journal of Studies in the New Testament: Supplement Series 253; London: T&T Clark International, 2003.

Bruce, F. F. *Second Thoughts on the Dead Sea Scrolls*. London: Paternoster Press, 1966.

———. *The Gospel of John: Introduction, Exposition and Notes*. Grand Rapids: Eerdmans, 1983.

———. *The Epistles of John: Introduction, Exposition and Notes*. Grand Rapids: Eerdmans, 1970.

Brueggemann, Walter. *A Commentary on Jeremiah: Exile and Homecoming*. Grand Rapids: Eerdmans, 1998.

———. ""Vine and Fig Tree": A Case Study in Imagination and Criticism." *Catholic Biblical Quarterly* 43 (1981): 188-204.

Bruner, Frederick Dale. *Matthew: A Commentary* Volume 2: The Churchbook. Revised and Expanded Edition. Michigan/Cambridge: Eerdmans, 1990.

Bryan, Steven M. *Jesus and Israel's Traditions of Judgement and Restoration.* Cambridge: Cambridge University Press, 2002.

———. "The Eschatological Temple in John 14." *Bulletin for Biblical Research* 15.2 (2005): 187-198.

Bultmann, Rudolph. *The Gospel of John: A Commentary*. Philadelphia: Westminster Press, 1971.

———. *The Johannine Epistles: A Commentary on the Johannine Epistles.* Hermeneia. Translated by R. Phillip O'Hara, Lane C. McGaughy and Robert W. Funk. Edited by Robert W. Funk. Philadelphia: Fortress, 1973.

Burge, Gary M. "Territorial Religion, Johannine Christology, and the Vineyard of John 15." Pages 384-396 in *Jesus of Nazareth Lord and Christ: Essays on the Historical Jesus and New Testament Christology.* Edited by Joel B. Green and Marx Turner. Grand Rapids: Eerdmans, 1994.

Burridge, Richard A. "Who writes, why, and for whom?" Pages 99-115 in *The Written Gospel*. Edited by Markus Bockmuehl and Donald A. Hagner. Cambridge: Cambridge University Press, 2005.

Cantarella, Tatiana. "Hospitality Language in the Gospel of John and Its Implications for Christian Community." M. A. diss., Nazarene Theological Seminary, 2006.

Carson, D. A. *The Gospel According to John*. Grand Rapids: Eerdmans, 1991.

Chaney, Marvin. "Whose Sour Grapes? The Addressees of Isaiah 5:1-7 in the Light of Political Economy." *Semeia* 87 (1999): 105-122.

Charlesworth, James H. *The Old Testament Pseudepigrapha: Apocalyptic Literature and the Testaments.* London: Darton, Longman & Todd, 1983.

———. *The Dead Sea Scrolls and the Historical Jesus.* London: Doubleday: 1992.

———. "Jesus as Son and the Righteous Teacher as Gardner." Pages 140-175 in *Jesus and the Dead Sea Scrolls.* Edited by James H. Charlesworth. New York: Doubleday, 1992.

Chennattu, Rekha M. *Johannine Discipleship as Covenant Relationship*. Peabody: Hendrickson, 2006.

Chilton, Bruce. *A Feast of Meanings: Eucharistic Theologies from Jesus through Johannine Circles*. Supplements to Novum Testamentum. Leiden; New York; Kohn: Brill, 1994.

Clendenin, Daniel B. *Eastern Orthodox Christianity: A Western Perspective*. Grand Rapids: Baker Books, 1994.

Cottrell, Leonard. *Life Under the Pharaohs*. London: Evans Brothers Limited, 1955.

Crump, David. "Re-examining the Johannine Trinity: Perichoresis or deification." *Scottish Journal of Theology* 59 (2006): 395-412.

Culpepper, R. Alan. *Anatomy of the Fourth Gospel: A Study in Literary Design*. Philadelphia: Fortress Press, 1983.

———. "Anti-Judaism in the Fourth Gospel as a Theological Problem for Christian Interpreters." Pages 61-83 in *Anti-Judaism and the Fourth Gospel: Papers for the eLeuven Colloquium, 2000*. Edited by R. Bieringer, D. Pollefeyt and F. Vandecasteele-Vannneuville. Assen, The Netherlands: Royal Van Gorcum, 2001.

———. "The Johannine Hypodeigma: A Reading of John 13." *Semeia* 53 (1991): 133-152.

———. "The Odes of Solomon and the Gospel of John." *Catholic Biblical Quarterly* 35 (1973): 298-322.

———. "The Pivot of John's Prologue." *New Testament Studies* 27 (1980): 1-31.

Cunningham, David S. *These Three are One: The Practice of Trinitarian Theology*. Oxford: Blackwell, 1998.

Curtis, Adrian. *Oxford Bible Atlas*. 4th ed. Oxford: Oxford University Press, 2007.

———. *Psalms*. Epworth Commentaries. Peterborough: Epworth Press, 2004.

D'Angelo, Mary Rose. "Abba and "Father": Imperial Theology and the Jesus Traditions." *Journal of Biblical Literature* 4 (1992): 611-630.

Davies, W. D. *The Gospel and the Land: Early Christianity and Jewish Territorial Doctrine*. Berkeley: U of California Press, 1974.

Deasley, Alex R. *The Shape of Qumran Theology*. Carlisle: Paternoster Press, 2000.

Deissmann, Adolf. *Light From the Ancient East: The New Testament Illustrated by Recently Discovered Texts of The Graeco-Roman World*. Trans. by Lionel R. M. Strachan. 4th ed. New York: George H. Doran Company, 1927.

Dennis, John A. *Jesus' Death and the Gathering of True Israel: The Johannine Appropriation of Restoration Theology in the Light of John 11:47-52.* Tubingen: Mohr Siebeck, 2006.

Dickson, Kwesi A. *Theology in Africa.* London: Darton, Longman and Todd, 1984.

Dlamini, Pauline. Interviewed on 23 December, 2008.

Dodd, C. H. "The First Epistle of John and the Fourth Gospel." *Bulletin of the John Rylands Library* 21 (1937): 129-156.

———. *Historical Tradition in the Fourth Gospel.* Cambridge: Cambridge University Press, 1963.

———. *The Interpretation of the Fourth Gospel.* Cambridge: Cambridge University Press, 1968.

Domeris, William R. "The Confession of Peter According to John 6:69." *Tyndale Bulletin* 44 (1993): 155-167.

Dunn, James D. G. "Let John Be John: A Gospel for Its Time." Pages 293-322 in *The Gospel and the Gospels.* Edited by Peter Stuhlmacher. Grand Rapids: Eerdmans, 1991.

———. "The Washing of the Disciples' Feet in John 13:1-20." *Zeitschrift für die Neutestamentliche Wissenschaft und die Kunde der Älteren Kirche* 61 (1970): 247-252.

Edwards, Ruth B. "The Christological Basis of Johannine Footwashing." Pages 367-383 in *Jesus of Nazareth Lord and Christ: Essays on the Historical Jesus and New Testament Christology.* Edited by Joel B. Green and Max Turner. Grand Rapids: Eerdmans, 1994.

Elliot, Mark A. *The Survivors of Israel: A Reconsideration of the Theology of Pre-Christian Judaism.* Grand Rapids; Cambridge: Eerdmans, 2000.

Erickson, Millard J. *God in Three Persons: A Contemporary Interpretation of the Trinity.* Grand Rapids: Baker Books, 1995.

Evans, Craig A. *Word and Glory: On the Exegetical and Theological Background of John's Prologue.* Sheffield: SAP, 1993.

Evans, M. J. "Blessing/curse." Pages 397-401 in *New Dictionary of Biblical Theology.* Edited by T. D. Alexander and Brian S. Rosner. Leicester: InterVarsity Press, 2000.

Evans-Pritchard, E. *Nuer Religion.* New York and Oxford: Oxford University Press, 1956.

Feliks, Jehuda. "Vine." Pages 155-157 in vol. 16 of the *Encyclopaedia Judaica. Supplementary Entries.* Edited by Cecil Roth. 16 vols. Jerusalem: Keter Publishing House, 1971-1972.

Fenton, J. C. *The Gospel According to John.* Clarendon, 1970.

Fogelqvist, Anders. "The Red-Dressed Zionists: Symbols of Power in a Swazi Independent Church." PhD diss., Uppsala University, 1986.

Ford, J. Massyngbaerde. *Redeemer, Friend, Mother: Salvation in Antiquity and in the Gospel of John.* Minneapolis: Fortress Press, 1997.

Frakel, Rafael. *Wine and Oil Production in Antiquity in Israel and Other Mediterranean Countries.* Sheffield: SAP, 1999.

Freedman, David Noel. "Divine Commitment and Human Obligation: The Covenant Theme." *Interpretation* 18 (1964): 419-431.

———— and David Miano. "People of the New Covenant." Pages 7-26 in *The Concept of the Covenant in the Second Temple Period.* Edited by Stanley E. Porter and Jacqueline C. R. de Roo. Leiden: Brill, 2003.

Freyne, Sean. *Galilee from Alexander the Great to Hadrian: A Study of Second Temple Judaism.* Wilmington: Michael Glazier, 1980.

————. *Galilee, Jesus and the Gospels: Literary Approaches and Historical Investigations.* Philadelphia: Fortress Press, 1988.

Friesen, Steven J. *Imperial Cults and the Apocalypse of John: Reading Revelation in the Ruins.* Oxford: Oxford University Press, 2001.

Fujita, Shozo. "The Metaphor of Plant in Jewish Literature of the Intertestamental Period." *Journal for the Study of Judaism* 7 (1976): 30-45.

Gager, John G. *Curse Tablets and Binding Spells from the Ancient World.* NY; Oxford: Oxford University Press, 1992.

————. *Kingdom and Community: The Social World of Early Christianity.* Englewood Cliffs, NJ: Prentice-Hall, 1975.

Gagne, Armand J. Joe Jr. *The Testimony of the Fourth Evangelist to the Johannine Community: We Know His Witness is True.* Crewe: Trafford Publishing, 2004.

Gaston, Lloyd. *No Stone on Another: Studies on the significance of the Fall of Jerusalem in the Synoptic Gospels.* Supplements to Novum Testamentum 23. Leiden: Brill, 1970.

Geller, Jeremy. "Wine making." Pages in *Encyclopaedia of the Archaeology of Ancient Egypt*. Edited by Kathryn A. Bard. London; New York: Routledge, 1999.

Goodenough, E. R. *Jewish Symbolism in the Greco-Roman Period*: 13 Volumes. New York: Pantheon, 1956.

Gorny, Ronald. "Viticulture and Ancient Anatolia." Pages 133-174 in *The Origins and Ancient History of Wine*. Edited by Patrick E. McGovern; Stuart M. Flemming and Solomon H. Katz. Luxembourg: Gordon and Breach Publishers, 1995.

Grenz, Stanley J. *Theology For The Community of God*. Grand Rapids; Cambridge: Eerdmans, 1994.

Griffith, Terry. ""The Jews Who Had Believed in Him" (8:31) and the Motif of Apostasy in the Gospel of John." Pages 183-192 in *The Gospel of John and Christian Theology*. Edited by Richard Bauckham and Carl Mosser. Grand Rapids: Eerdmans, 2008.

Gruenler, Royce Gordon. *The Trinity in the Gospel of John: A Thematic Commentary on the Fourth Gospel*. Grand Rapids: Baker Book House, 1986.

Gunton, Colin E. *Father, Son and Holy Spirit: Toward a Fully Trinitarian Theology*. London; New York: T&T Clark, 2003.

———. *The Promise of Trinitarian Theology*. 2nd ed. Edinburgh: T&T Clark, 1997.

———. *The Creator*. Edinburgh: Edinburgh University Press, 1998.

Guthrie, Donald. *New Testament Theology*. Leicester: InterVarsity Press, 1981.

Halliday, M. A. K. *Language and Social Semiotic: A Social Interpretation of Language as Meaning*. London: Edward Arnold, 1978.

Hammond-Tooke, W. D. *The Bantu Speaking Peoples of Southern Africa*. London: Routledge & Kegan Paul, 1937.

Harrill, Albert J. "Cannibalistic Language in the Fourth Gospel and Greco-Roman Polemics of Factionalism (John 6:52-66)." *Journal of Biblical Literature* 127 (2008): 133-158.

Haws, Charles G. "Suffering, hope and forgiveness: the ubuntu theology of Desmond Tutu." *Scottish Journal of Theology* 62 (2009): 477-489.

Hayward, Robert. "The Vine and its Products as Theological Symbols in First Century Palestinian Judaism." *The Durham University Journal* 82 (1990): 9-18.

Hengel, Martin. *Judaism and Hellenism : Studies in Their Encounter in Palestine During the Early Hellenistic Period.* 1st English ed. 2 vols. London: SCM Press, 1974.

———. "The Prologue of the Gospel of John as the Gateway to Christological Truth." Pages 265-294 in *The Gospel of John and Christian Theology.* Edited by Richard Bauckham and Carl Mosser. Grand Rapids: Eerdmans, 2008.

Hillers, D. G. *Covenant: The History of a Biblical Idea.* Baltimore: John Hopkins University Press, 1969.

Hoernle, A. Winifred. "Social Organization." Pages 67-94 in *The Bantu Speaking Tribes of South Africa: An Ethnological Survey.* Edited by I. Schapera. London: George Routledge & Sons, 1937.

Hoppe, O. F. M., Leslie J. *There Shall Be No Poor Among You: Poverty in the Bible.* Nashville: Abingdon, 2004.

Hoskyns, Edwyn Clement. *The Fourth Gospel.* Edited and completed by Francis Noel Davey. 2nd rev. ed. London: Faber and Faber, 1947.

Ihenacho, David Asonye. *The Community of Eternal Life: The Study of the Meaning of Life for the Johannine Community.* Lanham; New York; Oxford: University Press of America, 2001.

Jagt, Krijn van der. *Anthropological Approaches to the Interpretation of the Bible.* New York: United Bible Societies, 2002.

James, Michael. "Pruning Grape Vines." No pages. Cited 30 January 2008. Online: http://www.squidoo.com/pruning-grapes-vines.

———, T. G. H. "The Earliest History of Wine and its Importance in Ancient Egypt." Pages 197-214 in *The Origins and Ancient History of Wine.* Edited by Patrick E. McGovern, Stuart J. Fleming, and Solomon H. Katz. Luxembourg: Gordon and Breach Publishers, 1996.

Jensen, Alexander S. *John's Gospel as Witness: The Development of the Early Christian Language of Faith.* Aldershot: Ashgate, 2004.

Jeremias, Joachim. *The Eucharistic Words of Jesus.* Translated by Norman Perrin; London: SCM Press, 1966.

Jones, A. H. M. *The Herods of Judea.* Oxford: Oxford University Press, 1938.

Josephus. Translated by H. St. J. Thackeray et al. 10 vols. Loeb Classical Library. Cambridge, Mass.: Harvard University Press, 1926–1965.

Josephus, Flavius. *The Works of Josephus.* Complete and Unabridged. New Updated Edition. Translated by William Whiston. Peabody: Hendricksen Publishers, 1987.

Kanagaraj, Jey J. *"Mysticism" in the Gospel of John: An Inquiry into its Background.* Journal for the Study of the New Testament Series 158. Sheffield: SAP, 1998.

Karris, Robert J. *Jesus and the Marginalized in St. John's Gospel.* Collegeville: Liturgical Press, 1990.

Kee, Howard Clark. *Who Are the People of God? Early Christian Models of Community.* New Haven; London: Yale University Press, 1995.

Keener, Craig S. "Lamb." Pages 641-642 in *Dictionary of the Later New Testament and Its Developments.* Edited by Ralph P. Martin and Peter H. Davids. Downers Grove: InterVarsity Press, 1997.

———. The Gospel of John: *A Commentary.* 2 Vols. Peabody: Hendrickson Publishers, 2003.

Kees, H. *Ancient Egypt.* London: Faber & Faber, 1961.

Kerr, Alan R. *The Temple of Jesus' Body: The Temple Theme in the Gospel of John.* Journal for the Study of the New Testament Supplement Series 220. Sheffield: Sheffield Academic Press, 2002.

Kierspel, Lars. *The Jews and the World in the Fourth Gospel: Parallelism, Function, and Context.* Tübingen, Germany: Mohr Siebeck, 2006.

Kittel, G., and G. Friedrich, eds. *Theological Dictionary of the New Testament.* Translated by G. W. Bromiley. 10 vols. Grand Rapids: Eerdmans, 1964–1976.

Klauk, Hans-Joseph. *The Religious Context of Early Christianity: A Guide to Graeco-Roman Religions.* Trans. by Brian McNeil. Minneapolis: Fortress Press, 2003.

Klink, Edward W. III. *The Sheep of the Fold: The Audience and Origin of the Gospel of John.* Cambridge: Cambridge University Press, 2007.

Kloppenborg Verbin, John S. "Egyptian Viticultural Practices and the Citation of Isaiah 5:1-7 in Mark 12:1-9." *Novum Testamentum* 44 (2002): 134-159.

Knight, John A. *The Holiness Pilgrimage: Developing a Life-Style that Reflects Christ.* Kansas City: Beacon Hill Press of Kansas City, 1986.

Koenig, John. *New Testament Hospitality: Partnership with Strangers as Promise and Mission*. Philadelphia: Fortress Press, 1985.

Koester, Craig R. *Symbolism in the Fourth Gospel: Meaning, Mystery, Community*. 2nd ed. Minneapolis: Fortress Press, 2003.

———. *The Dwelling Place of God: The Tabernacle in the Old Testament, Intertestamental Jewish Literature, and the New Testament*. Catholic Biblical Quarterly Monograph Series 22. Washington D.C.: Catholic Biblical Association of America, 1989.

———. "The Savior of the World." *Journal of Biblical Literature* 4 (1990): 665-680.

Köstenberger, Andreas J. *Gospel of John*. Grand Rapids: Baker Academic, 2004.

———, and Scott R. Swain. *Father, Son and Spirit: The Trinity in John's Gospel*. NSBT; Downers Grove: InterVarsity Press, 2008.

Kruse, Colin G. *John*. Tyndale New Testament Commentaries 4. Nottingham: InterVarsity Press, 2003.

Kümmel, W. G. *Introduction to the New Testament*. 2nd ed. Trans. H. C. Kee; New York: Abingdon, 1975.

Kuper, Hilder. *The Swazi: A South African Kingdom*. 2nd ed. New York: Holt, Rinehart and Winston, 1963.

———. *An African Aristocracy: Rank Among the Swazi*. New York: Africana Publishing Company, 1980.

Kysar, Robert. "Johannine Metaphor—Meaning and Function: A Literary Case Study of John 10:1-8." *Semeia* 53 (1991): 81-111.

LaCugna, Cathrine. *God for Us: The Trinity and Christian Life*. San Francisco: Harper, 1991.

Lang, Bernhard. "Introduction: Anthropology as a new model for Biblical Studies." Pages 1-25 in *Anthropological Approaches to the Old Testament*. Edited by Bernhard Lang. London: SPCK, 1985.

Lesko, L. *King Tut's Wine Cellar*. Berkeley: B. C. Scribe, 1977.

Lightfoot, R. H. *St. John's Gospel: A Commentary*. Edited by C. F. Evans. London: Oxford University Press, 1960.

Lindars, Barnabas. *The Gospel of John*. The New Century Bible Commentary. London: Marshall & Morgan, & Scott, 1972.

Lossky, Vladimir. *The Mystical Theology of the Eastern Church*. London: James Clarke & Co., 1957.

Malatesta, Edward. *Interiority and Covenant: A Study of* εἶναι ἐν *and* μένειν ἐν *in the First Letter of Saint John*. Analecta Biblica 69. Rome: Biblical Institute Press, 1978.

Malbon, Elizabeth Struthers. "Ending at the Beginning: A Response." *Semeia* 52 (1990): 177-178.

Malina, Bruce J. "The Received View and What it Cannot Do: III John and Hospitality." *Semeia* 35 (1986): 171-194.

Malina Bruce J. and Richard L. Rohrbaugh. *Social-Science Commentary on the Gospel of John*. Minneapolis: Fortress Press, 1998.

Mandela, Nelson. "Ubuntu." No Pages. Cited 23 December, 2008. Online: http://ubuntu.wordpress.com/2006/06/01/the-meaning-of-ubuntu-explained -by-nelson-mandela/.

Marmon, Ellen L. "Teaching As Hospitality." *The Asbury Journal* 63 (2008): 33-40.

Marshall, I Howard. *Kept By The Power Of God: A Study of Perseverance and Falling Away*. Revised Edition. London: Epworth Press, 1995.

————. *New Testament Theology: Many Witnesses, One Gospel*. Downers Grove: InterVarsity Press, 2004.

Martinez, Florentino Garcia. *The Dead Sea Scrolls Translated*. Leiden: E. J. Brill, 1994.

Martyn, Louis J. *History and Theology in the Fourth Gospel*. 3rd ed. Louisville: Westminster John Knox, 2003.

Matsebula, J. S. M. *A History of Swaziland*. Cape Town: Longmans, Penguin, 1980.

Matsunaga, Kikuo. "Is John's Gospel Anti-Sacramental? A New Solution in the Light of the Evangelist's Milieu." *New Testament Studies* 27 (1981): 516-524.

Matthews, Victor H. "Treading the Winepress: Actual and Metaphorical Viticulture in the Ancient Near East." *Semeia* 86 (1999), 19-32.

Mays, James Luther. *Micah: A Commentary*. London: SCM Press, 1976.

Mbigi, Lovemore. *Ubuntu: The African Dream in Management*. Randburg: Knowledge Resources, 1997.

Mbiti, J. S. *African Religions and Philosophy*. London; Ibadan; Nairobi: Heinemann, 1969.

McCaffrey, James. *The House with Many Rooms: The Temple Theme in John 14:1-2*. Novum Testamentum Supplement Series 114. Roma: Editrice Pontificio Instituto Biblico, 1988.

McCarthy, D. J. "Covenant in the Old Testament." *Catholic Biblical Quarterly* 27 (1965): 217-240.

———. *Treaty and Covenant*. Rome: BIP, 1981.

McFall, L. "Serpent." Pages 773-75 in *New Dictionary of Biblical Theology*. Edited by T. D. Alexander and Brian S. Rosner. Leicester: InterVarsity Press, 2000.

McGovern, Patrick E. *Ancient Wine: The Search for the Origins of Viticulture*. Princeton and Oxford: Princeton University Press, 2003.

McLaughlin, G. A. *Commentary on the Gospel According to Saint John*. Salem: Convention Bookstore, 1973.

Meeks, Wayne. "The Ethics of the Fourth Evangelist." Pages 317-326 in *Exploring the GOJ: In Honor of D. Moody Smith*. Edited by R. Alan Culpepper and C. Clifton Black. Kentucky: John Knox Press, 1996.

———. "The Man From Heaven In Johannine Sectarianism." *Journal of Biblical Literature* 91 (1972): 44-72.

Meyers, Carol L. and Eric M. Meyers. *The Anchor Bible: Haggai, Zachariah 1-8: A New translation with Introduction and Commentary*. New York: Doubleday, 1987.

Miller, Ed. L. *Salvation-History in the Prologue of John: The Significance of John 1:3/4*. Leiden: Brill, 1989.

Milne, Bruce. *The Message of John*. The Bible Speaks Today: New Testament Series. Leicester: InterVarsity Press, 1993.

Miranda, Jose. *Being and the Messiah: The Message of St. John*. Translated by John Eagleson; New York: Orbis Books, 1977.

Moloney, Francis J. *Glory not Dishonor: Reading John 13-21*. Minneapolis: Fortress, 1998.

———. *The Gospel of John*. Sacra pagina 4. Collegeville: Liturgical Press, 1998.

Moltmann, Jürgen. *The Trinity and the Kingdom: The Doctrine of God*. Translated by Margaret Kohl. London: SPCK, 1981.

Morris, Leon. *Reflections on the Gospel of John.* 4 Vols; Grand Rapids: Baker Book House, 1986-1988.

————. *The Gospel According to John.* New International Commentary on the New Testament. Revised edition. Grand Rapids: Eerdmans, 1995.

————. *The Gospel According to John: The English Text with Introduction and Notes.* New International Commentary on the New Testament. Grand Rapids: Eerdmans, 1971.

————. *The Gospel According to Matthew.* Grand Rapids: Eerdmans, 1992.

Moule, C. F. D. "A Neglected Factor in the Interpretation of Johannine Eschatology." Pages 155-160 in *Studies in John Presented to Professor Dr. J. N. Sevenster on the Occasion of his Seventieth Birthday.* Supplements to Novum Testamentum 24; Leiden: Brill, 1970.

————. "The Individualism of the Fourth Gospel." *Novum Testamentum* 5 (1962): 171-186.

Mullins, Michael G., Alain Bouquet, and Larry E. Williams. *Biology of the Grapevine.* Cambridge: Cambridge University Press, 1992.

Negrul, M. A. "Evolution of cultivated forms of grapes." *Comptes rendues Academy of Science U. S. S. R.* 18 (1938): 585-88.

Nemet-Nejat, Karen Rhea. *Daily Life in Ancient Mesopotamia.* Westport; Connecticut; London: Greenwood Press, 1998.

Neyrey, Jerome H. "Worship in the Fourth Gospel: A Cultural Interpretation of John 14-17." *Biblical Theology Bulletin* 36 (2006), 107-117.

Ngewa, Samuel M. "John." Pages 1251-1296 in *Africa Bible Commentary: A One Volume Commentary Written by 70 African Scholars.* Edited by Tukunboh Adeyemo. Nairobi: WordAlive Publishers, 2006.

Nielsen, Kirsten. *There is Hope for a Tree: The Tree as Metaphor in Isaiah.* Journal of Studies in the Old Testament Supplement Series 65. Sheffield: Sheffield Academic Press, 1989.

Nyerere, Julius. "The Church's Role in Society." Pages 117-130 in *A Reader in African Christian Theology.* Edited by John Parratt. London: SPCK, 1987.

O'Day, Gail R. "Toward a Narrative-Critical Study of John." *Interpretation* 4 (1995): 341-346.

O'Grady, John F. "Shepherd and the Vine and the Branches." *Biblical Theology Bulletin* 8 (1978): 86-89.

Omer-Cooper, John. D. *The Zulu Aftermath: A 19th Century Revolution in Bantu Africa.* London: Longman, 1966.

Oswalt, John N. *Called to be Holy: A Biblical Perspective.* Nappanee: Evangel Publishing House, 1999.

Painter, John. *The Quest for the Messiah: The History, Literature and Theology of the Johannine Community.* 2nd ed. Edinburgh: T&T Clark, 2001.

Pamment, Margaret. "Path and Residence Metaphors in the Fourth Gospel." *Theology* 88 (1985): 118-124.

Pancaro, Severino. *The Law in the Fourth Gospel: The Torah and the Gospel Moses and Jesus, Judaism and Christianity.* Leiden: Brill, 1975.

Petersen, Norman. *The Gospel of John and the Sociology of Light: Language and Characterization in the Fourth Gospel.* Valley Forge: Trinity Press, 1993.

Phillips, Peter. *The Prologue of the Fourth Gospel: A Sequential Reading.* London: T&T Clark, 2006.

Pinnock, Clark D. *The Flame of Love.* Downer's Grove: InterVarsity Press, 1998.

Plantinga, Cornelius Jr., "The Fourth Gospel as Trinitarian Source Then and Now." Pages 303-321 in *Biblical Hermeneutics in Historical Perspective.* Edited by Mark S. Burrows and Paul Rorem. Grand Rapids: Eerdmans, 1991.

Poo, Mu-Chou. *Wine & Wine Offering in the Religion of Ancient Egypt.* London & New York: Kegan Paul International, 1995.

Powell, Marvin A. "Wine and the Vine in Ancient Mesopotamia: The Cuneiform Evidence." Pages 97-132 in *The Origins and Ancient History of Wine.* Edited by Patrick E. McGovern, Stuart J. Fleming, and Solomon H. Katz. Luxembourg: Gordon and Breach Publishers, 1996.

Porton, G. G. "The Grape Cluster in Jewish Literature and Art of Late Antiquity." *Journal of Jewish Studies* 27 (1976): 159-176.

Price, S. R. F. *Rituals and Power: The Roman Imperial Cult in Asia Minor.* Cambridge: Cambridge University Press, 1984.

Pritchard, James B., ed. *Ancient Near Eastern Texts Relating to the Old Testament.* 3rd ed. With Supplement, Princeton: Princeton University Press, 1969.

Pryor, John. *John: Evangelist of the Covenant People: The Narratives and Themes of the Fourth Gospel.* London: Darton, Longman & Todd, 1992.

Purkiser, W. T. *Exploring Christian Holiness* Vol. 1, Biblical Foundations. Kansas City: Beacon Hill of Kansas City, 1983.

Reed, David. "Rethinking John's Social Setting: Hidden Transcript, Antilanguage, and the Negotiation of the Empire." *Biblical Theology Bulletin* 36 (2006): 107-117.

Rensberger, David. *Johannine Faith and Liberating Community*. Philadelphia: Westminster Press, 1988.

Ring, Sharon H. *Wisdom's Friends: Community and Christology in the Fourth Gospel*. Louisville: Westminster John Knox, 1999.

Rose, Laurel L. *The Politics of Harmony: Land dispute strategies in Swaziland*. Cambridge: Cambridge University Press, 1992.

Ross, Cathy. "Creating Space: Hospitality as a Metaphor for Mission." *ANVIL* 25 (2008): 167-176.

Sanders, E. P. *Jesus and Judaism*. London: SCM, 1985.

Sanders, Jack T. *Ethics in the New Testament: Change and Development*. London: SCM, 1986.

Sasson, Jack M. "The Blood of Grapes: Viticulture and Intoxication in the Hebrew Bible." Pages 399-416 in *Drinking in Ancient Societies: History and Culture of Drinks in the Ancient Near East*. Edited by Lucio Milano. Padova: Sargon srl, 1994.

Schapera, I., ed. *The Bantu Speaking Tribes of South Africa: An Ethnological Survey*. London: George Routledge & Sons, 1937.

Schnackenburg, Rudolf. *The Gospel According to St. John*. 3 Volumes. Translated by Kevin Smyth. Edited by J. Massyngbaerde Ford and Kevin Smyth. Kent: Burns and Oates, 1968-1982.

———. *The Johannine Epistles: Introduction and Commentary*. Translated by Reginald and Ilse Fuller. New York: Crossroad, 1992.

Segovia, Fernando F. *Love Relationships in the Johannine Tradition: Agapē/Agapan in 1 John and the Fourth Gospel*. Society of Biblical Literature Dissertation Series 58. Chico: Scholars Press, 1982.

———. *The Farewell of the Word: The Johannine Call to Abide*. Minneapolis: Fortress, 1991.

———. "The Journeys of the Word of God: A Reading of the Plot of the Fourth Gospel." *Semeia* 53 (1991): 23-54.

———. "The Theology and Provenance of John 15:1-17." *Journal of Biblical Literature* 101 (1982): 115-128.

Seltan, Charles. *Wine in the Ancient World.* London: Routledge & Kegan Paul, 1957.

Semple, E. C. *The Geography of the Mediterranean: Its Relation to Ancient History.* New York: Henry Holt, 1931.

Shorter, Alan W. *Everyday Life in Ancient Egypt.* London: Sampson Low, Marston, 1923.

Singleton, Vernon L. "An Enologist's Commentary on Ancient Wine." Pages 67-76 in *The Origins and Ancient History of Wine.* Edited by Patrick E. McGovern, Stuart M. Flemming and Solomon H. Katz. Luxembourg: Gordon and Breach Publishers, 1995.

Smalley, Stephen S. "Diversity and Development in John." *New Testament Studies* 17 (1971): 276-292.

———. *John-Evangelist & Interpreter.* 2nd ed. Carlisle: Paternoster, 1998.

———. *1, 2, 3 John.* Word Biblical Commentary 51. Waco: Word Books, Publisher, Revised edition, 2007.

———. "New Light on the Fourth Gospel." *Tyndale Bulletin* 17 (1966): 35-62.

———. "The Christ-Christian Relationship in Paul and John." Pages 95-105 in *Pauline Studies: Essays presented to Professor F. F. Bruce on his 70th Birthday.* Edited by Donald A. Hagner and Murray J. Harris. Exeter: Paternoster, 1980.

———. "The Johannine Literature: A Sample of Recent Studies in English." *Theology* 103 (2000): 13-28.

Smith, D. Moody. *John.* Abingdon New Testament Commentaries. Nashville: Abingdon Press, 1999.

———. *The Theology of the Gospel of John.* Cambridge: Cambridge University Press, 1995.

Smith, Ralph L. *Micah – Malachi*: Word Biblical Commentary 32. Waco: Word Books Publisher, 1984.

Staley, Jeffrey L. "The Politics of Place and the Place of Politics in the Gospel of John." Pages 265-277 in *What is John? Vol. II: Literary and Social Readings of the Fourth Gospel.* Edited by Fernando F. Segovia. Society of Biblical Literature Symposium Series. Atlanta: Scholars Press, 1998.

Stansell, Gary. *Micah and Isaiah: A form and Tradition Historical Comparison.* Atlanta: Scholars Press, 1988.

Strecker, Georg. *Theology of the New Testament.* Translated by M. Eugene Boring. Berlin: Walter de Gruyter, 1996.

Swanson, Dwight. "Holiness in the Dead Sea Scrolls: The Priorities of Faith." Pages 19-39 in *Holiness and Ecclesiology in the New Testament.* Edited by Kent E. Brower and Andy Johnson. Grand Rapids; Cambridge: Eerdmans, 2007.

Swarup, Paul. *The Self-understanding of the Dead Sea Scrolls Community: An Eternal Planting, A House of Holiness.* Library of Second Temple Studies 59. London/New York: T&T Clark, 2006.

Talbert, Charles H. *Reading John: A Literary and Theological Commentary on the Fourth Gospel and the Johannine Epistles.* London: SPCK, 1992.

Taylor, A. Wingrove. "Holiness Values from the Heavenly Vine." *Wesleyan Theological Journal* 37 (2002): 219-223.

Thatcher, Tom. *The Riddles of Jesus in John: A Study in Tradition and Folklore.* Society of Biblical Literature Monograph Series 53. Atlanta: Society of Biblical Literature, 2000.

Thomas, J. C. *Footwashing in John 13 and the Johannine Community.* Sheffield: Journal for the Study of the Old Testament, 1991.

Tiemeyer, Lena Sofia. "The Guilty Priesthood (Zech 3)." Pages 1-19 in *The Book of Zechariah and its Influence.* Edited by Christopher Tuckett. Aldershot: Ashgate Publishing, 2003.

Trebilco, Paul. *The Early Christians in Ephesus from Paul to Ignatius.* Wissenschaftliche Untersuchungen zum Neuen Testament 166. Tübingen: Mohr Siebeck, 2004.

Tukasi, Emmanuel O. *Determinism and Petitionary Prayer in John and the Dead Sea Scrolls: An Ideological Reading of John and the Rule of the Community* (1QS). Edited by L. Grabbe; London: T&T Clarke International, 2008.

Tutu, Desmond. "Ubuntu." *Wikipedia.* Cited 23 December, 2008.

Unwin, Tim. *Wine and the vine: An Historical Geography of Viticulture and the Wine Trade.* London & New York: Routledge, 2003.

Van De Mieroop, Marc. *A History of the Ancient Near East ca. 3000-323 BC.* Oxford: Blackwell Publishing Company, 2004.

Van Tilborg, Sjef. *Reading John in Ephesus*. Supplements to Novum Testamentum 83. Leiden: Brill, 1996.

VanderKam, James C. *The Book of Jubilees*. Sheffield: Sheffield Academic Press, 2001.

Vavilov, Nikolai I. "Studies on the Origin of Cultivated Plants." *Bulletin of Applied Botany* 16 (1926): 1-148.

Verbin, John S. Kloppenborg. "Egyptian Viticulture and the Citation of Isaiah 5:1-7 in Mark 12:1-9." *Novum Testamentum* 44 (2002): 134-159.

Vermes, Geza. *The Dead Sea Scrolls in English*. Third, revised and augmented edition, including the Temple Scroll and other recently published manuscripts. London: Penguin Books, 1987.

Volf, Miroslav. *After our Likeness: The Church as the Image of the Trinity*. Grand Rapids: Eerdmans, 1998.

Waetjen, Herman C. *The Gospel of the Beloved Disciple: A Work in Two Editions*. New York; London: T & T Clark, 2005.

Walker, Peter. *Jesus and the Holy City: New Testament Perspectives on Jerusalem*. Grand Rapids: Eerdmans, 1996.

Walsh, Carey Ellen. *The Fruit of the Vine: Viticulture In Ancient Israel*. Eisenbraus: Winoma Lake, 2000.

Ware, Bruce A. *Father, Son and Holy Spirit: Relationship, Roles and Relevance*. Wheaton: Crossway Books, 2005.

———. Kallistos. *Orthodox Way*. London: Mowbray, 1979.

Werblowsky, R. J. Zwi and Geoffrey Wigoder, eds. *The Encyclopedia of the Jewish Religion*. London: Pheonix House, 1967.

Wesley, John. *The Poetical Works of John & Charles Wesley*. 13 vols.; Reprinted from the originals, with the last corrections of the authors; Together with the Poems of Charles Wesley not before published; Collected and arranged by G. Osborne; London: Parternoster-Row, 1868.

Westcott, B. F. *The Gospel According to John: The Authorized Version with Introduction and Notes*. London: John Murray, 1908.

———. *The Gospel According to St. John: The Authorized Version with Introduction and Notes*. Grand Rapids: Eerdmans, 1881.

Whitacre, Rodney A. *Johannine Polemic: The Role of Tradition and Theology*. Chico, California: Scholars Press, 1982.

Wigoder, Geoffrey. Ed-in-Chief. *The New Encyclopedia of Judaism*. New York: New York University Press, 1989, 2002.

Williamson, H. G. M. *The International Critical Commentary: Isaiah 1-5* Vol. 1. London: T & T Clark, 2006.

Williamson, Paul R. *Abraham, Israel and the Nations: The Patriarchal Promise and its Covenantal Development in Genesis*. Edited by David J. A. Clines and Philip R. Davies. Sheffield: SAP, 2000.

Woll, Bruce D. *Johannine Christianity in Conflict: Authority, Rank, and Succession in the First Farewell Discourse*. Chico, California: Scholars Press, 1981.

Wright, N. T. *Jesus and the Victory of God*. Minneapolis: Fortress, 1996.

———. *Surprised by Hope*. London: SPCK, 2007.

Yak-Hwee, Tan. *Re-resenting The Johannine Community: A Postcolonial Perspective*. Society of Biblical Literature 107; NY: Peter Lang, 2008.

Yarbrough, O. Larry. "Parents and Children in the Jewish Family of Antiquity." Pages 41-49 in *The Jewish Family in Antiquity*. Edited by Shaye J. D. Cohen. Atlanta: Scholars Press, 1993.

Yee, Gale A. "A Form-Critical Study of Isaiah 5:1-7 as a Song and Juridical Parable." *Catholic Biblical Quarterly* 43 (1981): 30-40.

Zizioulas, John. *Being as Communion*. New York: St. Vladimir Seminary Press, 1985.

Zohary, Daniel. "The Domestication of the Grapevine Vitis Vinifera L. in the Near East." Pages 23-43 in *The Origins and Ancient History of Wine*. Edited by Patrick E. McGovern, Stuart M. Flemming and Solomon H. Katz. Luxembourg: Gordon and Breach Publishers, 1995.